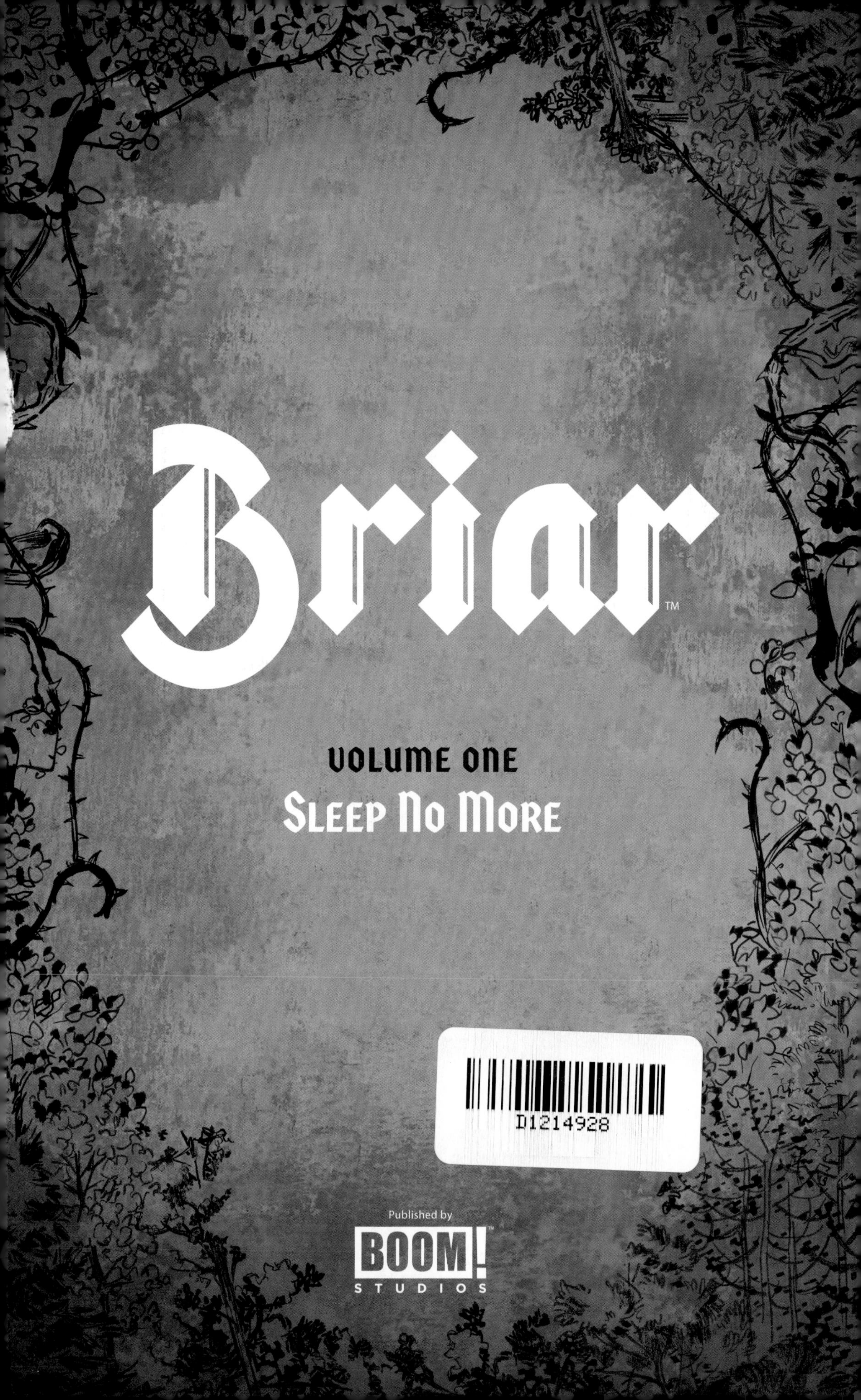

Briar™

VOLUME ONE
Sleep No More

Published by
BOOM! STUDIOS

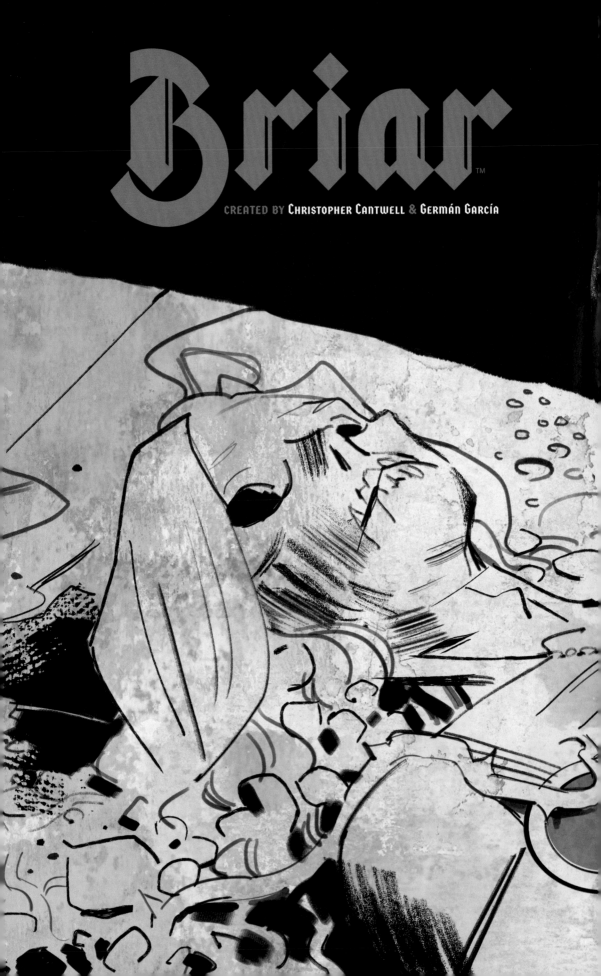

Briar™

CREATED BY CHRISTOPHER CANTWELL & GERMÁN GARCÍA

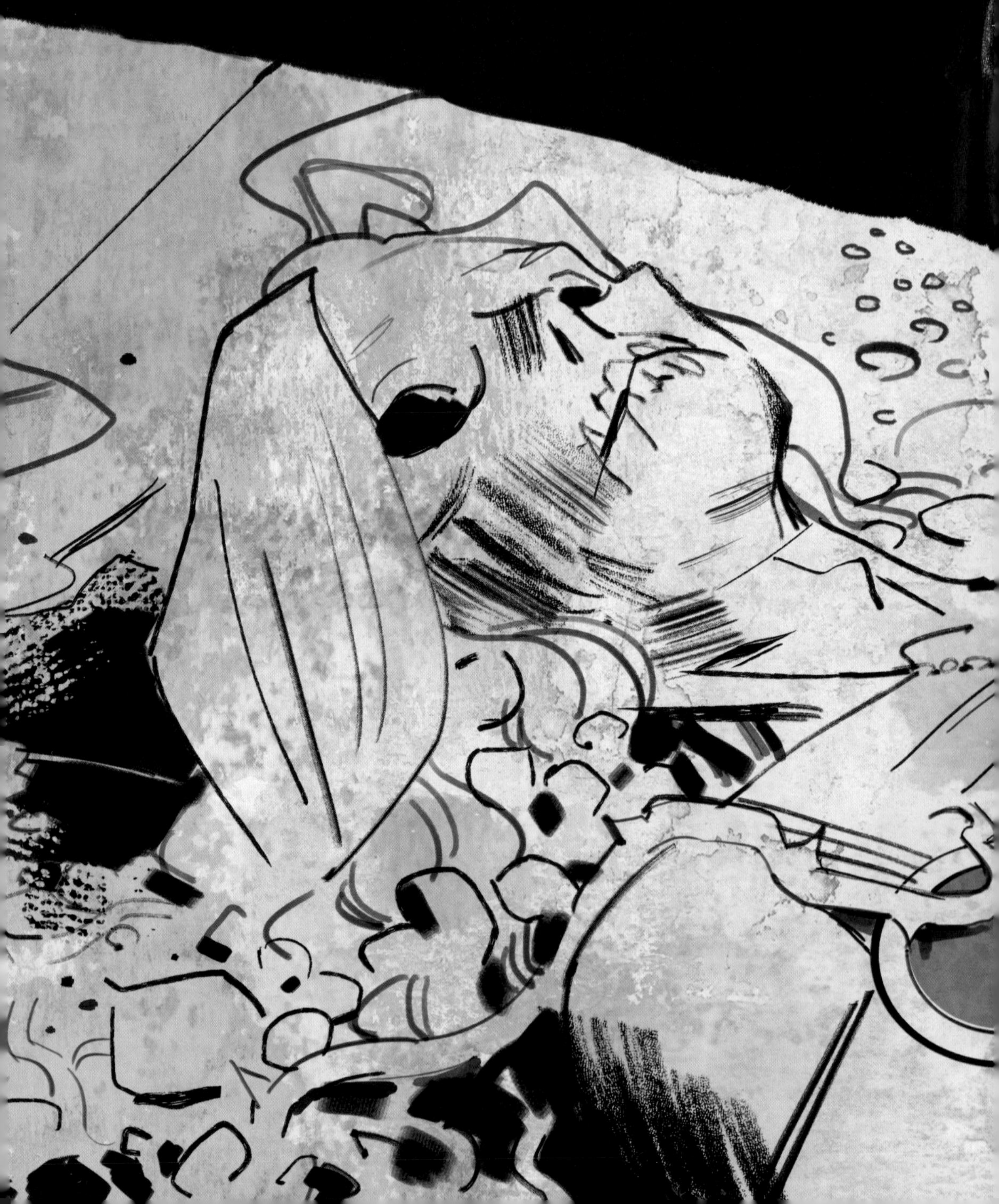

WRITTEN BY
CHRISTOPHER CANTWELL

ILLUSTRATED BY
GERMÁN GARCÍA

COLORED BY
MATHEUS LOPES

LETTERED BY
ANDWORLD DESIGN

COVER BY
GERMÁN GARCÍA

BOOM! STUDIOS
EXCLUSIVE COVER BY
JUNGGEUN YOON

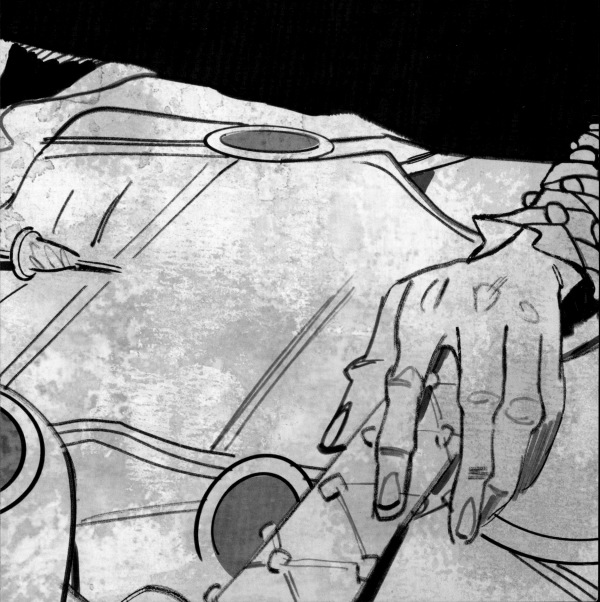

BRIAR Volume One, May 2023. Published by BOOM! Studios, a division of Boom Entertainment, Inc. Briar is ™ & © 2023 Ocean Breeze Soap Company and Germán García. Originally published in single magazine form as BRIAR No. 1-4. ™ & © 2022, 2023 Ocean Breeze Soap Company and Germán García. All rights reserved. BOOM! Studios™ and the BOOM! Studios logo are trademarks of Boom Entertainment, Inc., registered in various countries and categories. All characters, events, and institutions depicted herein are fictional. Any similarity between any of the names, characters, persons, events, and/or institutions in this publication to actual names, characters, and persons, whether living or dead, events, and/or or institutions is unintended and purely coincidental. BOOM! Studios does not read or accept unsolicited submissions of ideas, stories, or artwork.

BOOM! Studios, 6920 Melrose Ave, Los Angeles, CA 90038-3306. Printed in Canada. First Printing.

ISBN: 978-1-68415-900-0
eISBN: 978-1-64668-872-2

Boom! Studios Exclusive
ISBN: 978-1-60886-170-5

Logo Designer
Fernando Rosales

Designer
Madison Goyette

Editor
Allyson Gronowitz

Executive Editor
Eric Harburn

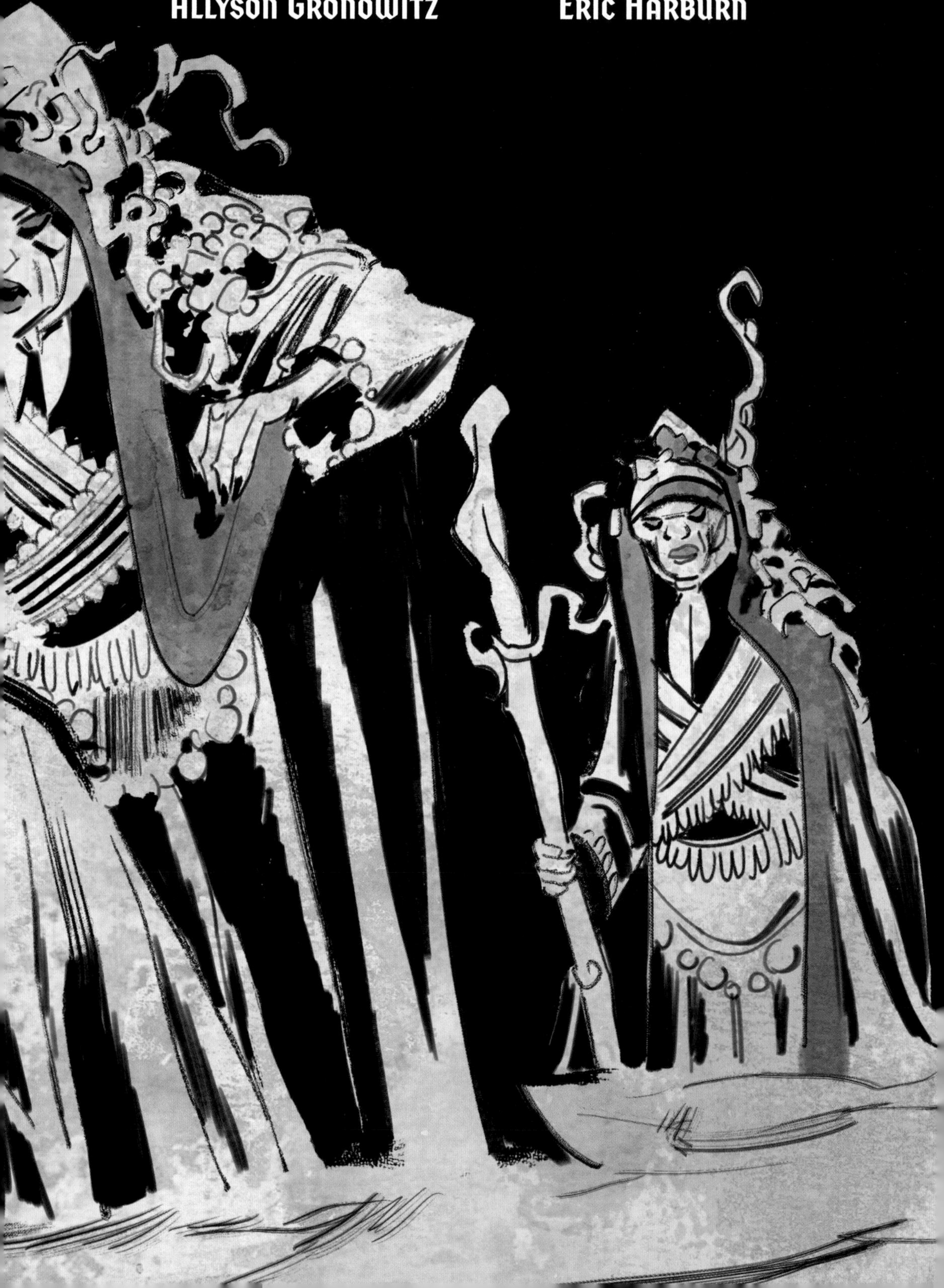

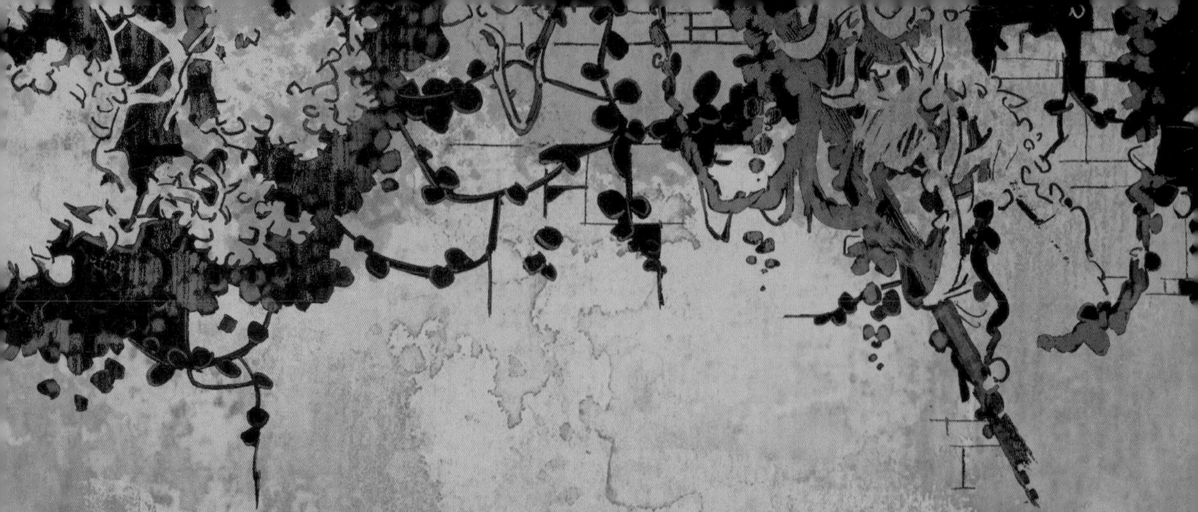

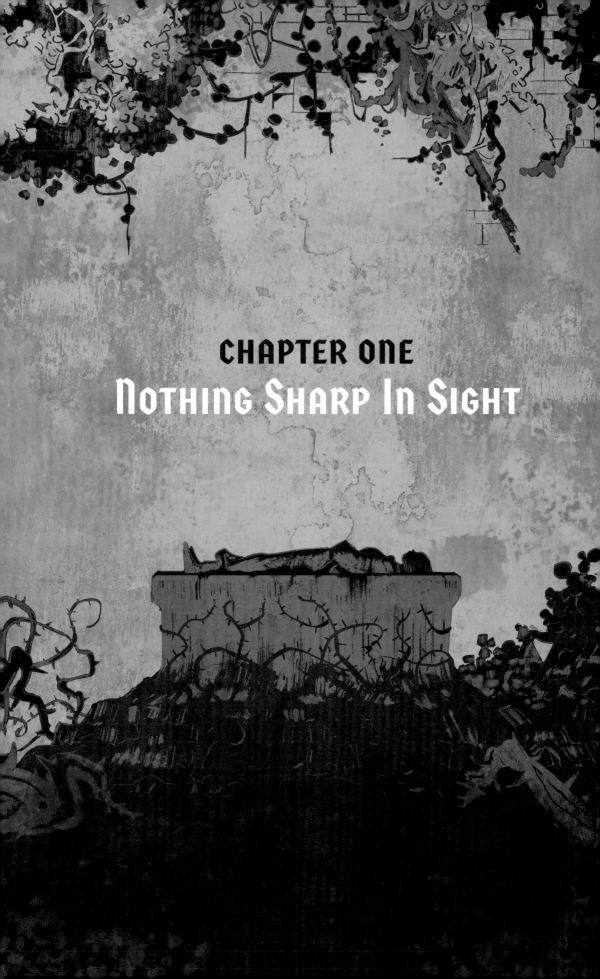

CHAPTER ONE

Nothing Sharp In Sight

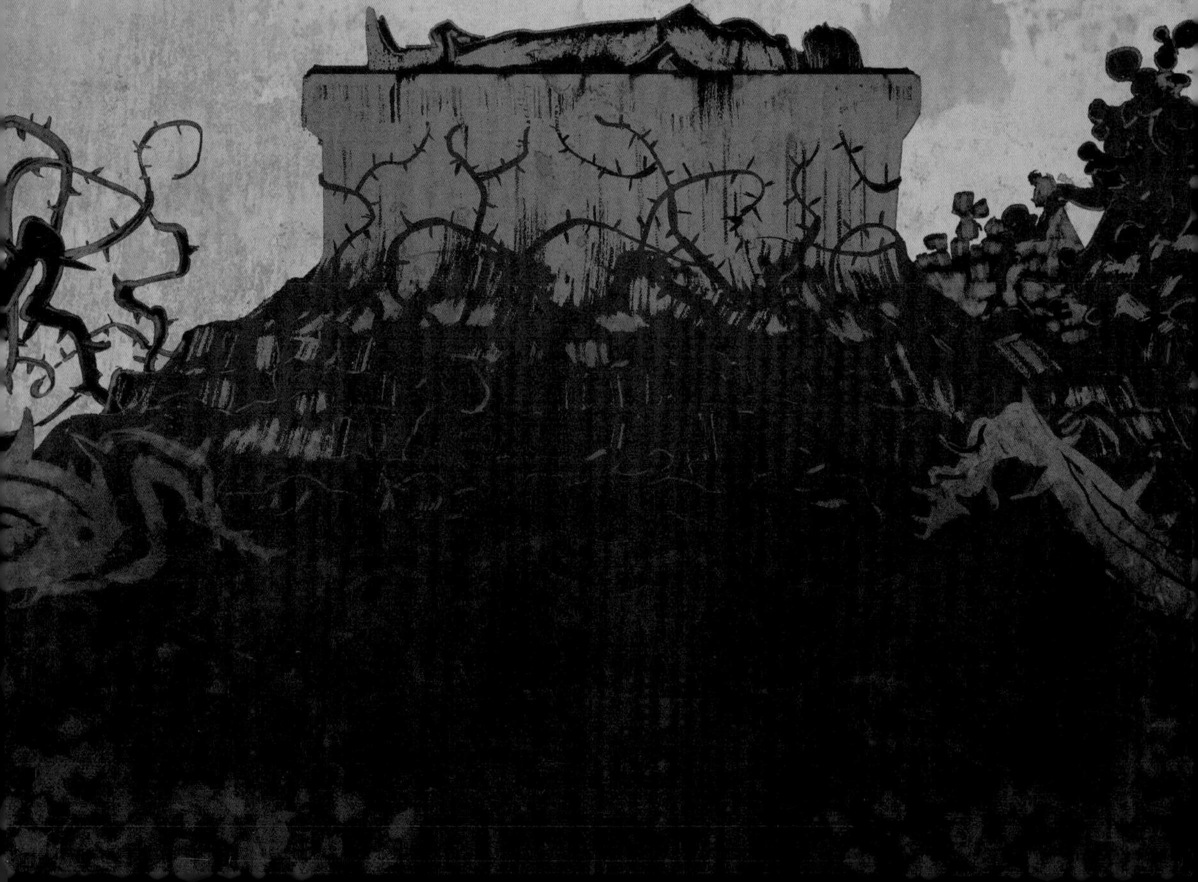

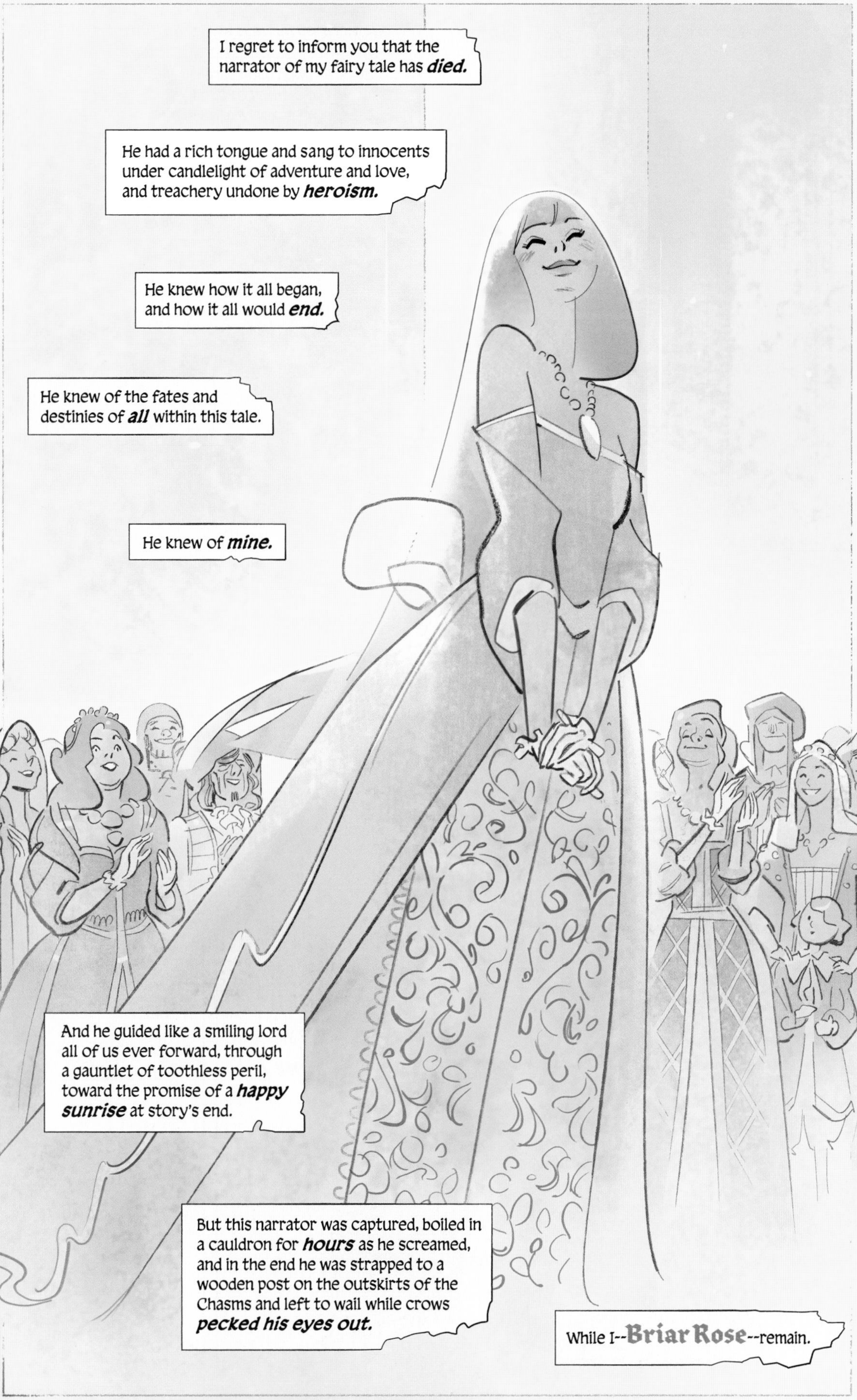
I regret to inform you that the narrator of my fairy tale has *died.*
He had a rich tongue and sang to innocents under candlelight of adventure and love, and treachery undone by *heroism.*
He knew how it all began, and how it all would *end.*
He knew of the fates and destinies of *all* within this tale.
He knew of *mine.*
And he guided like a smiling lord all of us ever forward, through a gauntlet of toothless peril, toward the promise of a *happy sunrise* at story's end.
But this narrator was captured, boiled in a cauldron for *hours* as he screamed, and in the end he was strapped to a wooden post on the outskirts of the Chasms and left to wail while crows *pecked his eyes out.*
While I--Briar Rose--remain.

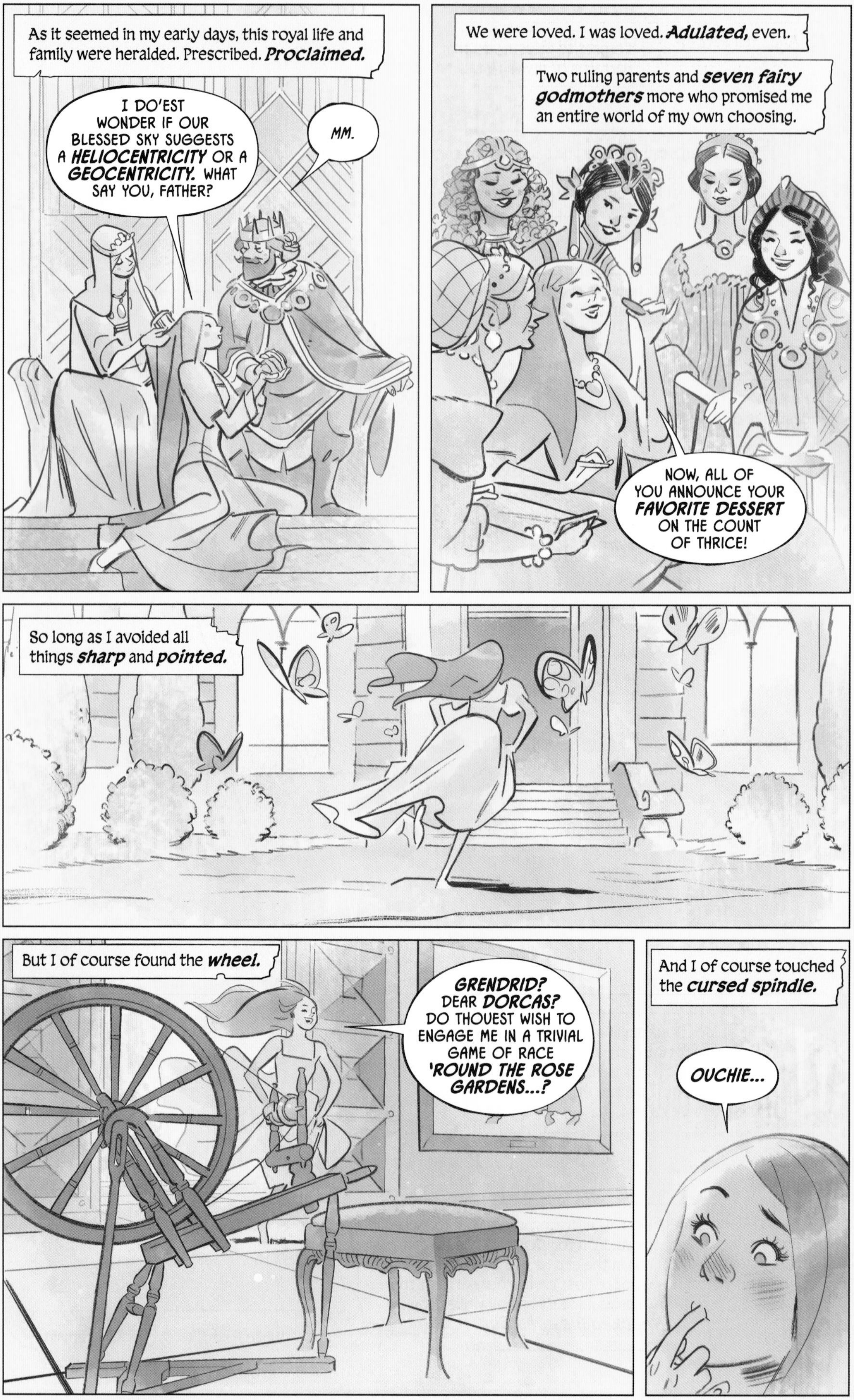
As it seemed in my early days, this royal life and family were heralded. Prescribed. *Proclaimed.*
I DO'EST WONDER IF OUR BLESSED SKY SUGGESTS A *HELIOCENTRICITY* OR A *GEOCENTRICITY.* WHAT SAY YOU, FATHER?
MM.
We were loved. I was loved. *Adulated,* even.
Two ruling parents and *seven fairy godmothers* more who promised me an entire world of my own choosing.
NOW, ALL OF YOU ANNOUNCE YOUR *FAVORITE DESSERT* ON THE COUNT OF THRICE!
So long as I avoided all things *sharp* and *pointed.*
But I of course found the *wheel.*
GRENDRID? DEAR *DORCAS?* DO THOUEST WISH TO ENGAGE ME IN A TRIVIAL GAME OF RACE *'ROUND THE ROSE GARDENS...?*
And I of course touched the *cursed spindle.*
OUCHIE...

And I fell *asleep.* Not unto death as I was forewarned, but into a slumber so deep I vanished even from myself.

My godmothers all mourned dutifully, following the *sacrosanct script.*

My father warred with all--avenging me as a victim claimed in truth by none he slew--and his kingdom *increased.*

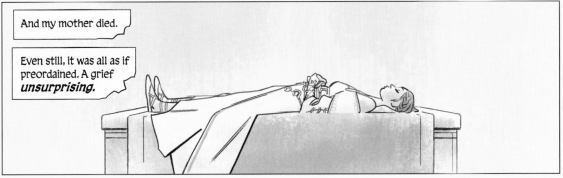

And my mother died.

Even still, it was all as if preordained. A grief *unsurprising.*

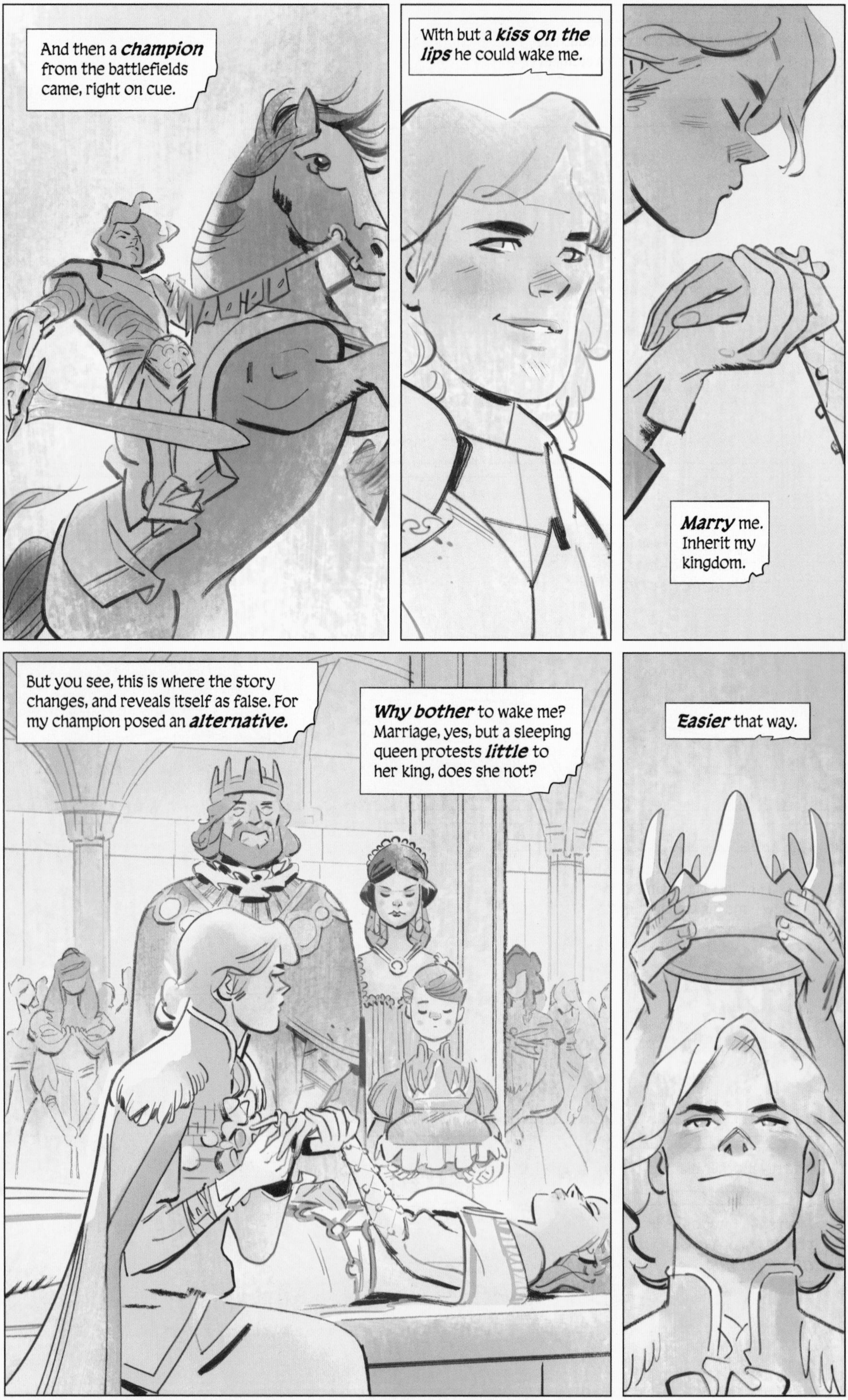
And then a *champion* from the battlefields came, right on cue.
With but a *kiss on the lips* he could wake me.
Marry me. Inherit my kingdom.
But you see, this is where the story changes, and reveals itself as false. For my champion posed an *alternative.*
Why bother to wake me? Marriage, yes, but a sleeping queen protests *little* to her king, does she not?
Easier that way.

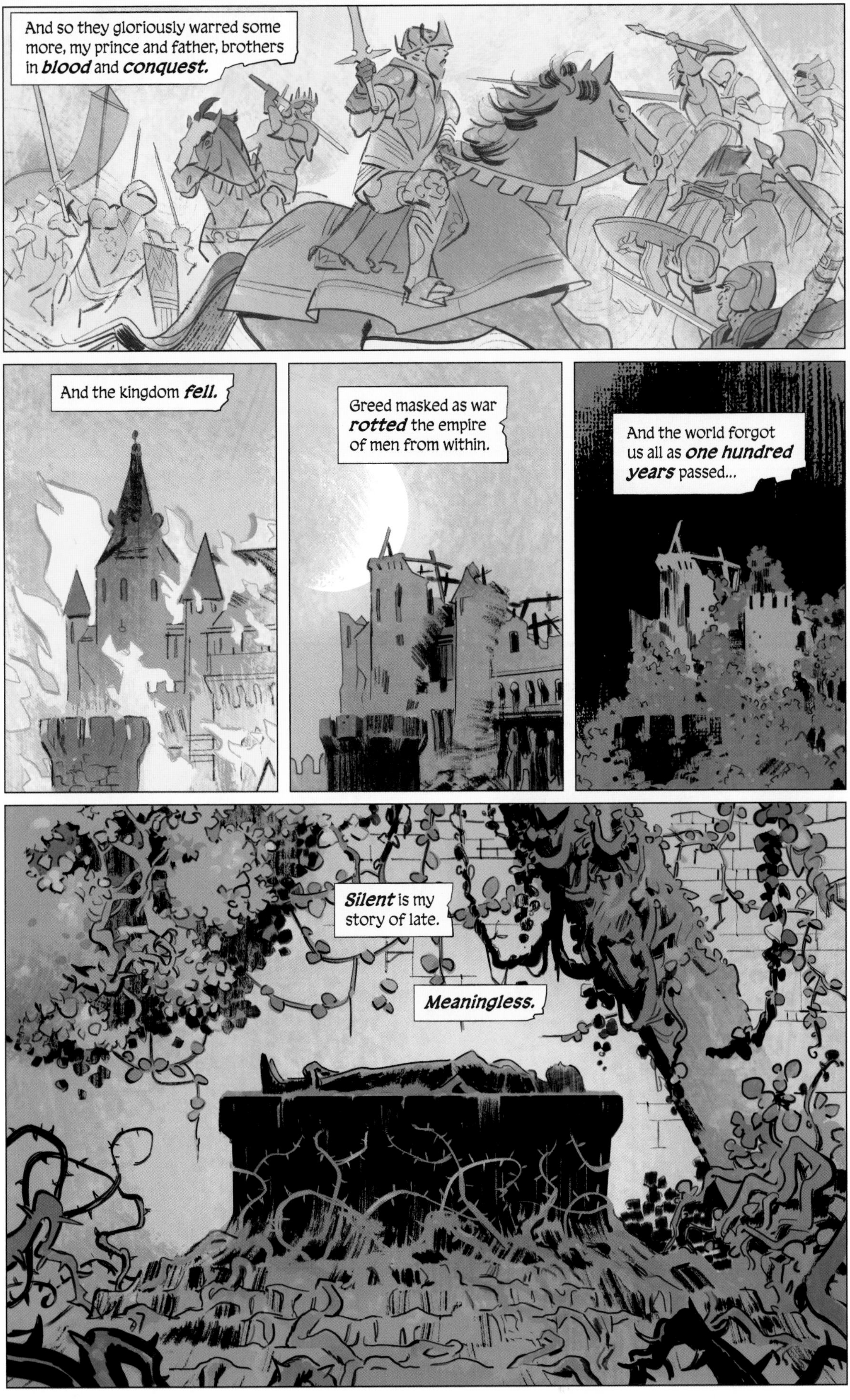
And so they gloriously warred some more, my prince and father, brothers in **blood** and **conquest.**
And the kingdom **fell.**
Greed masked as war **rotted** the empire of men from within.
And the world forgot us all as **one hundred years** passed...
Silent is my story of late.
Meaningless.

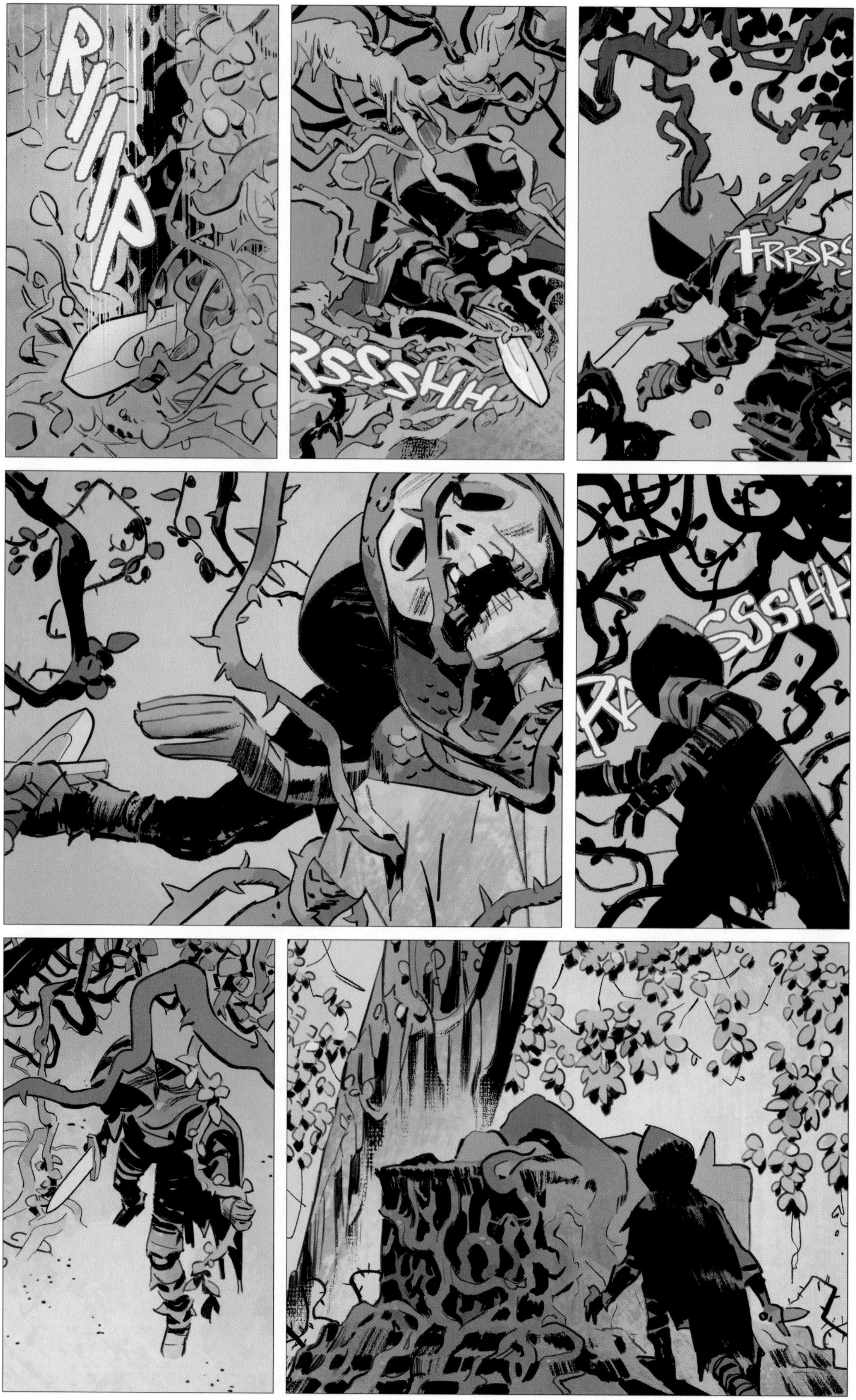
RIIIP
RSSSHH
FRRSRS
RASSSH

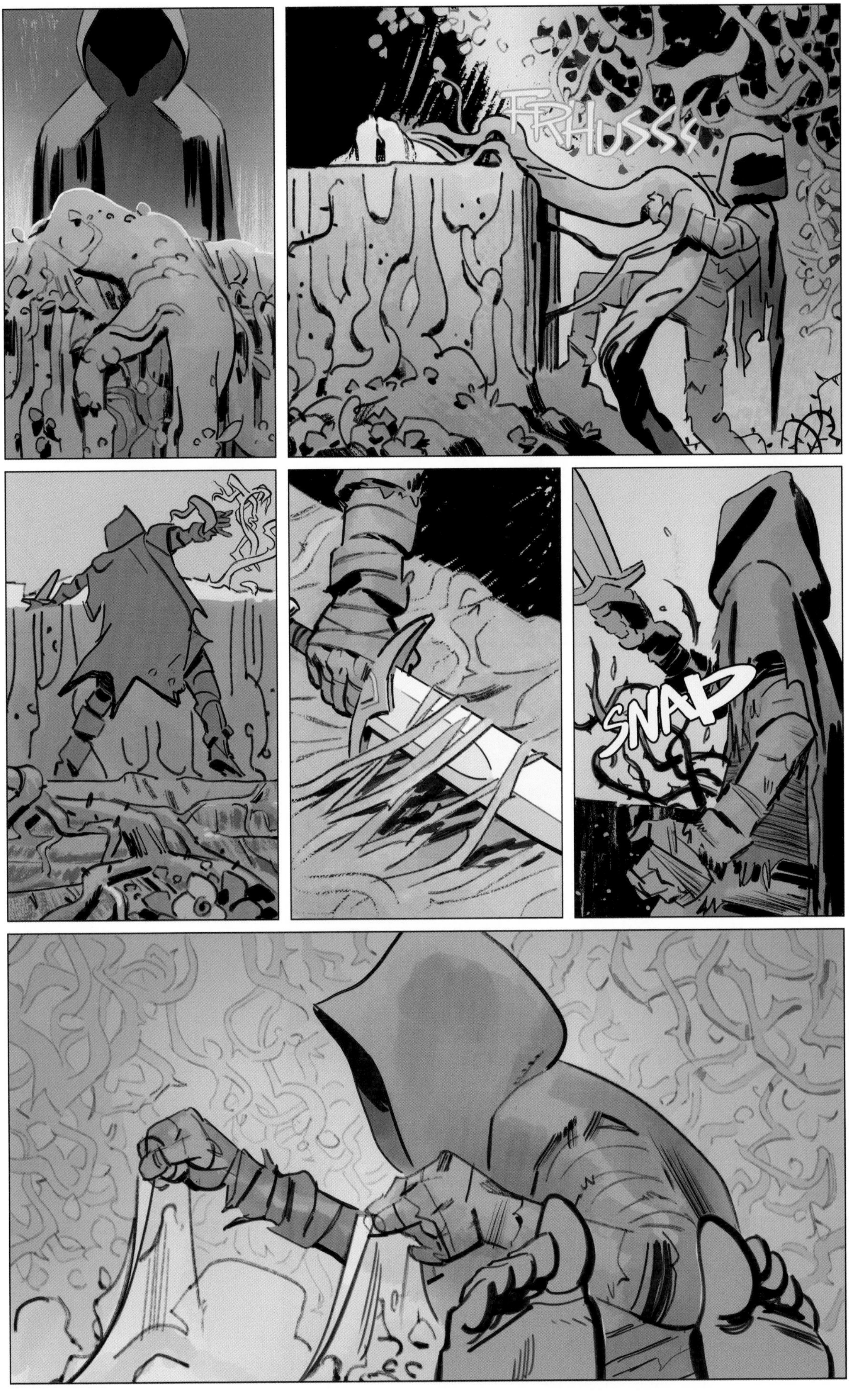
FRHUSSS
SNAP

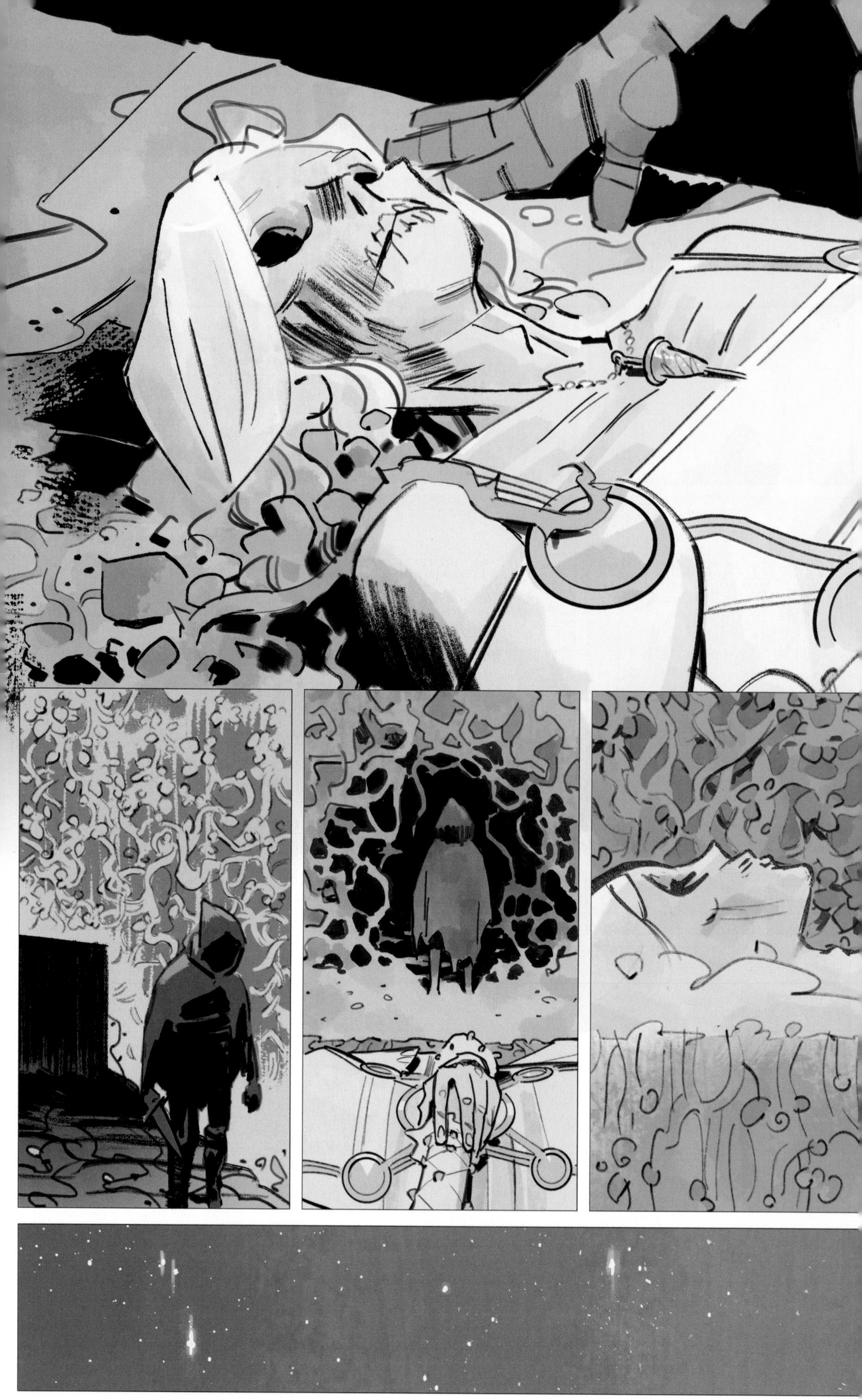

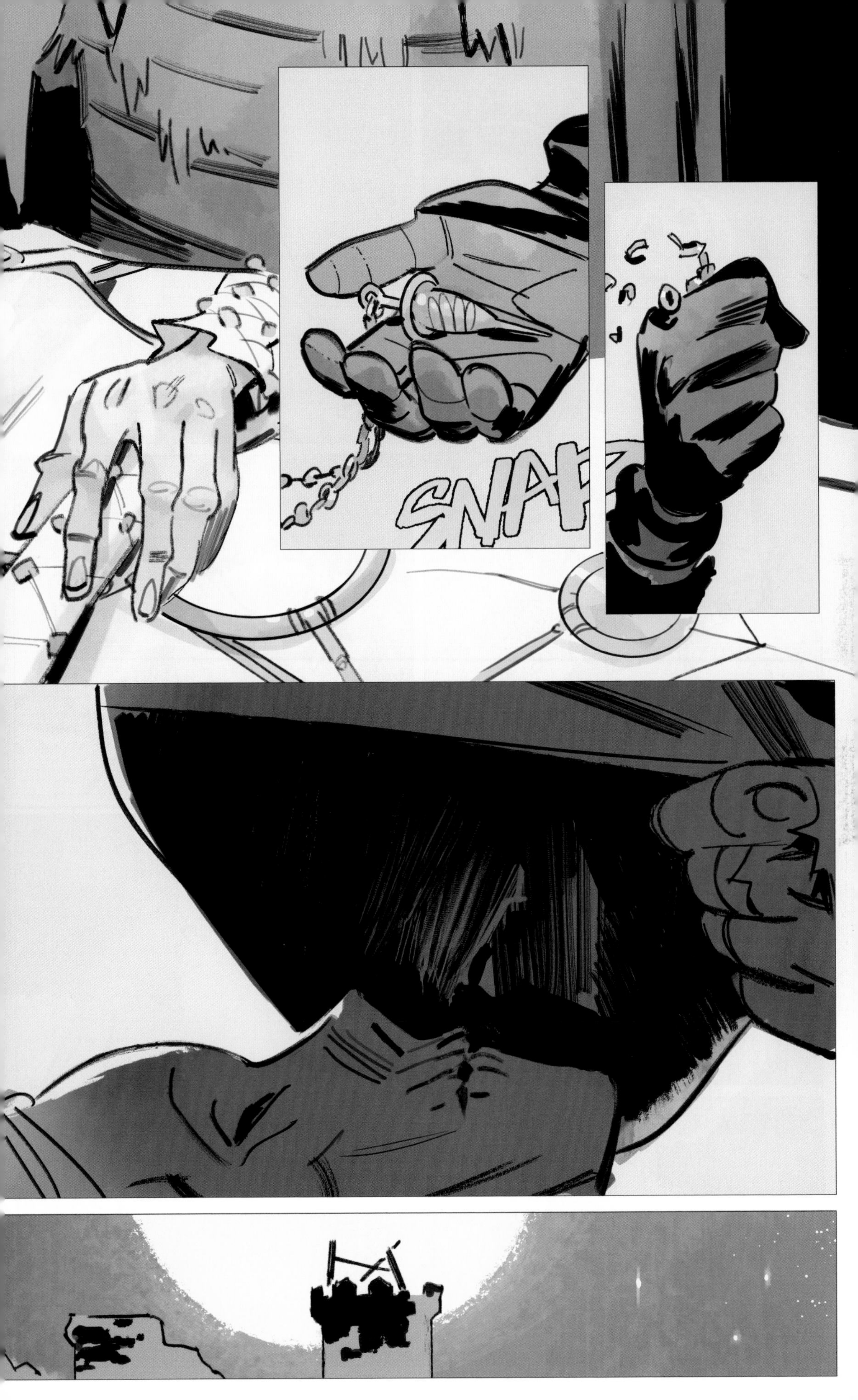
SNAP

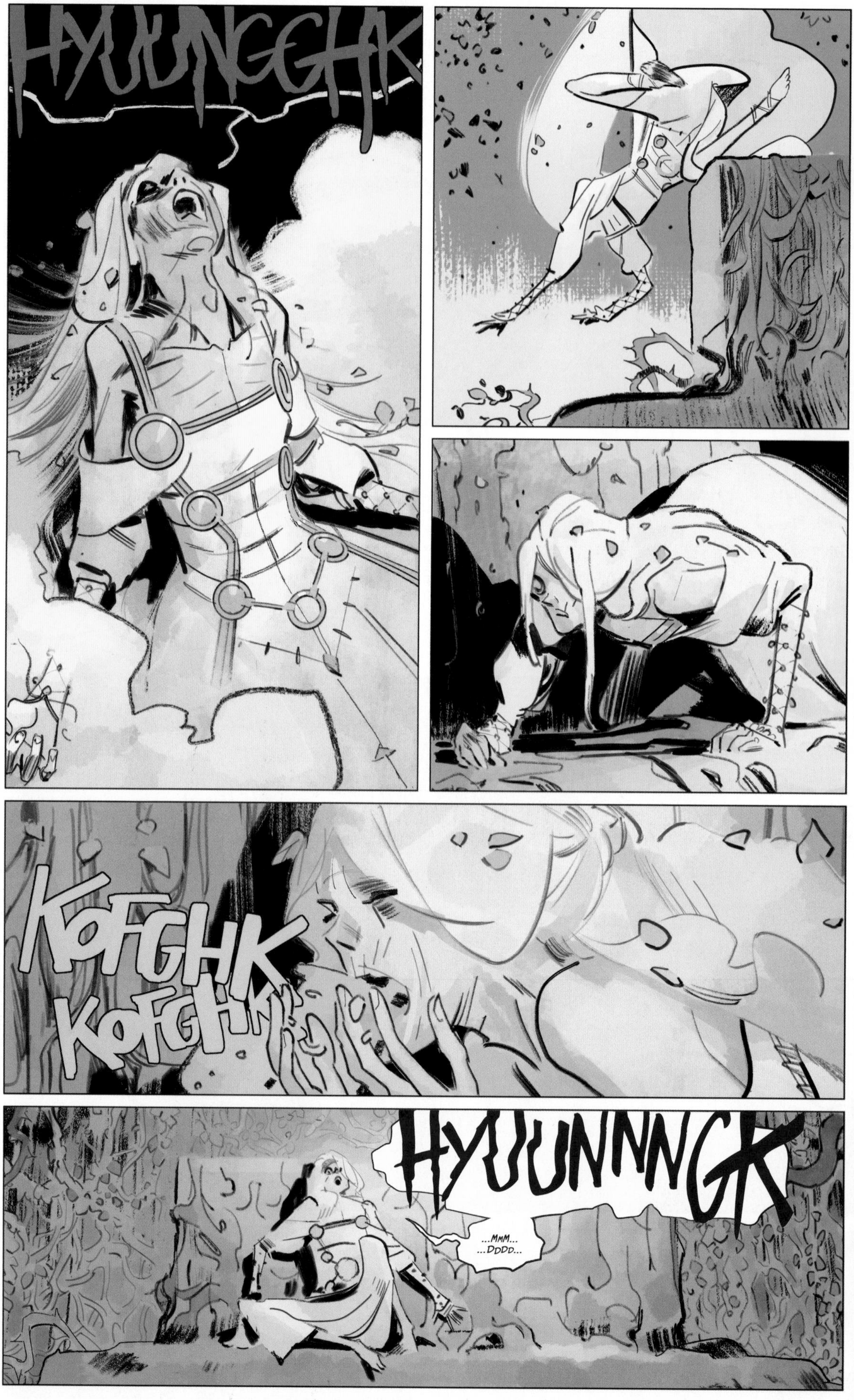
HYUUNGGHK
KOFGHK
KOFGHK
HYUUNNNGK
...MMM...
...DDDD...

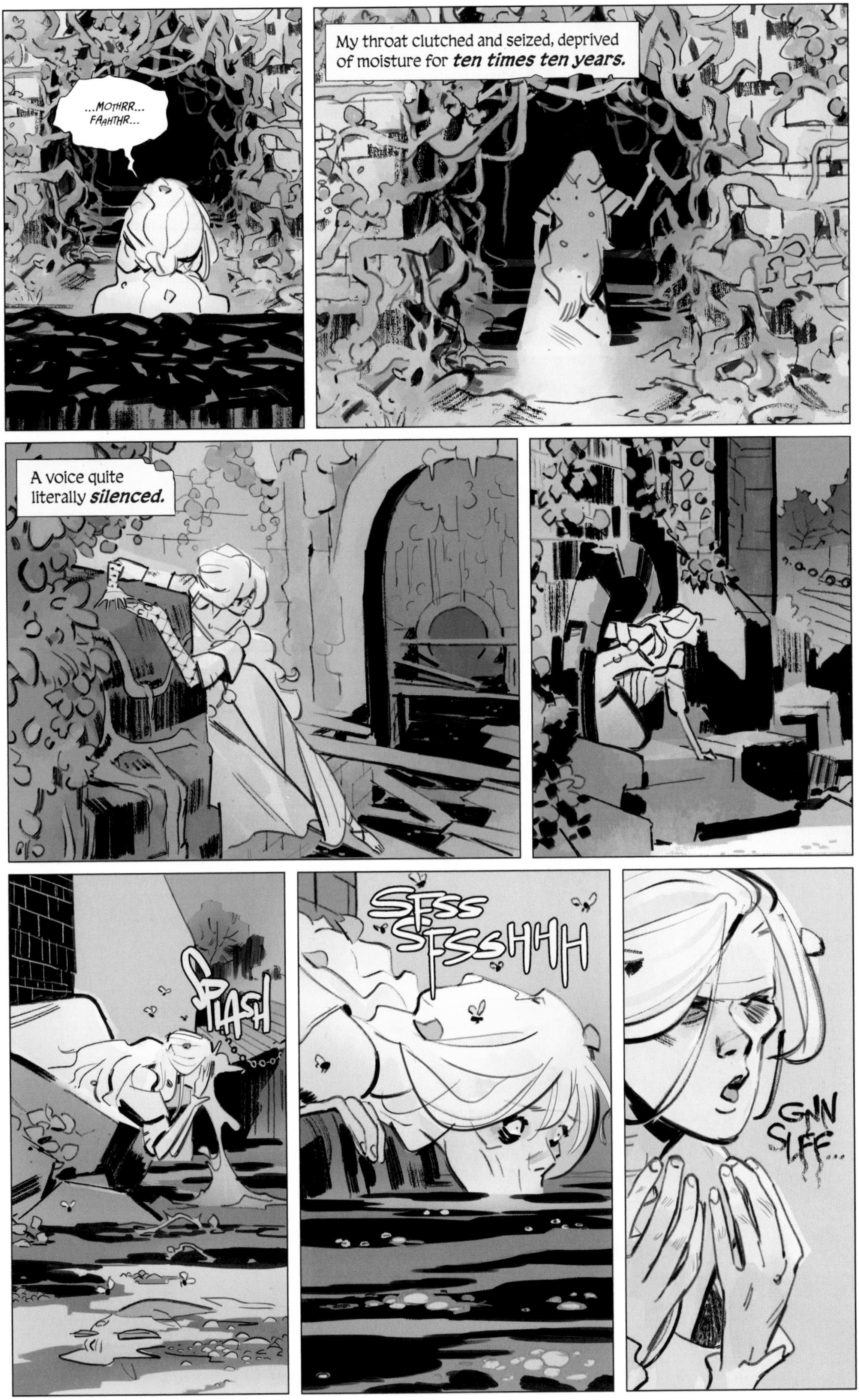
...MOTHRR...
FAAHTHR...
My throat clutched and seized, deprived of moisture for ten times ten years.
A voice quite literally silenced.
SPLASH
SFSS
SFSSHHH
GNN
SLFF...

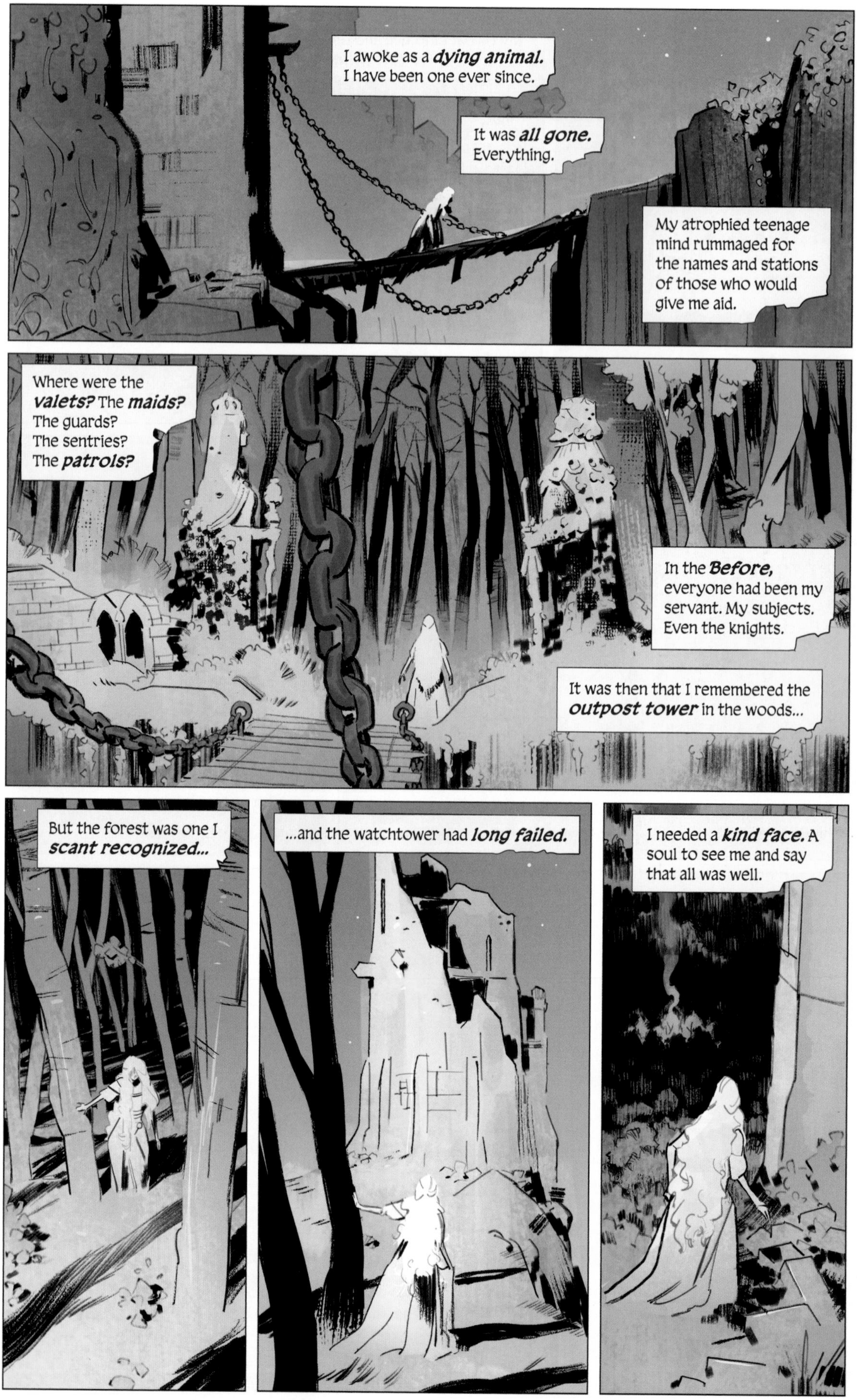
I awoke as a dying animal. I have been one ever since.
It was all gone. Everything.
My atrophied teenage mind rummaged for the names and stations of those who would give me aid.
Where were the valets? The maids? The guards? The sentries? The patrols?
In the Before, everyone had been my servant. My subjects. Even the knights.
It was then that I remembered the outpost tower in the woods...
But the forest was one I scant recognized...
...and the watchtower had long failed.
I needed a kind face. A soul to see me and say that all was well.

But there *are* no more kind faces in this world.

They have all been eaten away by the *hideous darkness.*

BLEEUERG

PHRSSK GHRSCH

CRICUS SKRCH GHRSCH

Woe is the damsel of *this* story. Oh, *woe. Boo hoo.*

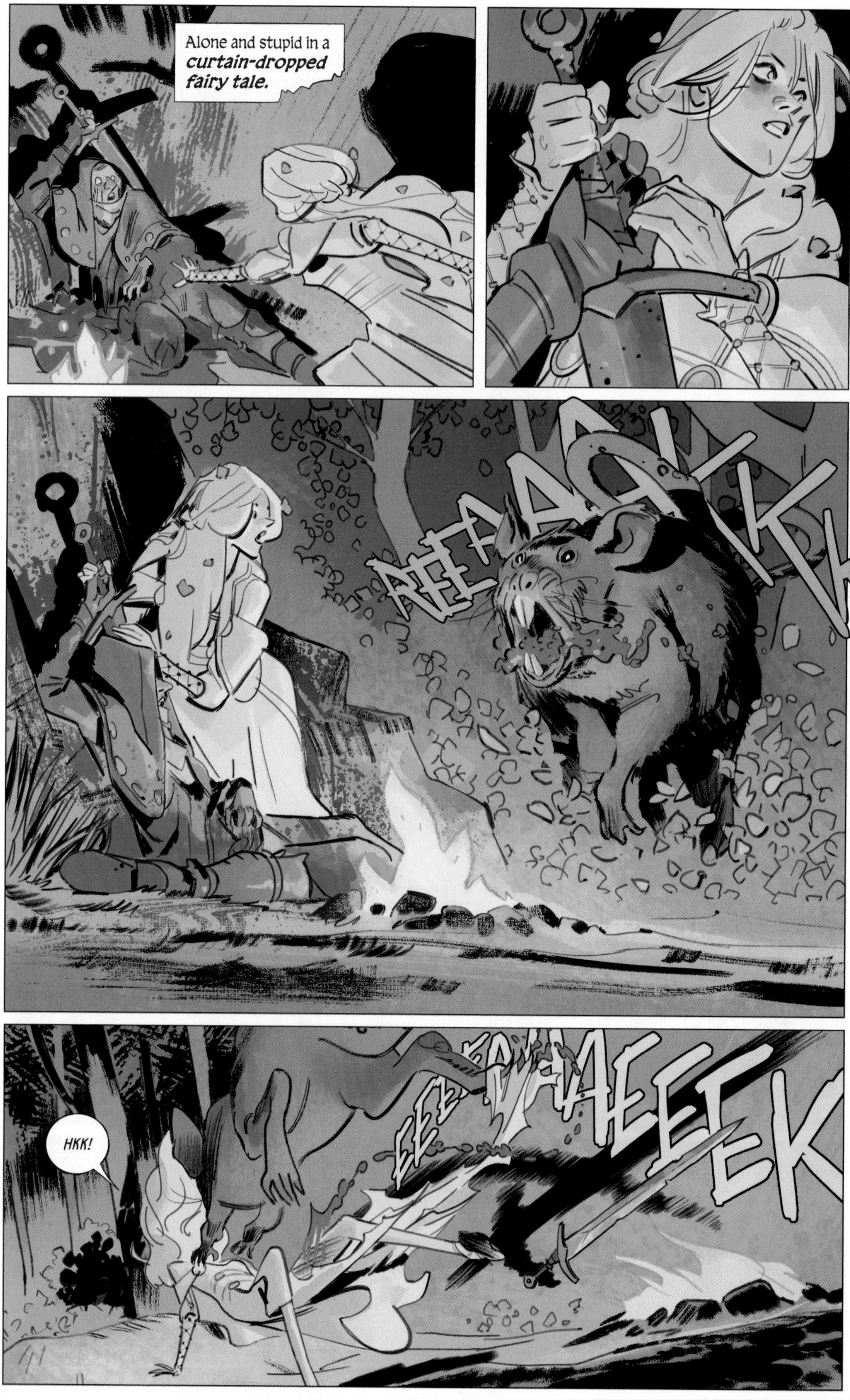
Alone and stupid in a *curtain-dropped fairy tale.*
REEAAAAKKKK
HKK!
EEEAAAEEEEK

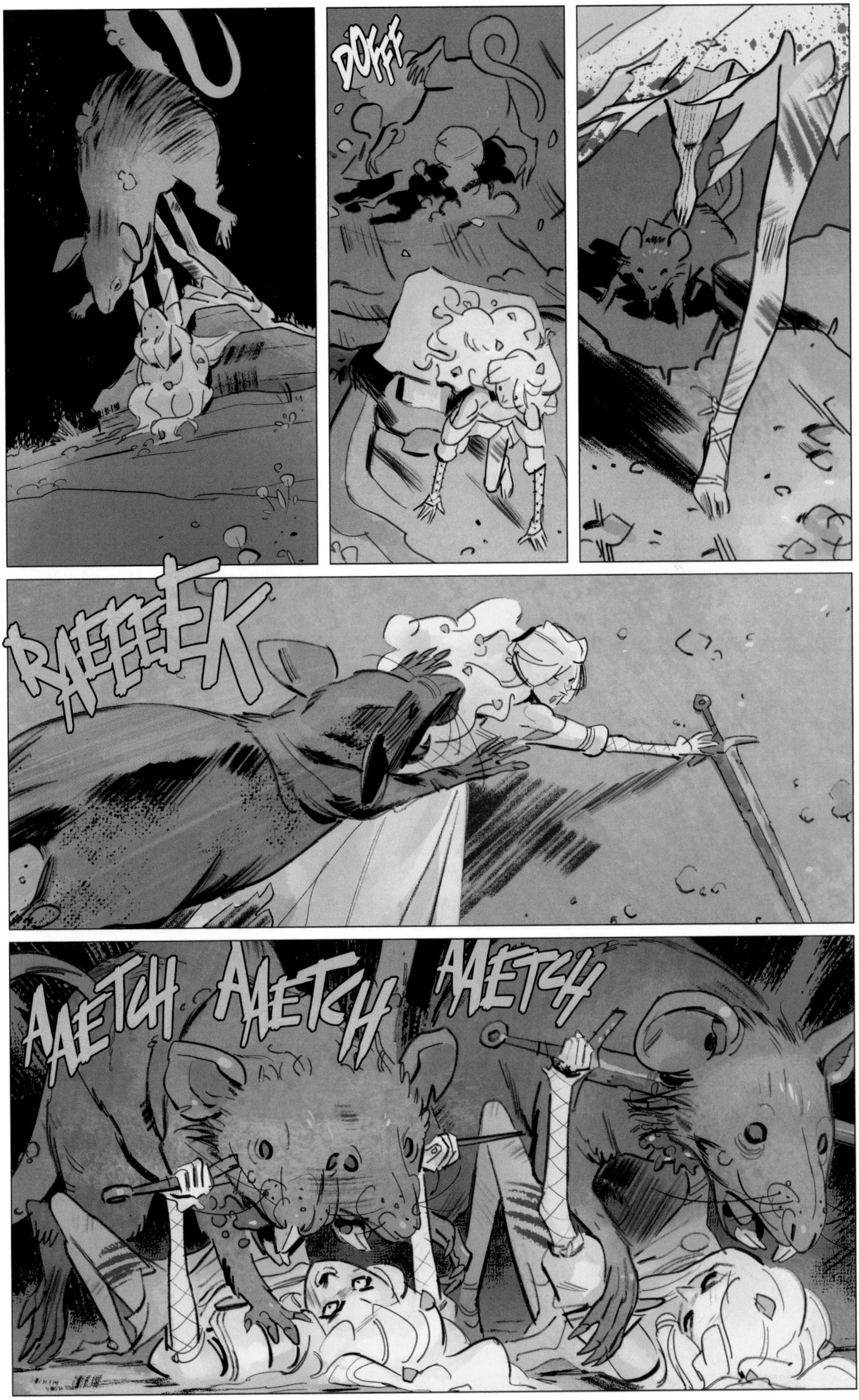
DOFF
RAEEEEK
AAETCH
AAETCH
AAETCH

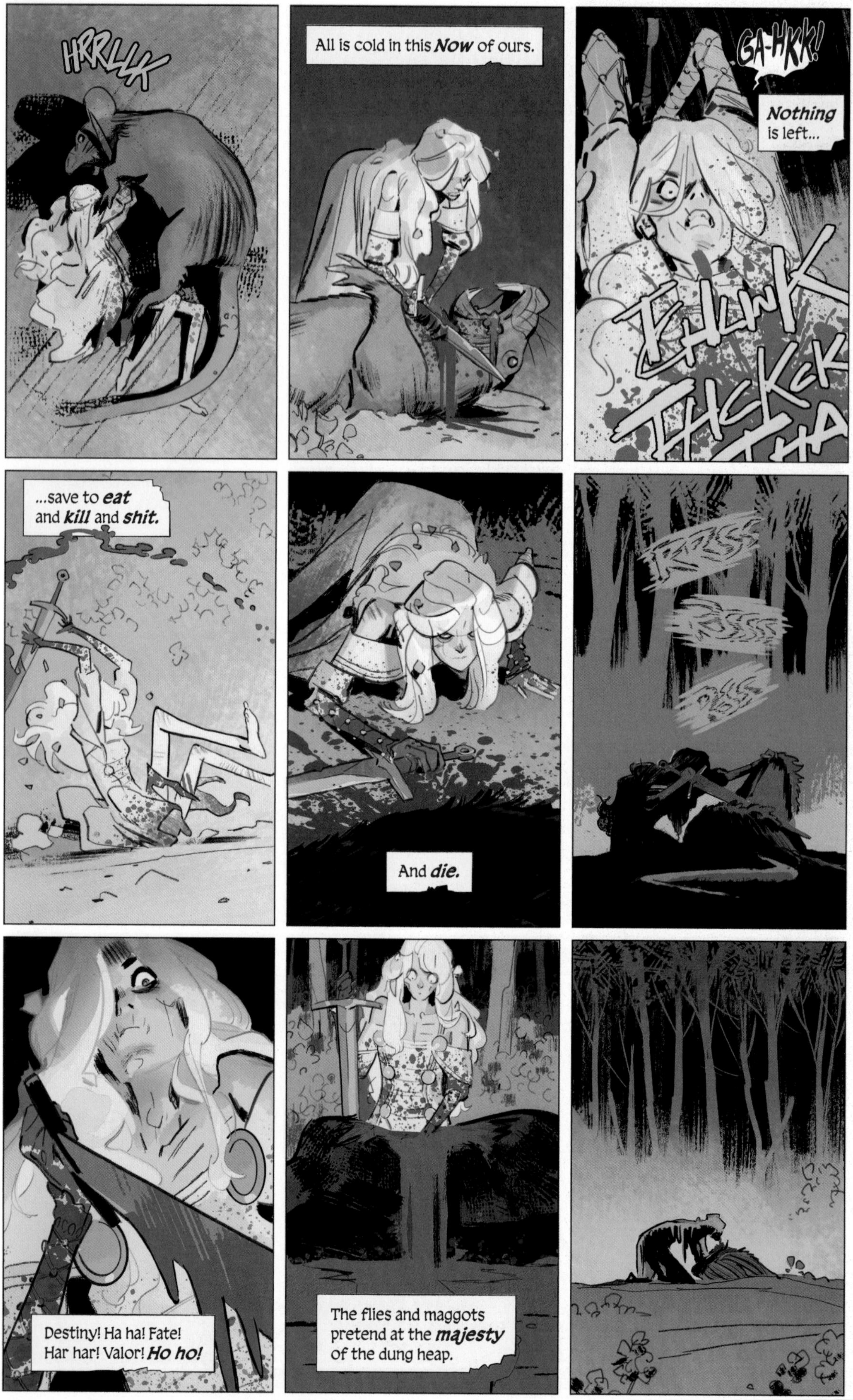
HRRLLK
All is cold in this *Now* of ours.
GA-HKK!
Nothing is left...
THUNK
THCKCK
...save to *eat* and *kill* and *shit.*
And *die.*
Destiny! Ha ha! Fate! Har har! Valor! *Ho ho!*
The flies and maggots pretend at the *majesty* of the dung heap.

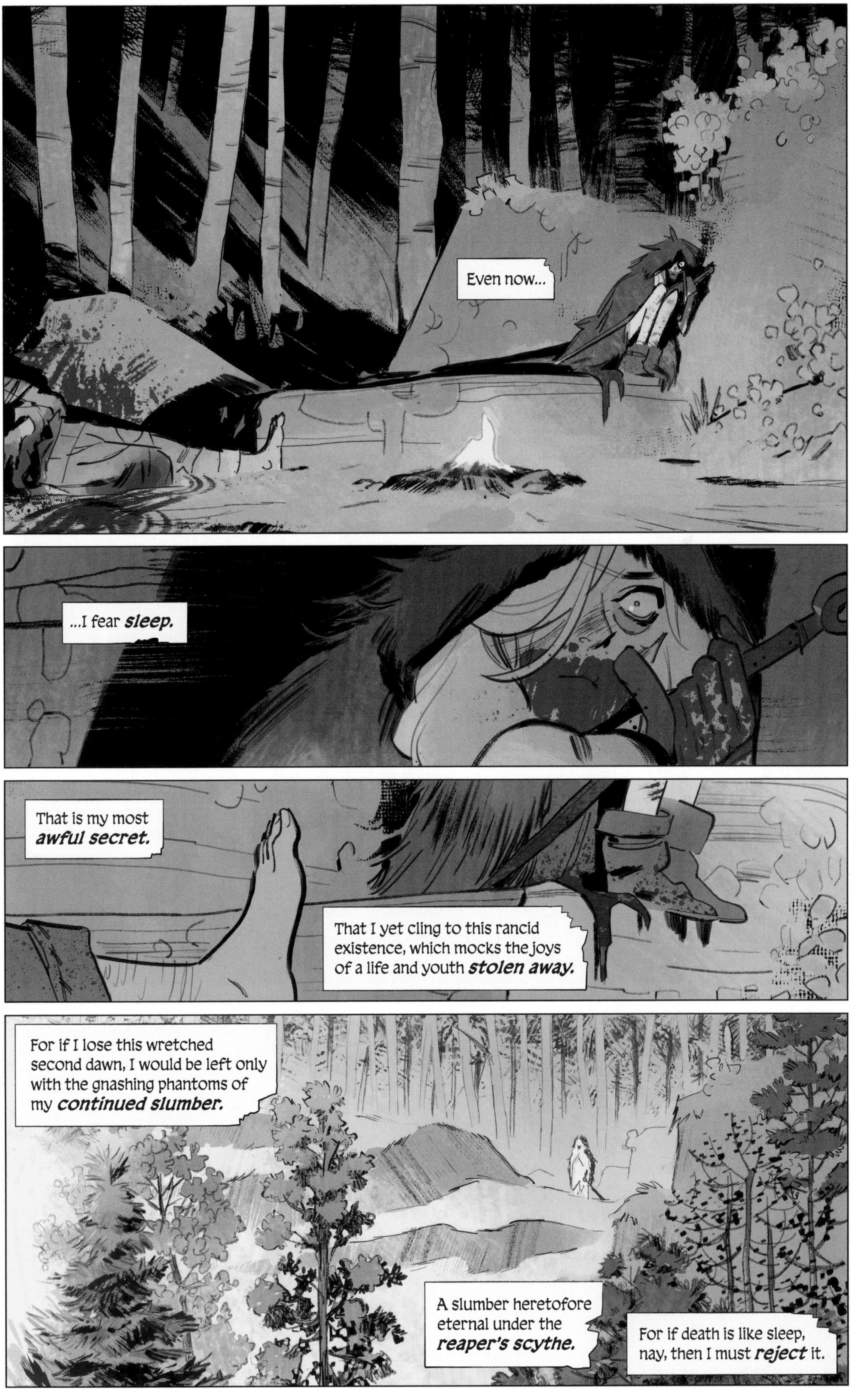
Even now...
...I fear sleep.
That is my most awful secret.
That I yet cling to this rancid existence, which mocks the joys of a life and youth stolen away.
For if I lose this wretched second dawn, I would be left only with the gnashing phantoms of my continued slumber.
A slumber heretofore eternal under the reaper's scythe.
For if death is like sleep, nay, then I must reject it.

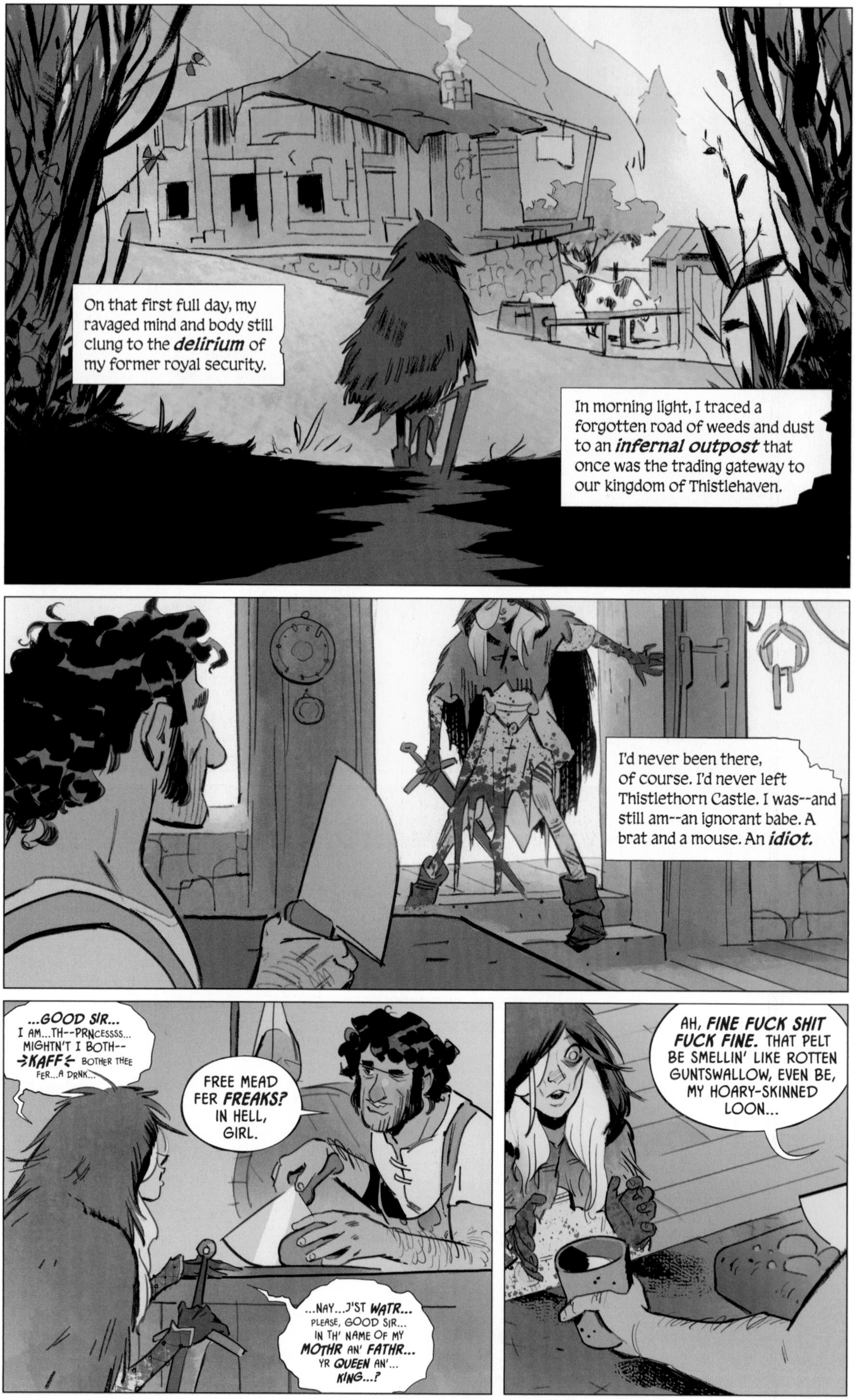
On that first full day, my ravaged mind and body still clung to the *delirium* of my former royal security.
In morning light, I traced a forgotten road of weeds and dust to an *infernal outpost* that once was the trading gateway to our kingdom of Thistlehaven.
I'd never been there, of course. I'd never left Thistlethorn Castle. I was--and still am--an ignorant babe. A brat and a mouse. An *idiot.*
...GOOD SIR... I AM...TH--PRNCESSSS... MIGHTN'T I BOTH-- ⇛KAFF⇚ BOTHER THEE FER...A DRNK...
FREE MEAD FER *FREAKS?* IN HELL, GIRL.
...NAY...J'ST *WATR...* PLEASE, GOOD SIR... IN TH' NAME OF MY *MOTHR* AN' *FATHR...* YR *QUEEN* AN'... *KING...?*
AH, *FINE FUCK SHIT FUCK FINE.* THAT PELT BE SMELLIN' LIKE ROTTEN GUNTSWALLOW, EVEN BE, MY HOARY-SKINNED LOON...

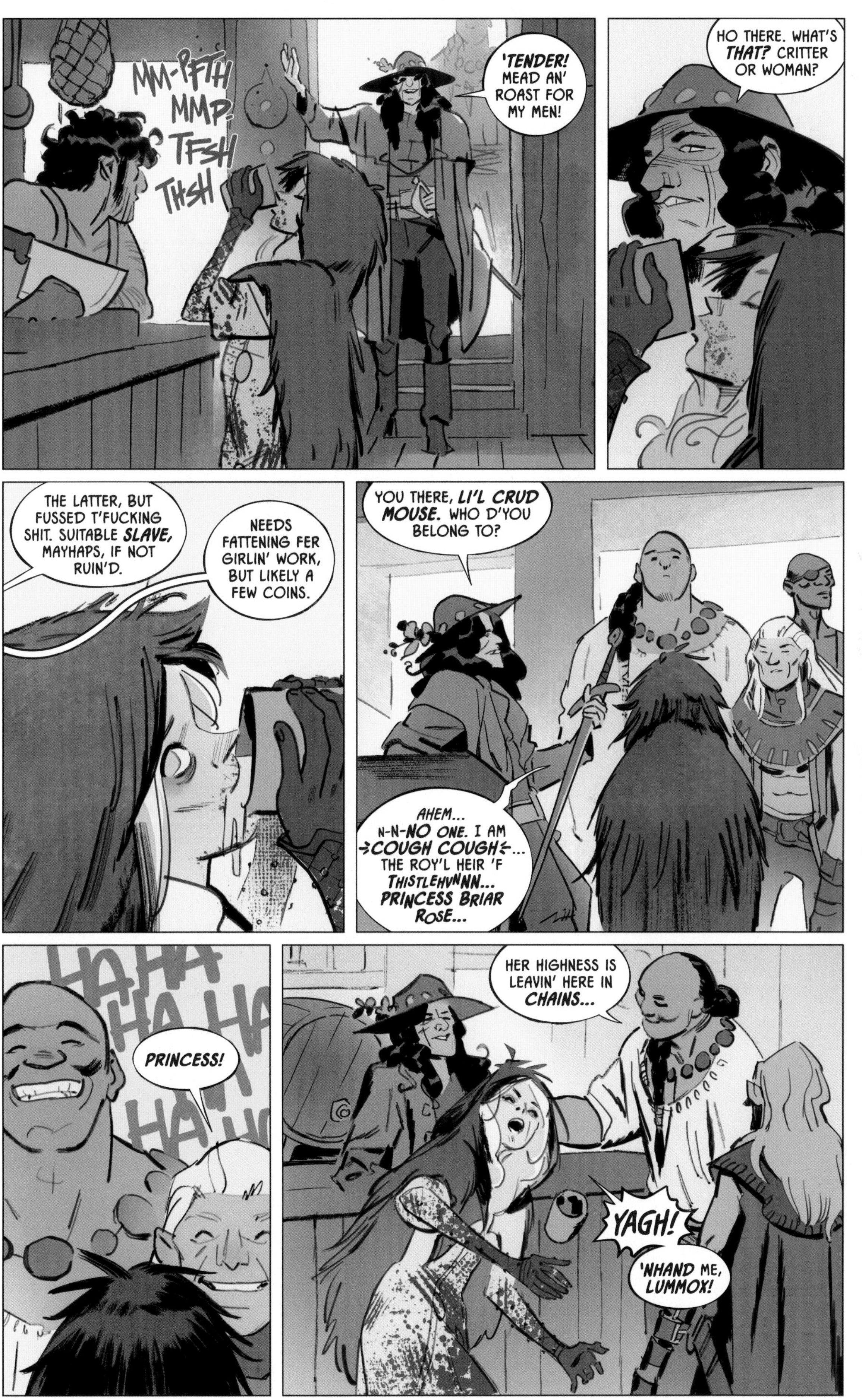
MM-PFTH
MMP-
TFSH
THSH
'TENDER! MEAD AN' ROAST FOR MY MEN!
HO THERE. WHAT'S THAT? CRITTER OR WOMAN?
THE LATTER, BUT FUSSED T'FUCKING SHIT. SUITABLE SLAVE, MAYHAPS, IF NOT RUIN'D.
NEEDS FATTENING FER GIRLIN' WORK, BUT LIKELY A FEW COINS.
YOU THERE, LI'L CRUD MOUSE. WHO D'YOU BELONG TO?
AHEM... N-N-NO ONE. I AM COUGH COUGH... THE ROY'L HEIR 'F THISTLEHVNNN... PRINCESS BRIAR ROSE...
HA HA HA HA HA
PRINCESS!
HER HIGHNESS IS LEAVIN' HERE IN CHAINS...
YAGH!
'NHAND ME, LUMMOX!

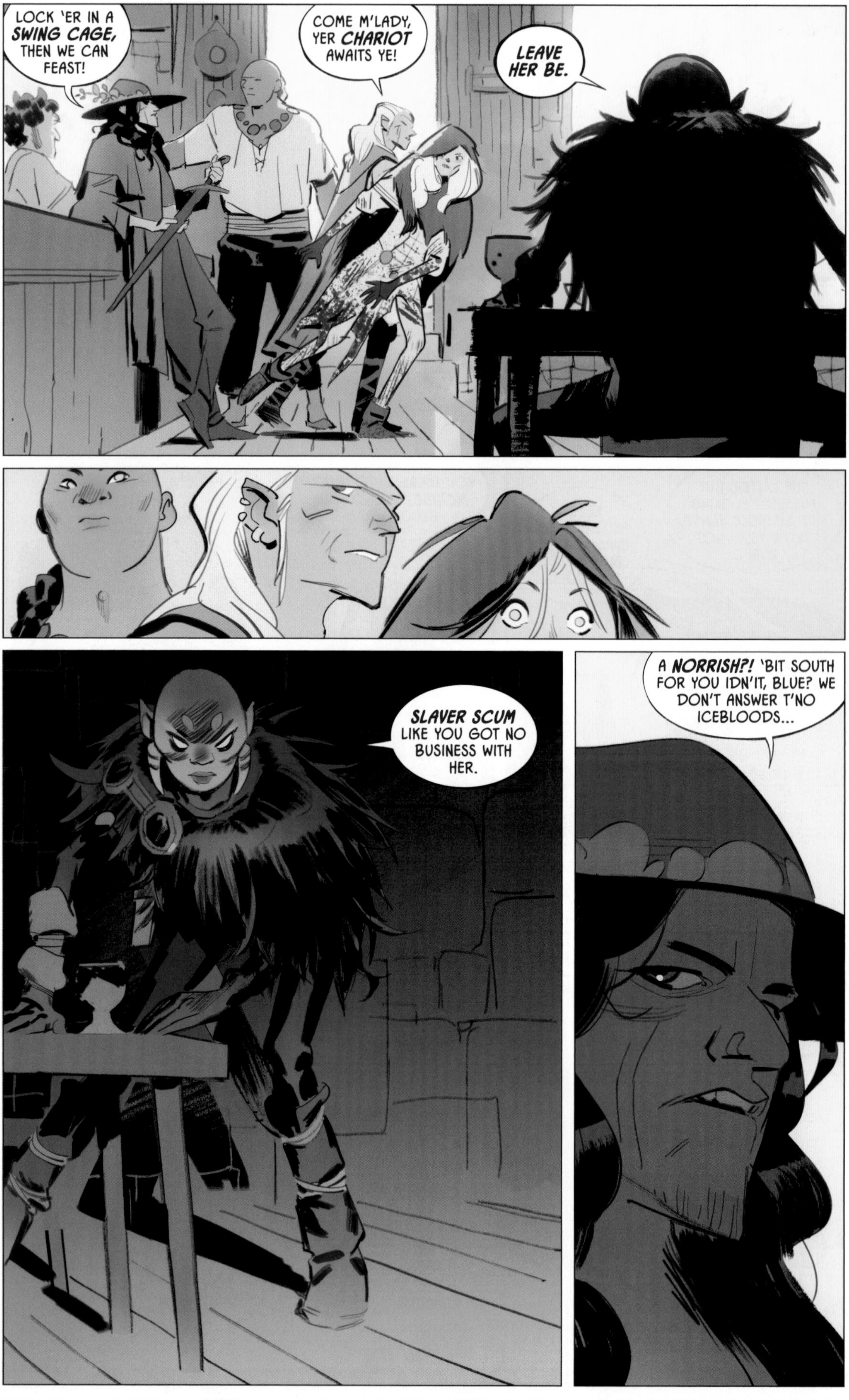
LOCK 'ER IN A SWING CAGE, THEN WE CAN FEAST!
COME M'LADY, YER CHARIOT AWAITS YE!
LEAVE HER BE.
SLAVER SCUM LIKE YOU GOT NO BUSINESS WITH HER.
A NORRISH?! 'BIT SOUTH FOR YOU IDN'IT, BLUE? WE DON'T ANSWER T'NO ICEBLOODS...

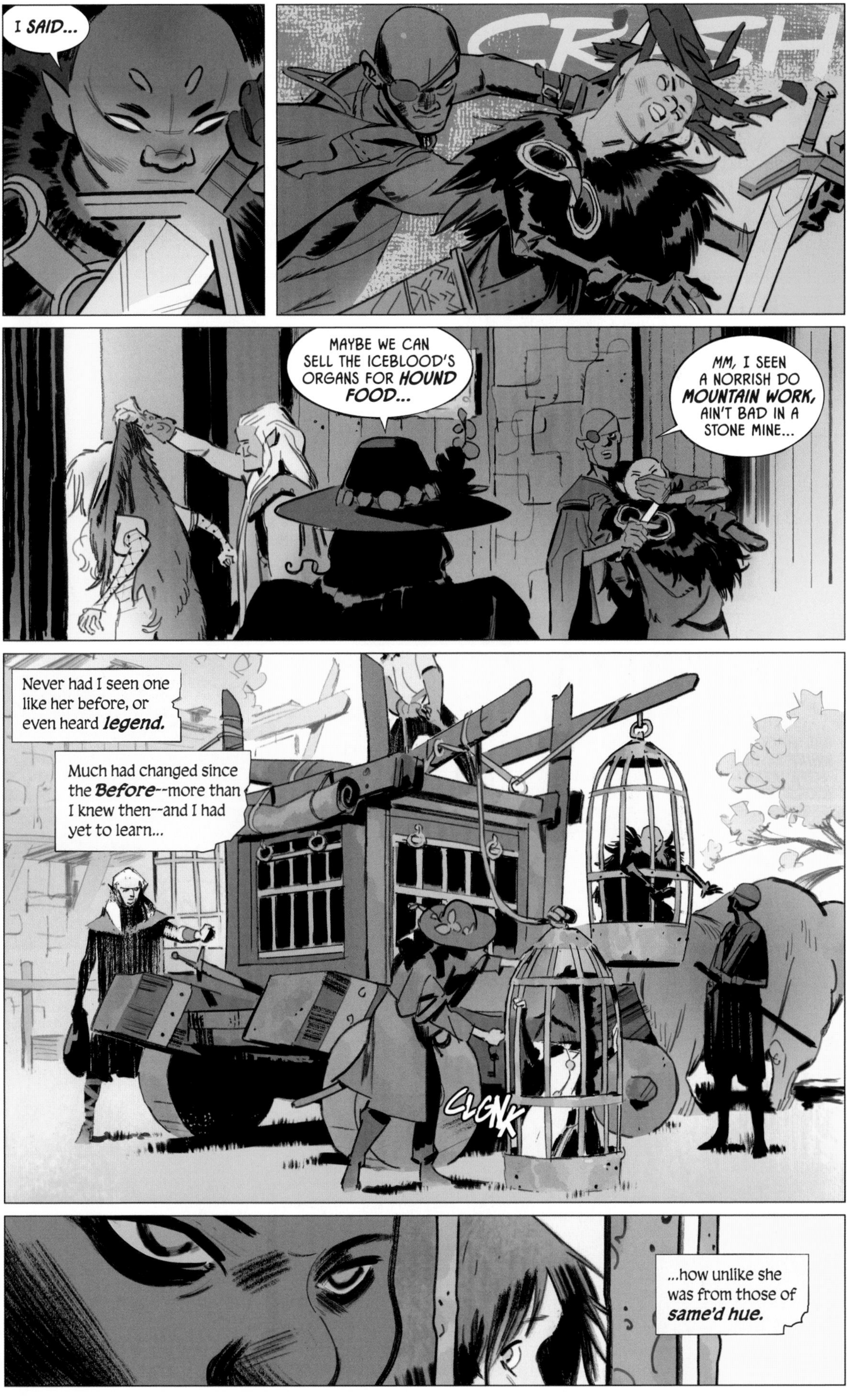
I SAID...
CRASH
MAYBE WE CAN SELL THE ICEBLOOD'S ORGANS FOR HOUND FOOD...
MM, I SEEN A NORRISH DO MOUNTAIN WORK, AIN'T BAD IN A STONE MINE...
Never had I seen one like her before, or even heard legend.
Much had changed since the Before--more than I knew then--and I had yet to learn...
CLGNK
...how unlike she was from those of same'd hue.

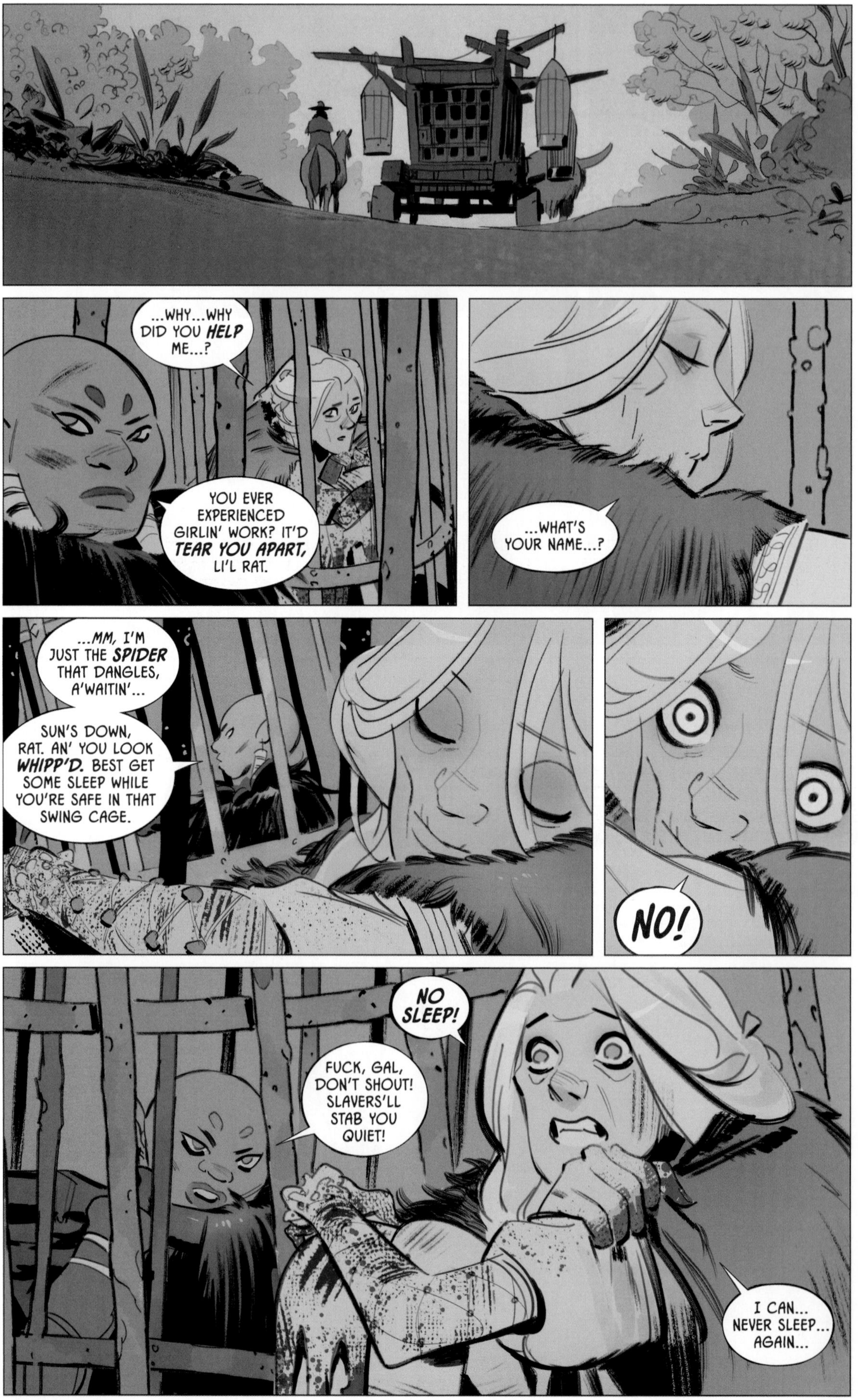

...WHY...WHY DID YOU HELP ME...?
YOU EVER EXPERIENCED GIRLIN' WORK? IT'D TEAR YOU APART, LI'L RAT.
...WHAT'S YOUR NAME...?
...MM, I'M JUST THE SPIDER THAT DANGLES, A'WAITIN'...
SUN'S DOWN, RAT. AN' YOU LOOK WHIPP'D. BEST GET SOME SLEEP WHILE YOU'RE SAFE IN THAT SWING CAGE.
NO!
NO SLEEP!
FUCK, GAL, DON'T SHOUT! SLAVERS'LL STAB YOU QUIET!
I CAN... NEVER SLEEP... AGAIN...

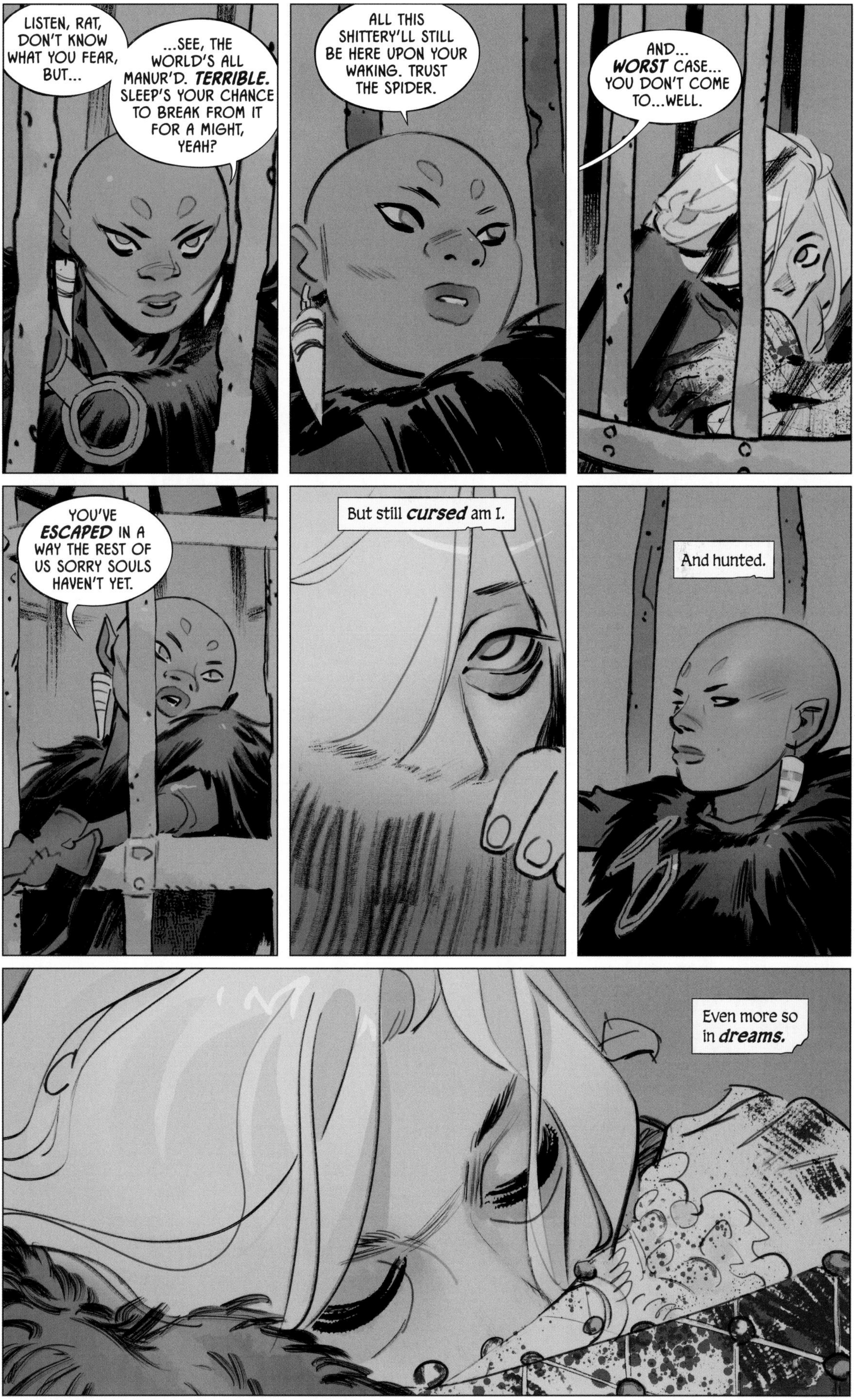
LISTEN, RAT, DON'T KNOW WHAT YOU FEAR, BUT...
...SEE, THE WORLD'S ALL MANUR'D. TERRIBLE. SLEEP'S YOUR CHANCE TO BREAK FROM IT FOR A MIGHT, YEAH?
ALL THIS SHITTERY'LL STILL BE HERE UPON YOUR WAKING. TRUST THE SPIDER.
AND... WORST CASE... YOU DON'T COME TO...WELL.
YOU'VE ESCAPED IN A WAY THE REST OF US SORRY SOULS HAVEN'T YET.
But still cursed am I.
And hunted.
Even more so in dreams.

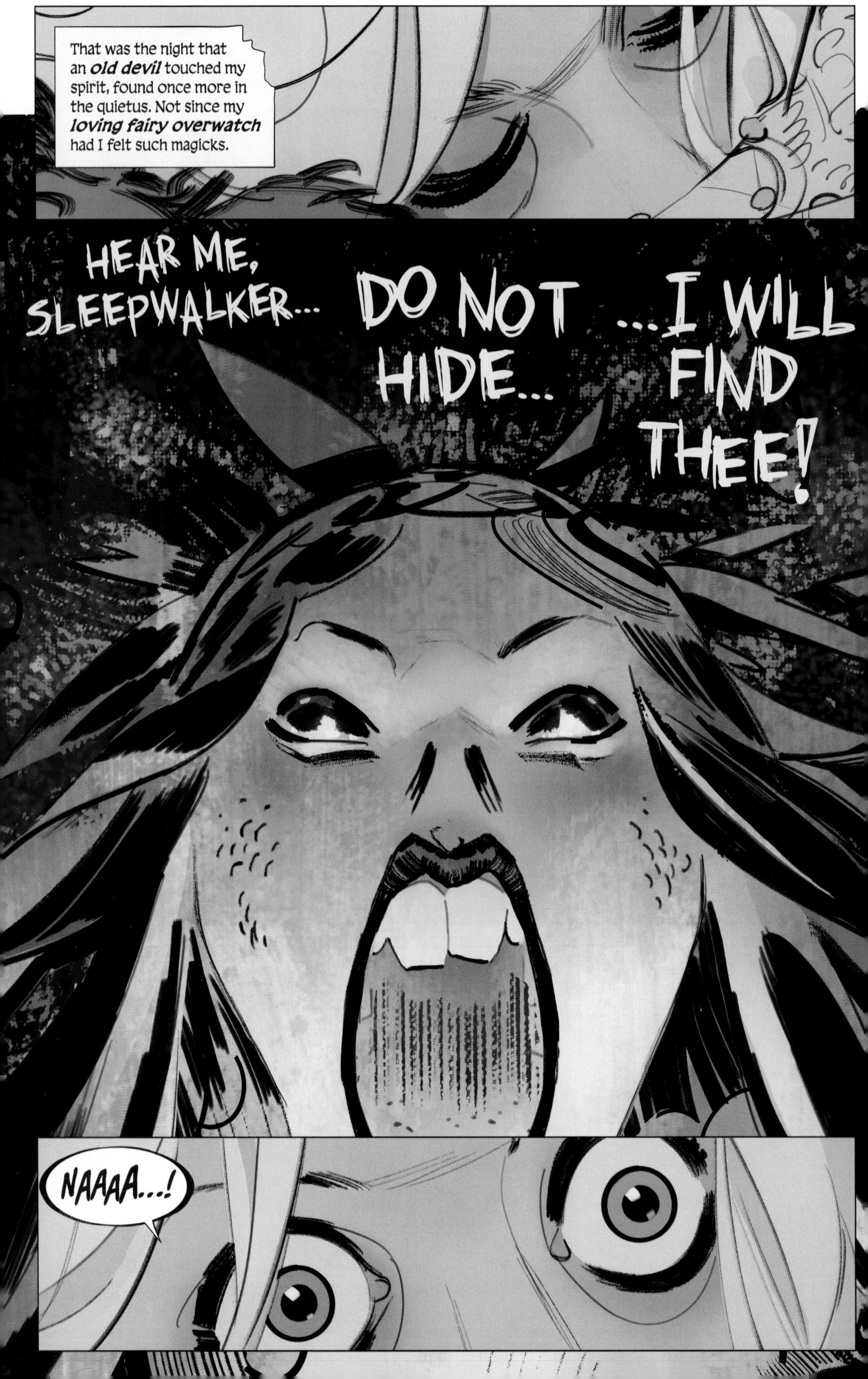

That was the night that an ***old devil*** touched my spirit, found once more in the quietus. Not since my ***loving fairy overwatch*** had I felt such magicks.
HEAR ME, SLEEPWALKER...
DO NOT HIDE...
...I WILL FIND THEE!
NAAAA...!

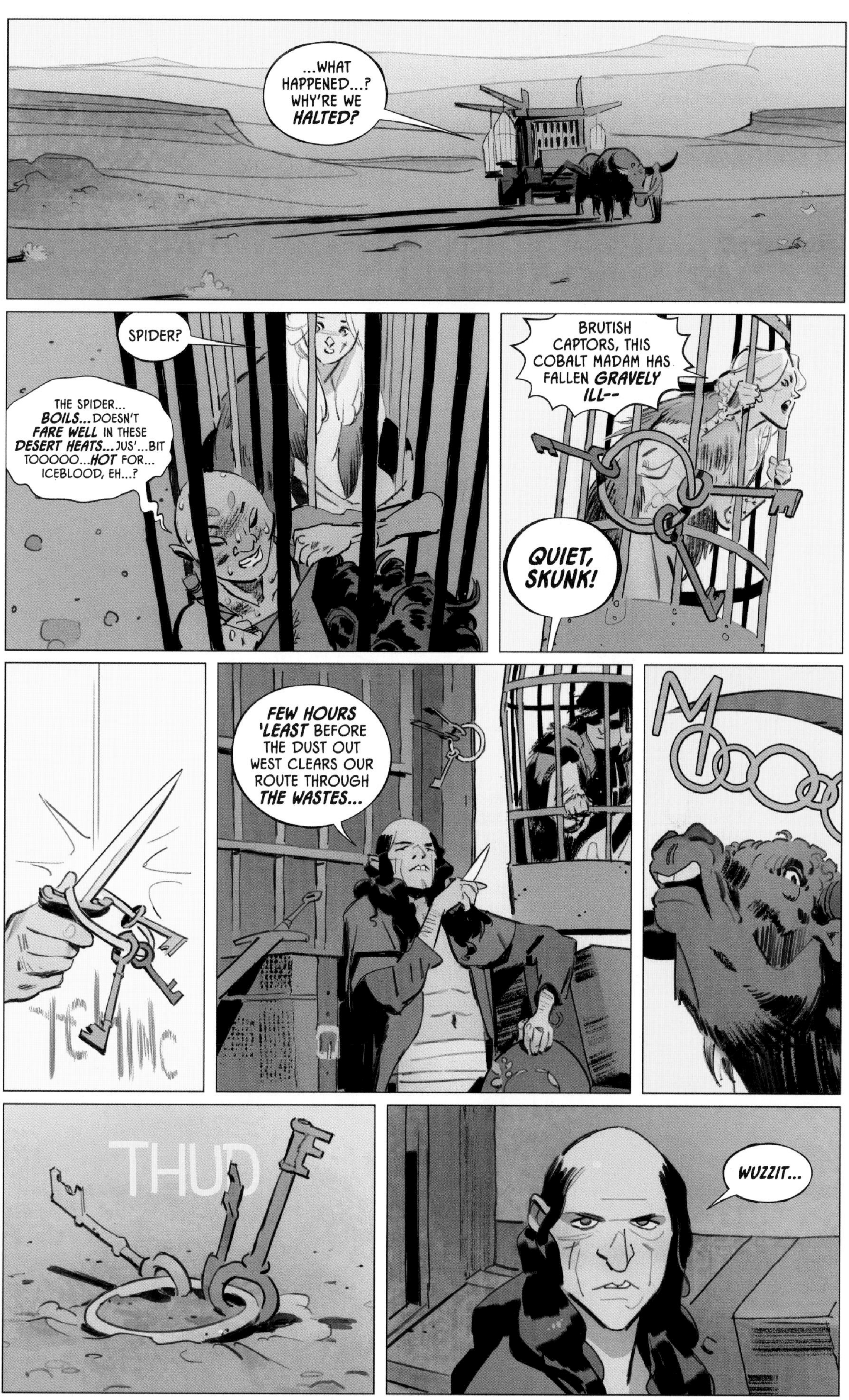
...WHAT HAPPENED...? WHY'RE WE HALTED?
SPIDER?
THE SPIDER... BOILS...DOESN'T FARE WELL IN THESE DESERT HEATS...JUS'...BIT TOOOOO...HOT FOR... ICEBLOOD, EH...?
BRUTISH CAPTORS, THIS COBALT MADAM HAS FALLEN GRAVELY ILL--
QUIET, SKUNK!
TCHINC
FEW HOURS 'LEAST BEFORE THE DUST OUT WEST CLEARS OUR ROUTE THROUGH THE WASTES...
MOOOOO
THUD
WUZZIT...

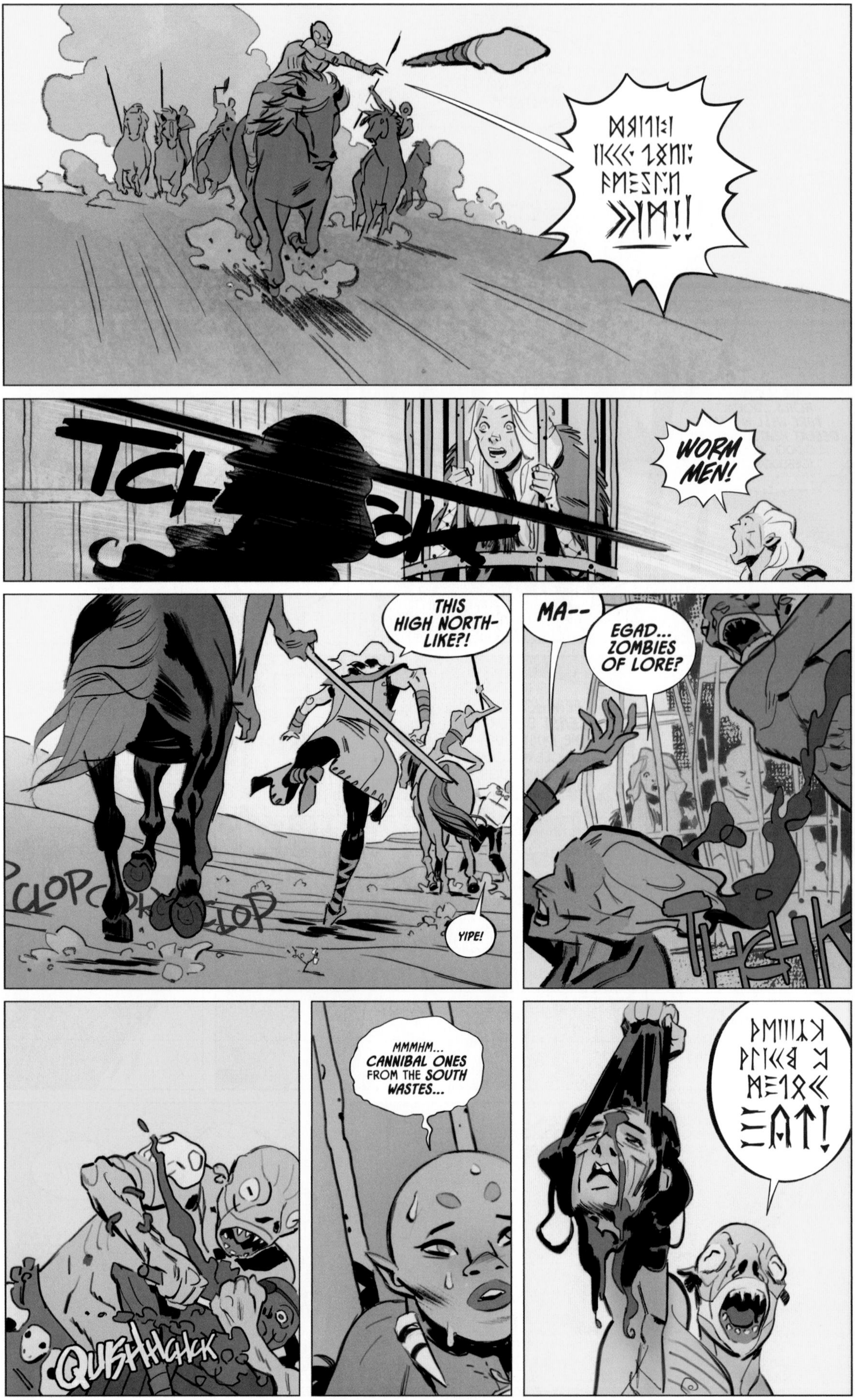
WORM MEN!
THIS HIGH NORTH-LIKE?!
YIPE!
MA--
EGAD... ZOMBIES OF LORE?
MMMHM... CANNIBAL ONES FROM THE SOUTH WASTES...

...NOW THEY'LL CARRY OFF THEIR FEASTS TO THE TAR PITS...
...BOILED SPIDER...
WAIT!!
HELLLLP! SOMEONE!!!
...TOL' YOU THE SHITTERY PREVAILS... ...MUS' BE QUITE A SHOCK T'YER FRAGILE HIGHNESS...
WHY NOT... WHY NOT EAT US...?
T'THEM, NORRISH MEAT'S POISONOUS... AND YOU'RE JUS' BONES...
CLICK

HOW DID YOU... WITHOUT THE KEYS INSIDE YOUR OWN CAGE...?

DUFF

CLACLK

I CAN *AID* YOU...

...NAY...

YES. AS YOU AIDED ME...

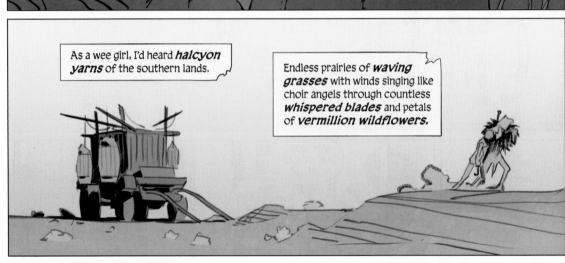

As a wee girl, I'd heard *halcyon yarns* of the southern lands.

Endless prairies of *waving grasses* with winds singing like choir angels through countless *whispered blades* and petals of *vermillion wildflowers*.

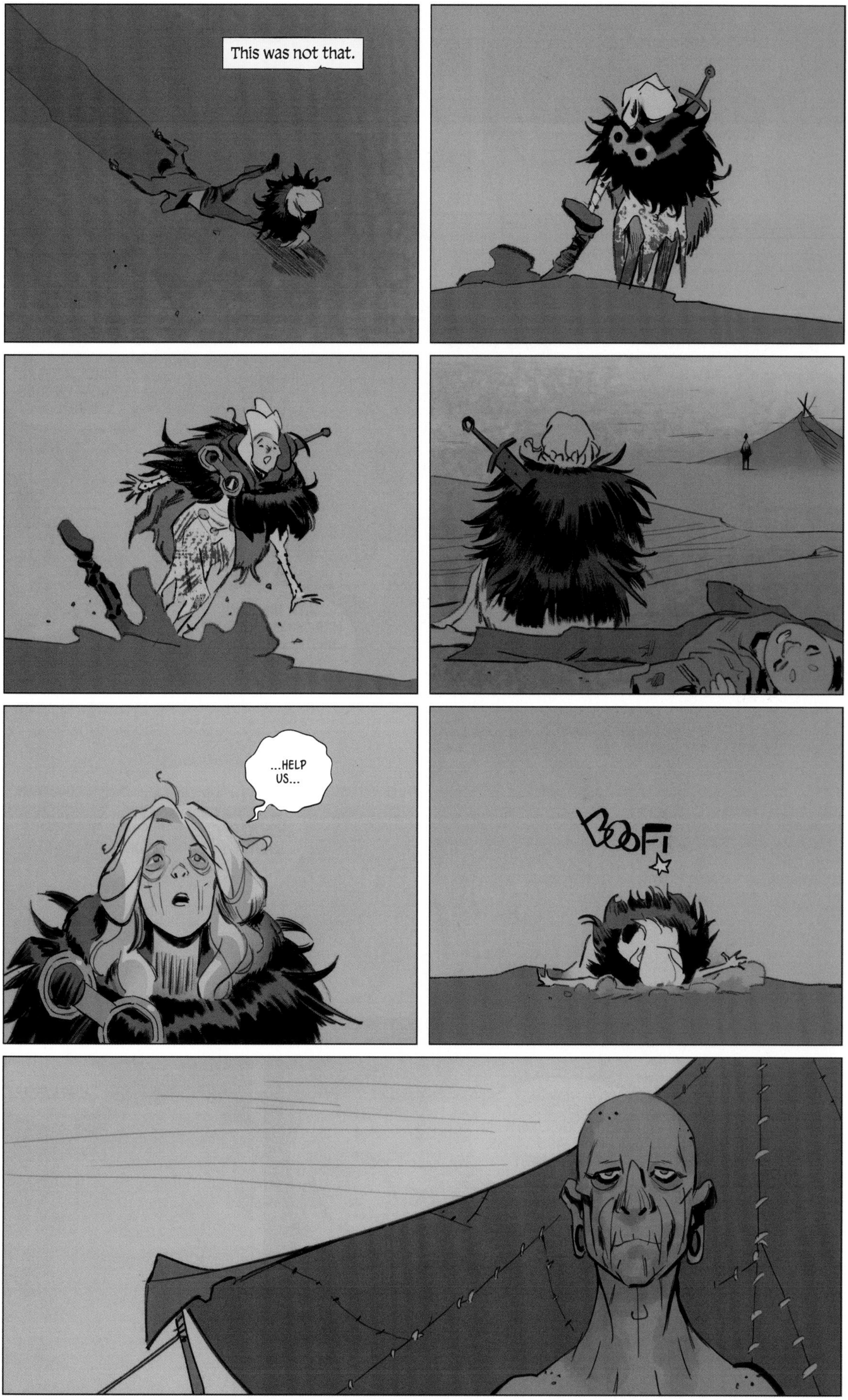

This was not that.
...HELP US...
BOOF!

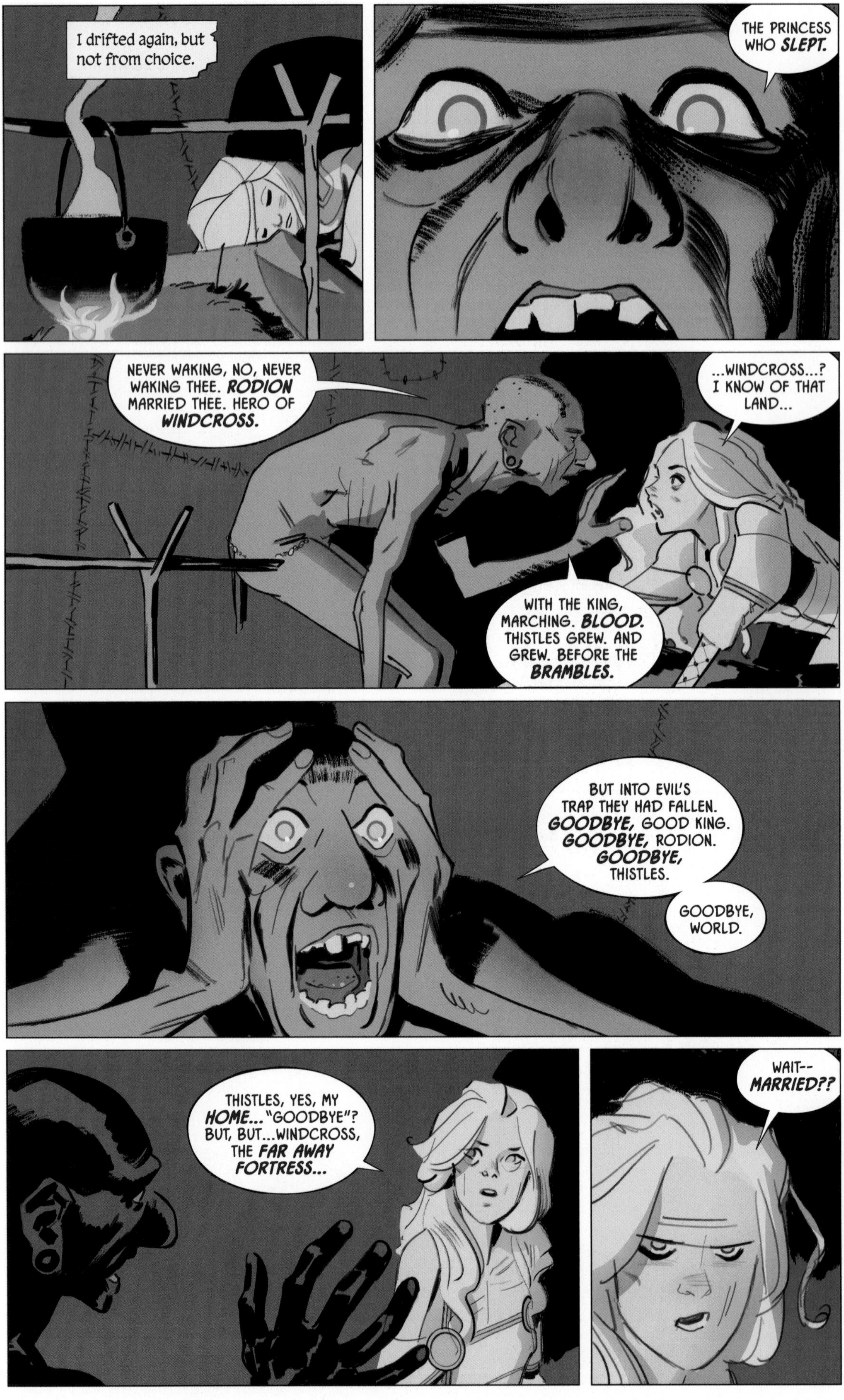
I drifted again, but not from choice.
THE PRINCESS WHO *SLEPT.*
NEVER WAKING, NO, NEVER WAKING THEE. *RODION* MARRIED THEE. HERO OF *WINDCROSS.*
...WINDCROSS...? I KNOW OF THAT LAND...
WITH THE KING, MARCHING. *BLOOD.* THISTLES GREW. AND GREW. BEFORE THE *BRAMBLES.*
BUT INTO EVIL'S TRAP THEY HAD FALLEN. *GOODBYE,* GOOD KING. *GOODBYE,* RODION. *GOODBYE,* THISTLES.
GOODBYE, WORLD.
THISTLES, YES, MY *HOME...* "GOODBYE"? BUT, BUT...WINDCROSS, THE *FAR AWAY FORTRESS...*
WAIT-- *MARRIED??*

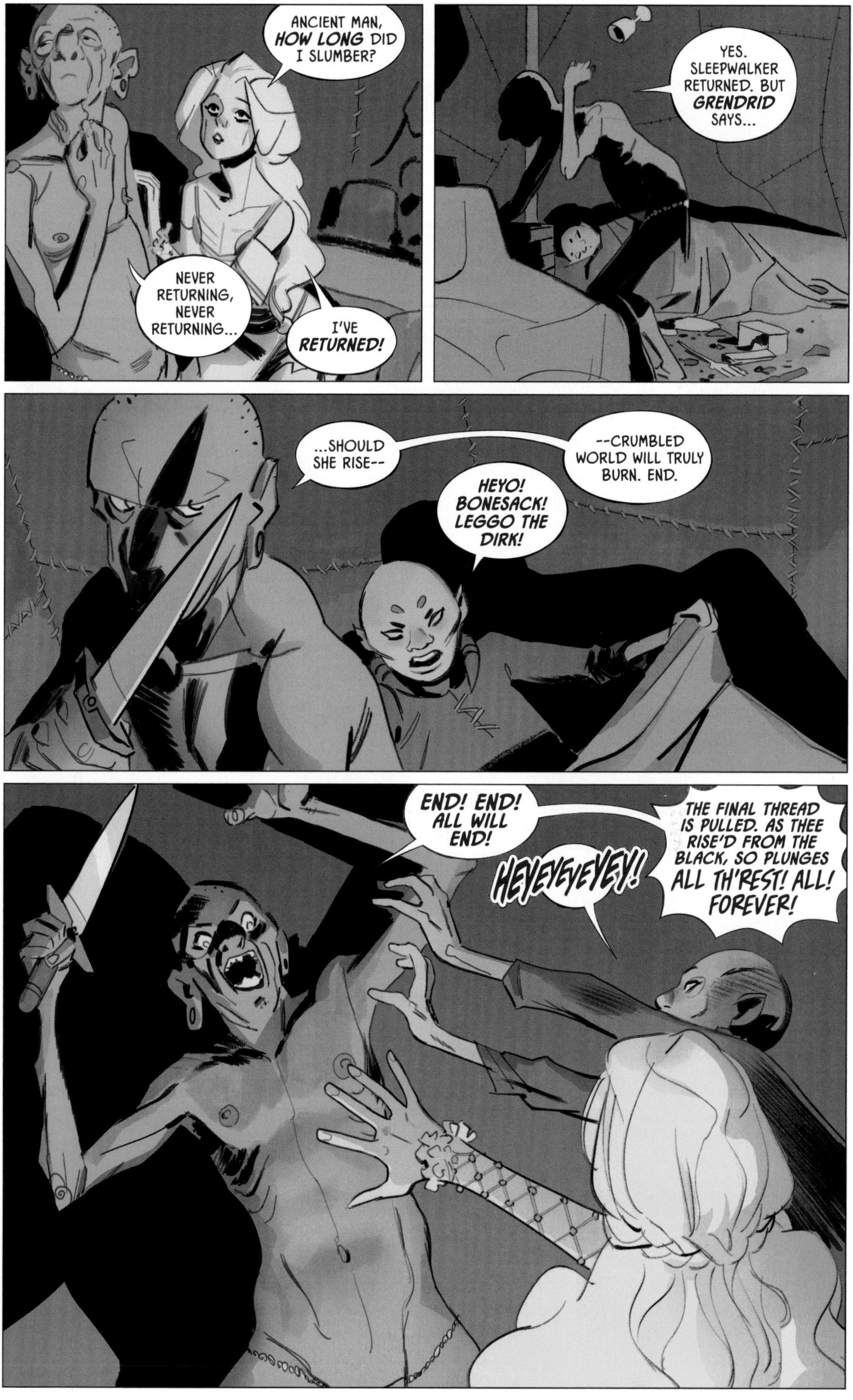
ANCIENT MAN, HOW LONG DID I SLUMBER?
NEVER RETURNING, NEVER RETURNING...
I'VE RETURNED!
YES. SLEEPWALKER RETURNED. BUT GRENDRID SAYS...
...SHOULD SHE RISE--
--CRUMBLED WORLD WILL TRULY BURN. END.
HEYO! BONESACK! LEGGO THE DIRK!
END! END! ALL WILL END!
HEYEYEYEYEY!
THE FINAL THREAD IS PULLED. AS THEE RISE'D FROM THE BLACK, SO PLUNGES ALL TH'REST! ALL! FOREVER!

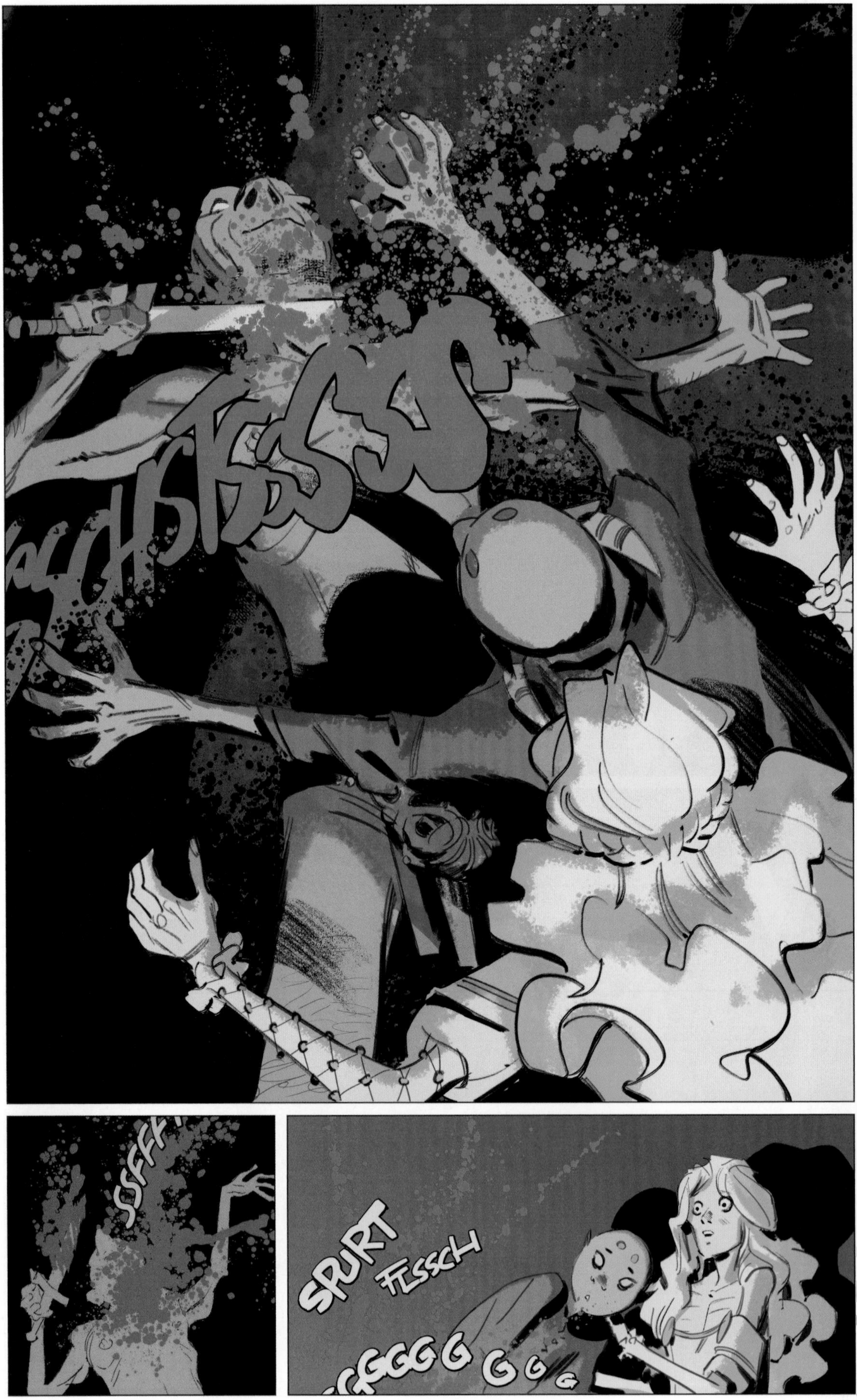
SPURT
FSSCH

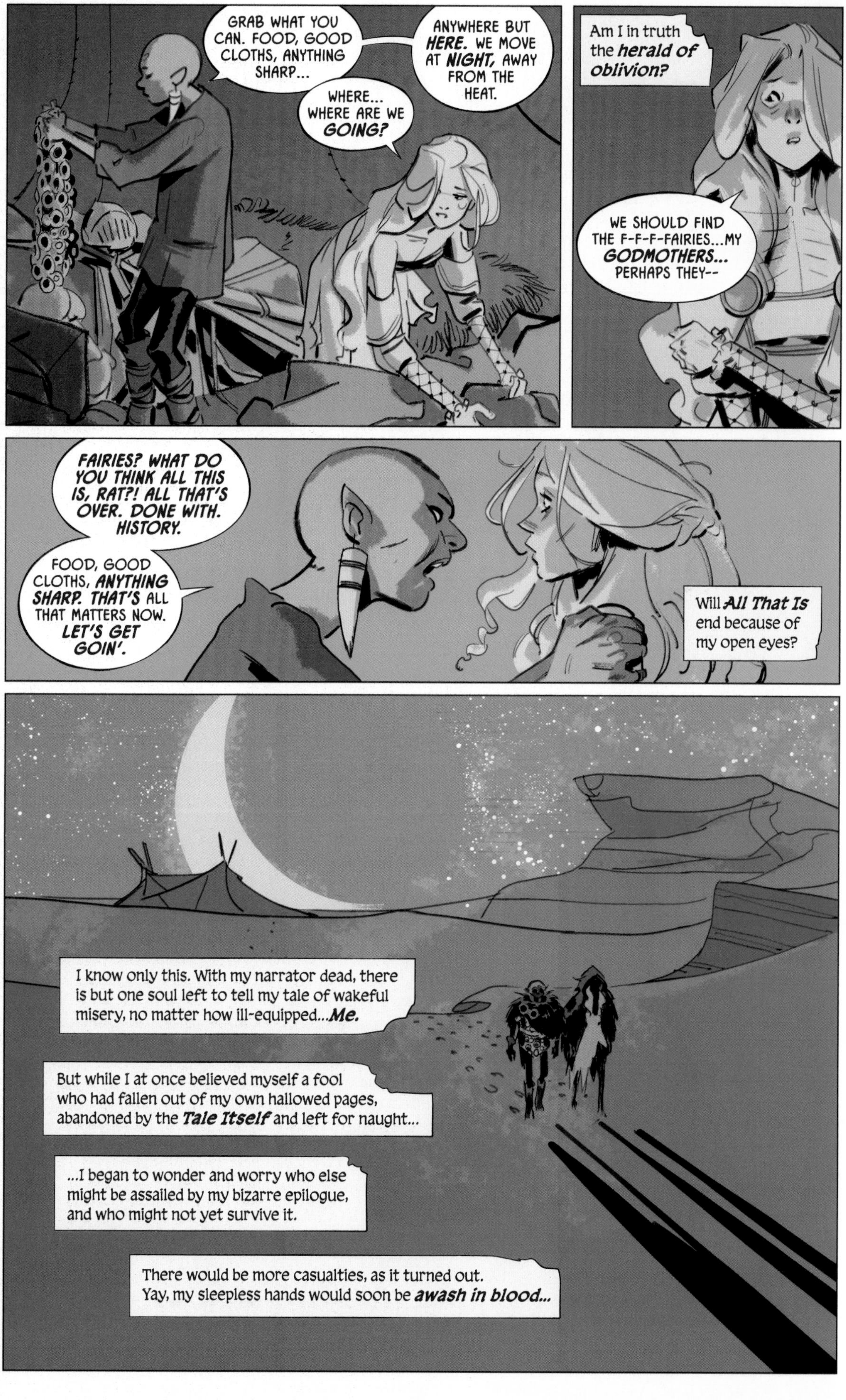
GRAB WHAT YOU CAN. FOOD, GOOD CLOTHS, ANYTHING SHARP...
WHERE... WHERE ARE WE GOING?
ANYWHERE BUT HERE. WE MOVE AT NIGHT, AWAY FROM THE HEAT.
Am I in truth the herald of oblivion?
WE SHOULD FIND THE F-F-F-FAIRIES...MY GODMOTHERS... PERHAPS THEY--
FAIRIES? WHAT DO YOU THINK ALL THIS IS, RAT?! ALL THAT'S OVER. DONE WITH. HISTORY.
FOOD, GOOD CLOTHS, ANYTHING SHARP. THAT'S ALL THAT MATTERS NOW. LET'S GET GOIN'.
Will All That Is end because of my open eyes?
I know only this. With my narrator dead, there is but one soul left to tell my tale of wakeful misery, no matter how ill-equipped...Me.
But while I at once believed myself a fool who had fallen out of my own hallowed pages, abandoned by the Tale Itself and left for naught...
...I began to wonder and worry who else might be assailed by my bizarre epilogue, and who might not yet survive it.
There would be more casualties, as it turned out. Yay, my sleepless hands would soon be awash in blood...

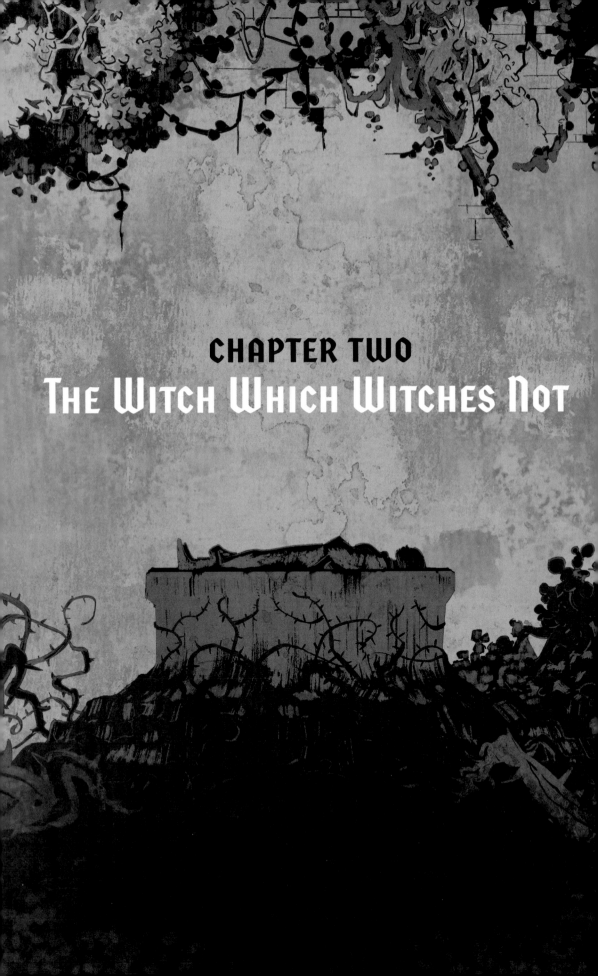

CHAPTER TWO
THE WITCH WHICH WITCHES NOT

Why was it that a *spindle* pronounced my destiny?

Well, it is said that a spindle winds the *threads of fate* on *life's fulminous loom.*

SPAATCH

Or so I was told in *childish stories.*

For now, it seems that *all* the great fabric woven is *unraveling.*

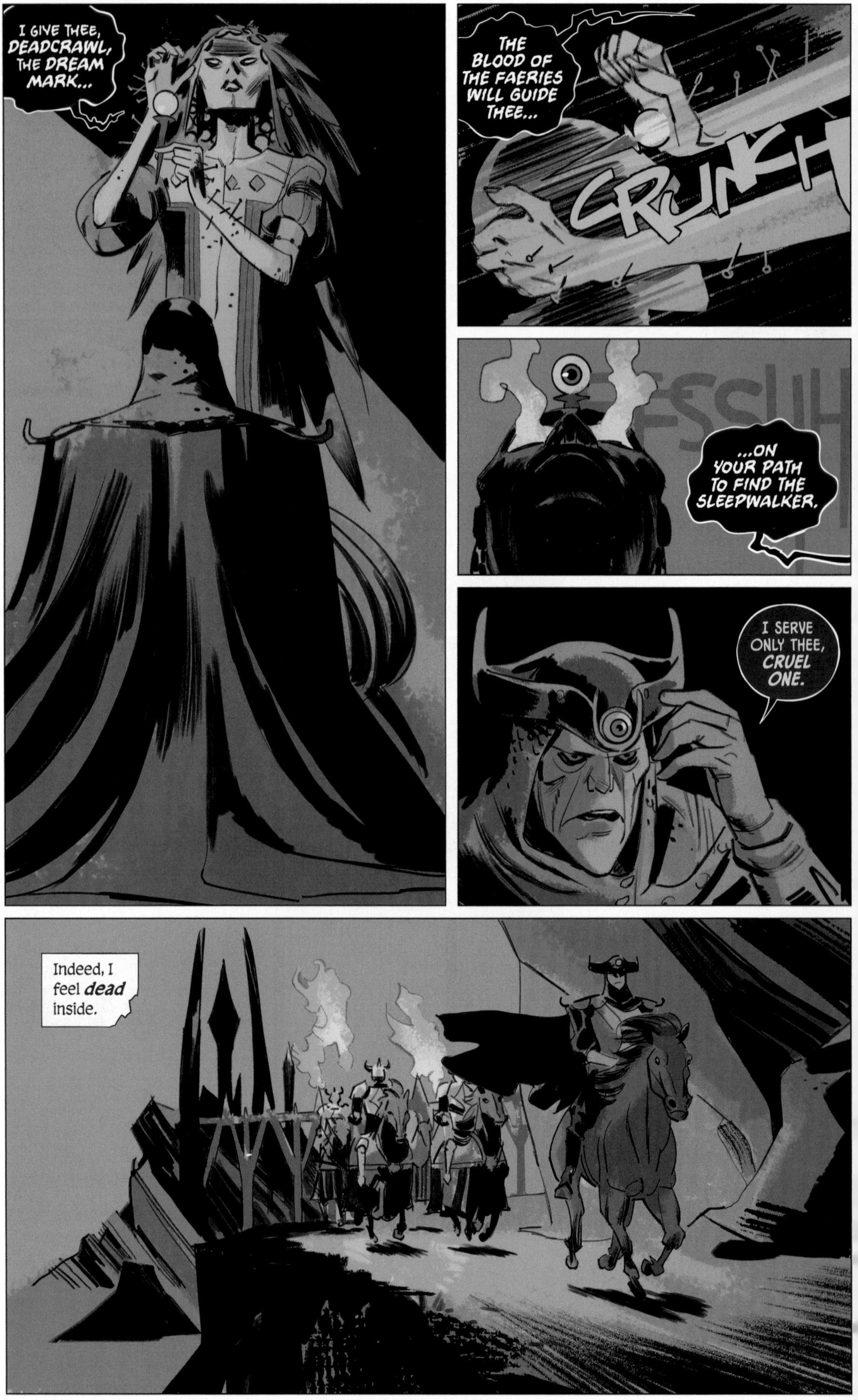

I GIVE THEE, DEADCRAWL, THE DREAM MARK...
THE BLOOD OF THE FAERIES WILL GUIDE THEE...
CRUNCH
...ON YOUR PATH TO FIND THE SLEEPWALKER.
I SERVE ONLY THEE, CRUEL ONE.
Indeed, I feel *dead* inside.

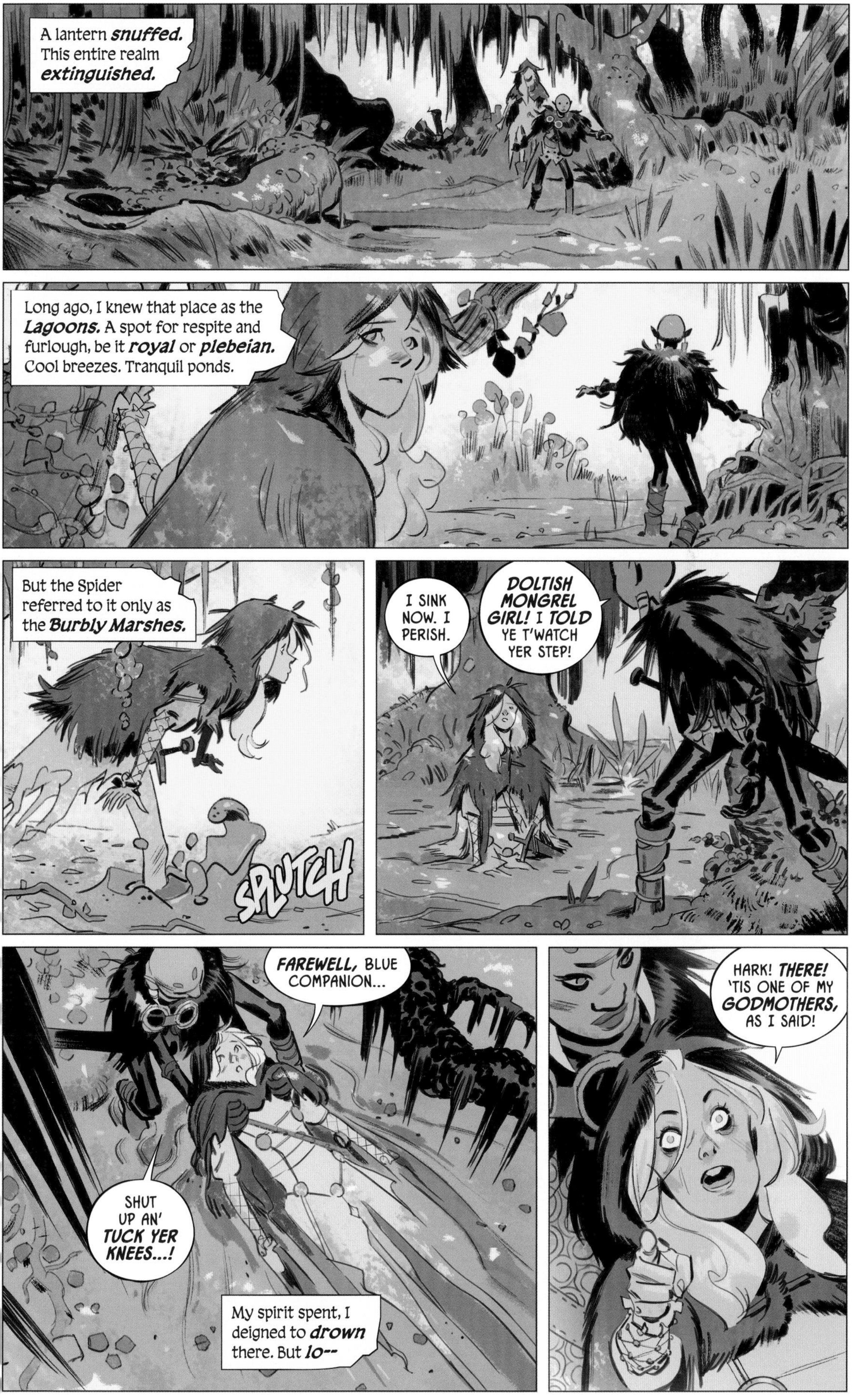

A lantern snuffed. This entire realm extinguished.
Long ago, I knew that place as the Lagoons. A spot for respite and furlough, be it royal or plebeian. Cool breezes. Tranquil ponds.
But the Spider referred to it only as the Burbly Marshes.
SPLUTCH
I SINK NOW. I PERISH.
DOLTISH MONGREL GIRL! I TOLD YE T'WATCH YER STEP!
FAREWELL, BLUE COMPANION...
SHUT UP AN' TUCK YER KNEES...!
My spirit spent, I deigned to drown there. But lo--
HARK! THERE! 'TIS ONE OF MY GODMOTHERS, AS I SAID!

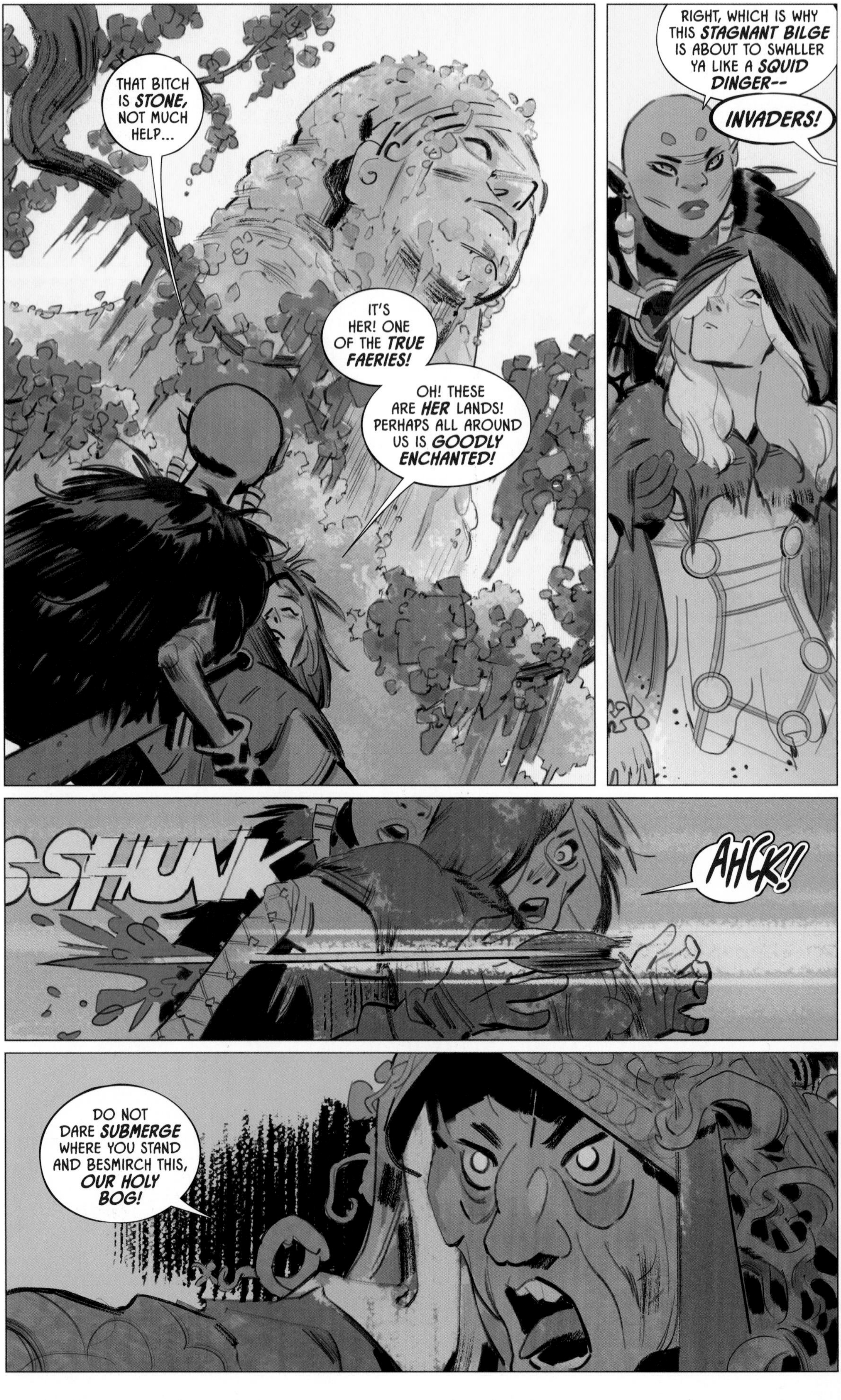
THAT BITCH IS STONE, NOT MUCH HELP...
IT'S HER! ONE OF THE TRUE FAERIES!
OH! THESE ARE HER LANDS! PERHAPS ALL AROUND US IS GOODLY ENCHANTED!
RIGHT, WHICH IS WHY THIS STAGNANT BILGE IS ABOUT TO SWALLER YA LIKE A SQUID DINGER--
INVADERS!
SSHUNK
AHCK!!
DO NOT DARE SUBMERGE WHERE YOU STAND AND BESMIRCH THIS, OUR HOLY BOG!

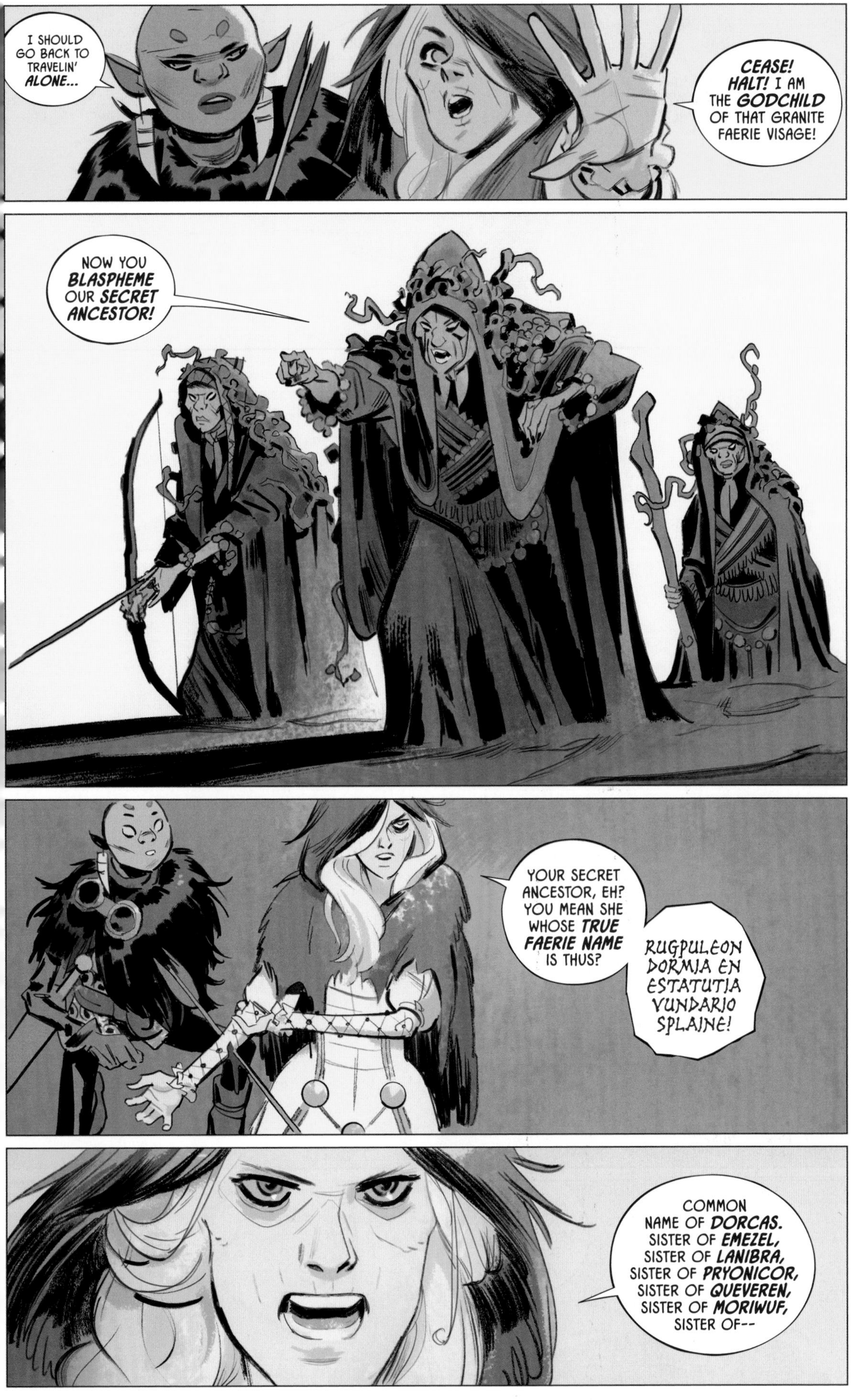
I SHOULD GO BACK TO TRAVELIN' ALONE...
CEASE! HALT! I AM THE GODCHILD OF THAT GRANITE FAERIE VISAGE!
NOW YOU BLASPHEME OUR SECRET ANCESTOR!
YOUR SECRET ANCESTOR, EH? YOU MEAN SHE WHOSE TRUE FAERIE NAME IS THUS?
RUGPULEON DORMJA EN ESTATUTJA VUNDARJO SPLAJNE!
COMMON NAME OF DORCAS. SISTER OF EMEZEL, SISTER OF LANIBRA, SISTER OF PRYONICOR, SISTER OF QUEVEREN, SISTER OF MORIWUF, SISTER OF--

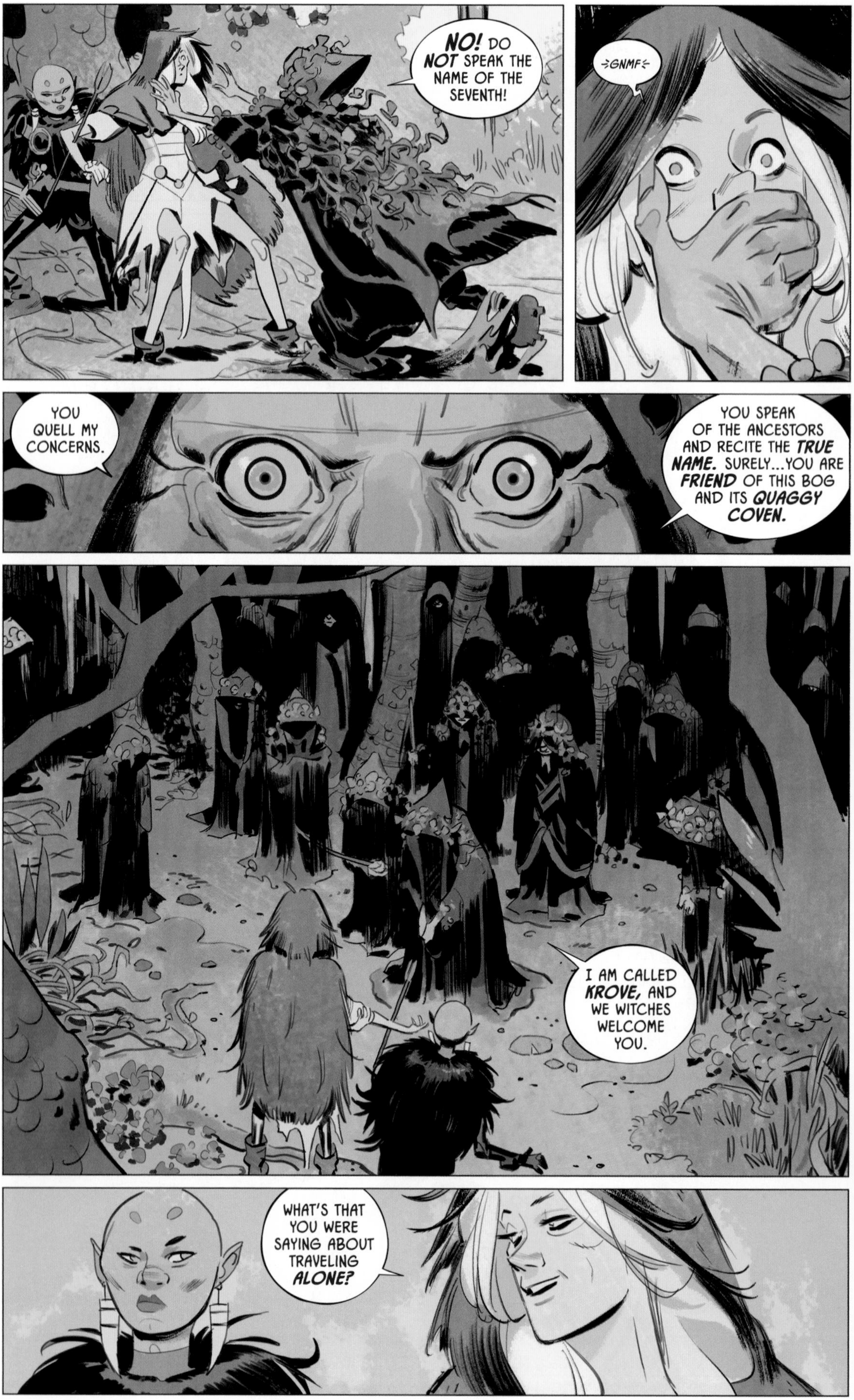
NO! DO NOT SPEAK THE NAME OF THE SEVENTH!
GNMF
YOU QUELL MY CONCERNS.
YOU SPEAK OF THE ANCESTORS AND RECITE THE TRUE NAME. SURELY...YOU ARE FRIEND OF THIS BOG AND ITS QUAGGY COVEN.
I AM CALLED KROVE, AND WE WITCHES WELCOME YOU.
WHAT'S THAT YOU WERE SAYING ABOUT TRAVELING ALONE?

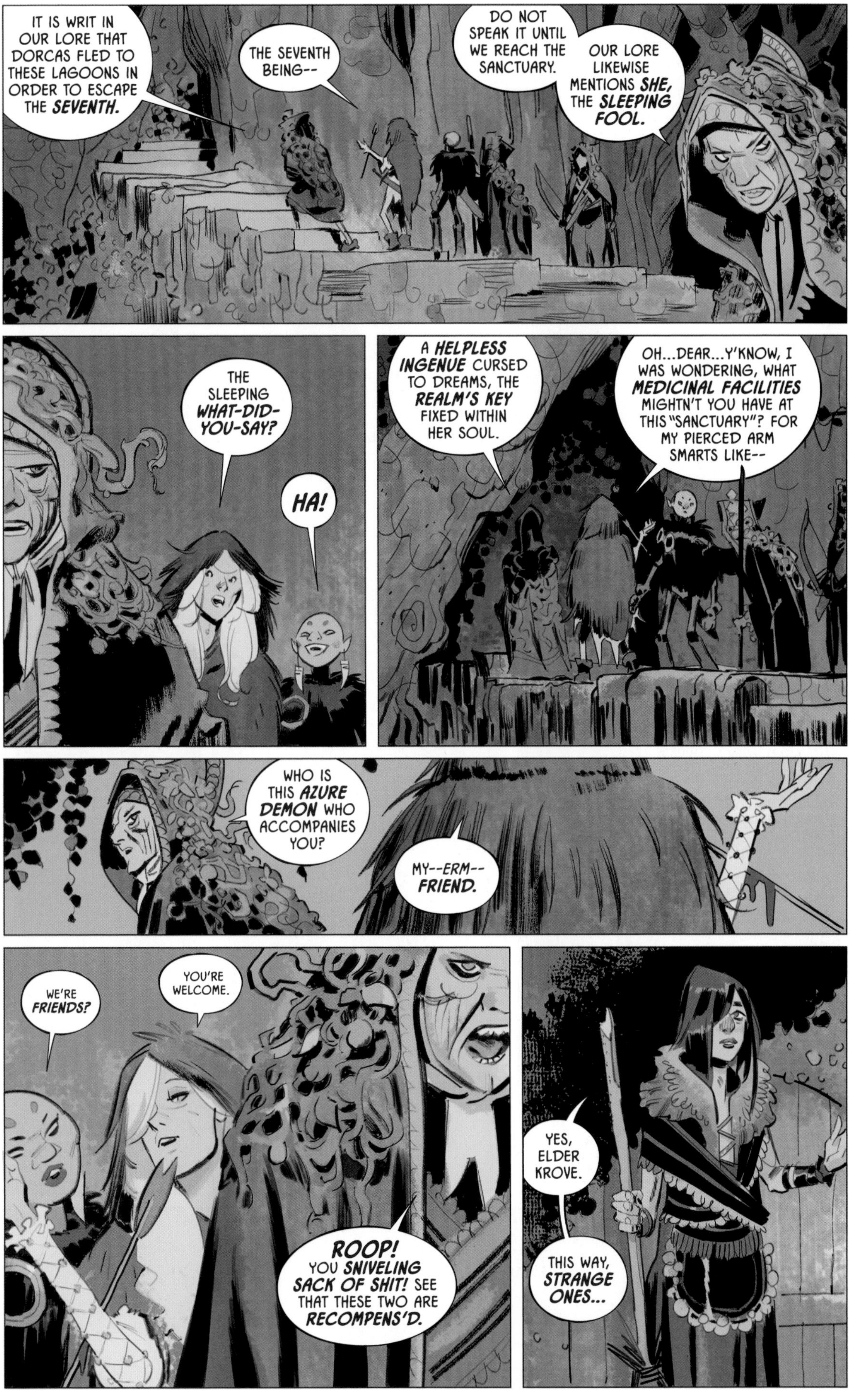
IT IS WRIT IN OUR LORE THAT DORCAS FLED TO THESE LAGOONS IN ORDER TO ESCAPE THE SEVENTH.
THE SEVENTH BEING--
DO NOT SPEAK IT UNTIL WE REACH THE SANCTUARY.
OUR LORE LIKEWISE MENTIONS SHE, THE SLEEPING FOOL.
THE SLEEPING WHAT-DID-YOU-SAY?
HA!
A HELPLESS INGENUE CURSED TO DREAMS, THE REALM'S KEY FIXED WITHIN HER SOUL.
OH...DEAR...Y'KNOW, I WAS WONDERING, WHAT MEDICINAL FACILITIES MIGHTN'T YOU HAVE AT THIS "SANCTUARY"? FOR MY PIERCED ARM SMARTS LIKE--
WHO IS THIS AZURE DEMON WHO ACCOMPANIES YOU?
MY--ERM--FRIEND.
WE'RE FRIENDS?
YOU'RE WELCOME.
ROOP! YOU SNIVELING SACK OF SHIT! SEE THAT THESE TWO ARE RECOMPENS'D.
YES, ELDER KROVE.
THIS WAY, STRANGE ONES...

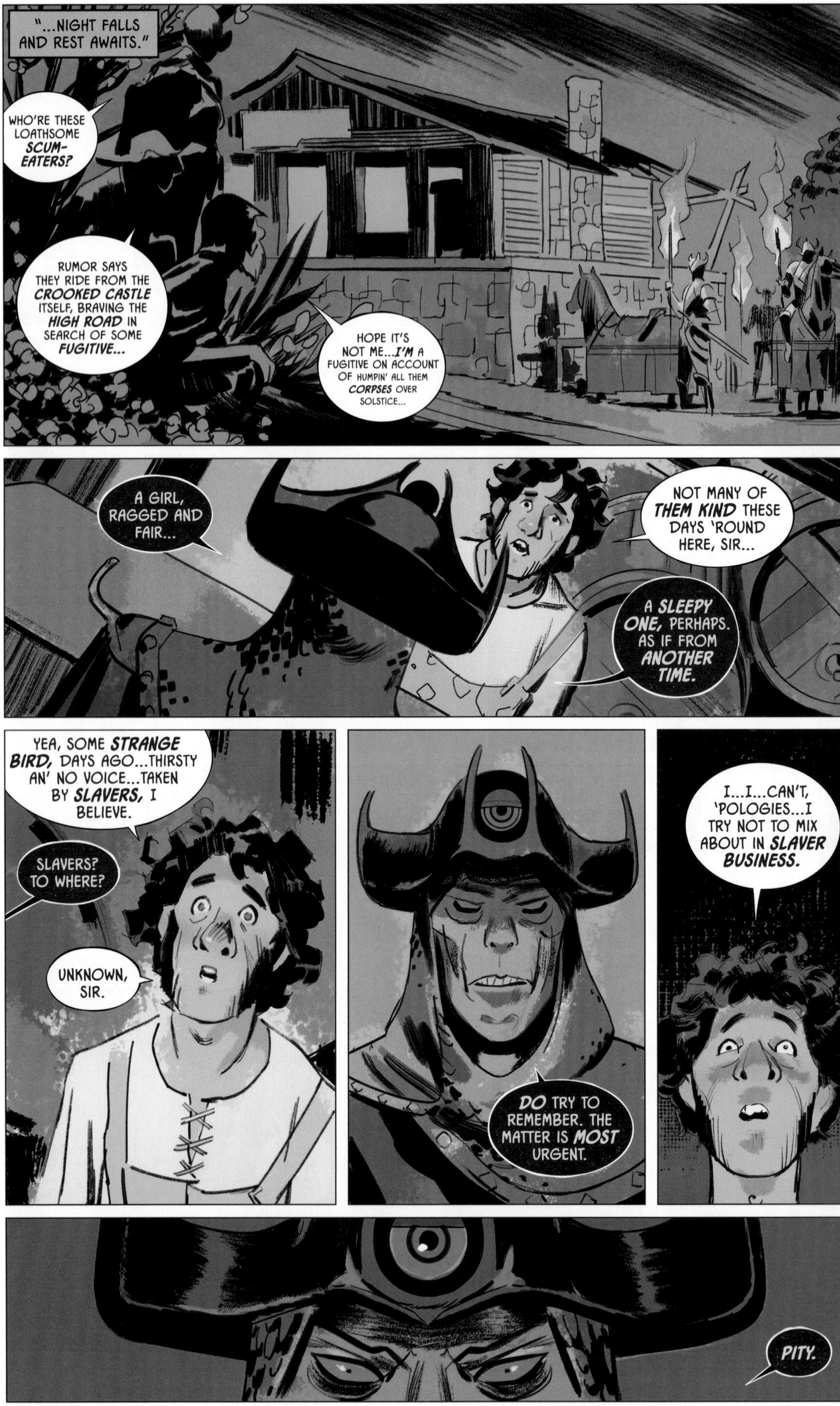
"...NIGHT FALLS AND REST AWAITS."
WHO'RE THESE LOATHSOME SCUM-EATERS?
RUMOR SAYS THEY RIDE FROM THE CROOKED CASTLE ITSELF, BRAVING THE HIGH ROAD IN SEARCH OF SOME FUGITIVE...
HOPE IT'S NOT ME...I'M A FUGITIVE ON ACCOUNT OF HUMPIN' ALL THEM CORPSES OVER SOLSTICE...
A GIRL, RAGGED AND FAIR...
NOT MANY OF THEM KIND THESE DAYS 'ROUND HERE, SIR...
A SLEEPY ONE, PERHAPS. AS IF FROM ANOTHER TIME.
YEA, SOME STRANGE BIRD, DAYS AGO...THIRSTY AN' NO VOICE...TAKEN BY SLAVERS, I BELIEVE.
SLAVERS? TO WHERE?
UNKNOWN, SIR.
DO TRY TO REMEMBER. THE MATTER IS MOST URGENT.
I...I...CAN'T, 'POLOGIES...I TRY NOT TO MIX ABOUT IN SLAVER BUSINESS.
PITY.

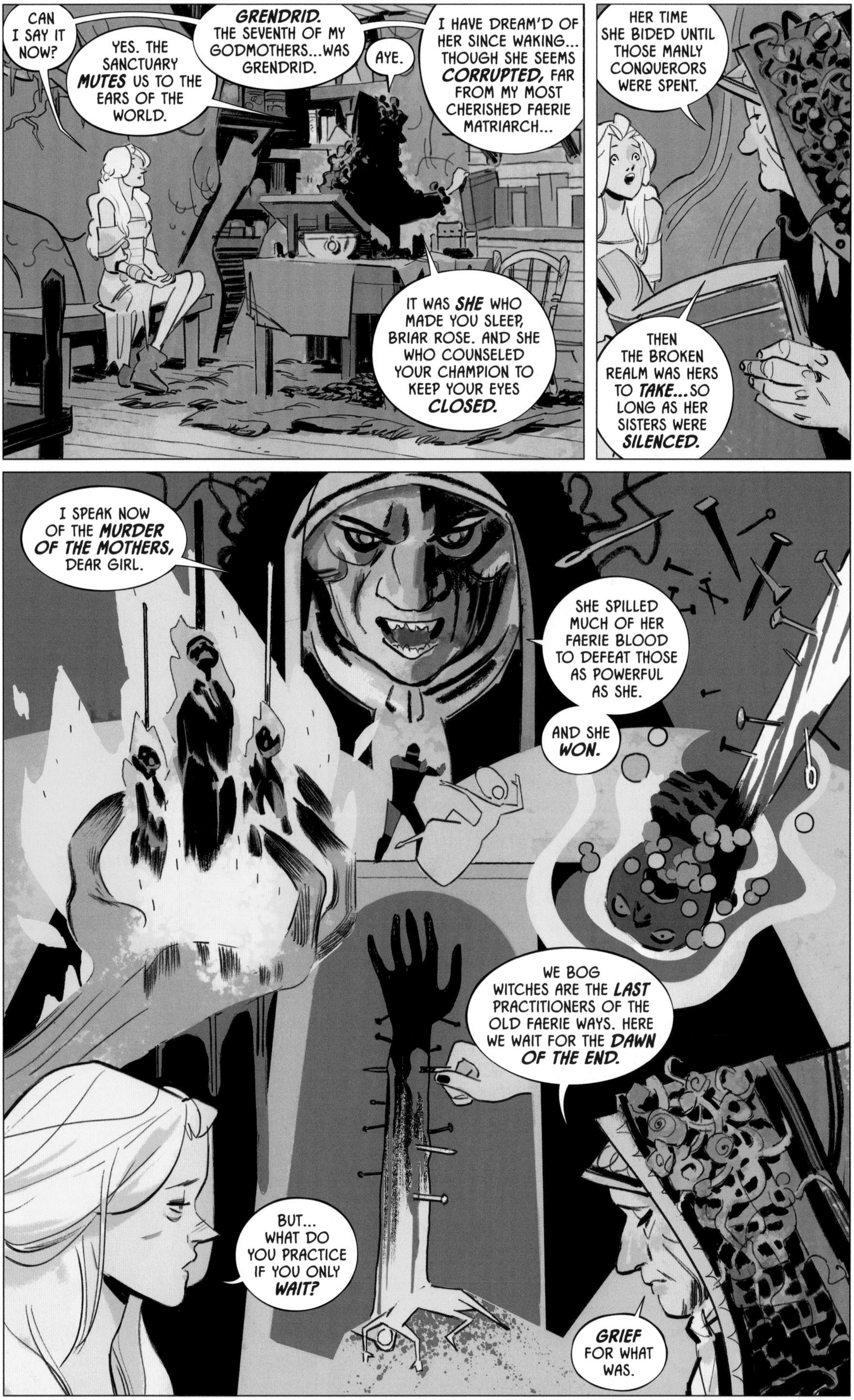
CAN I SAY IT NOW?
YES. THE SANCTUARY MUTES US TO THE EARS OF THE WORLD.
GRENDRID. THE SEVENTH OF MY GODMOTHERS...WAS GRENDRID.
AYE.
I HAVE DREAM'D OF HER SINCE WAKING... THOUGH SHE SEEMS CORRUPTED, FAR FROM MY MOST CHERISHED FAERIE MATRIARCH...
IT WAS SHE WHO MADE YOU SLEEP, BRIAR ROSE. AND SHE WHO COUNSELED YOUR CHAMPION TO KEEP YOUR EYES CLOSED.
HER TIME SHE BIDED UNTIL THOSE MANLY CONQUERORS WERE SPENT.
THEN THE BROKEN REALM WAS HERS TO TAKE...SO LONG AS HER SISTERS WERE SILENCED.
I SPEAK NOW OF THE MURDER OF THE MOTHERS, DEAR GIRL.
SHE SPILLED MUCH OF HER FAERIE BLOOD TO DEFEAT THOSE AS POWERFUL AS SHE.
AND SHE WON.
WE BOG WITCHES ARE THE LAST PRACTITIONERS OF THE OLD FAERIE WAYS. HERE WE WAIT FOR THE DAWN OF THE END.
BUT... WHAT DO YOU PRACTICE IF YOU ONLY WAIT?
GRIEF FOR WHAT WAS.

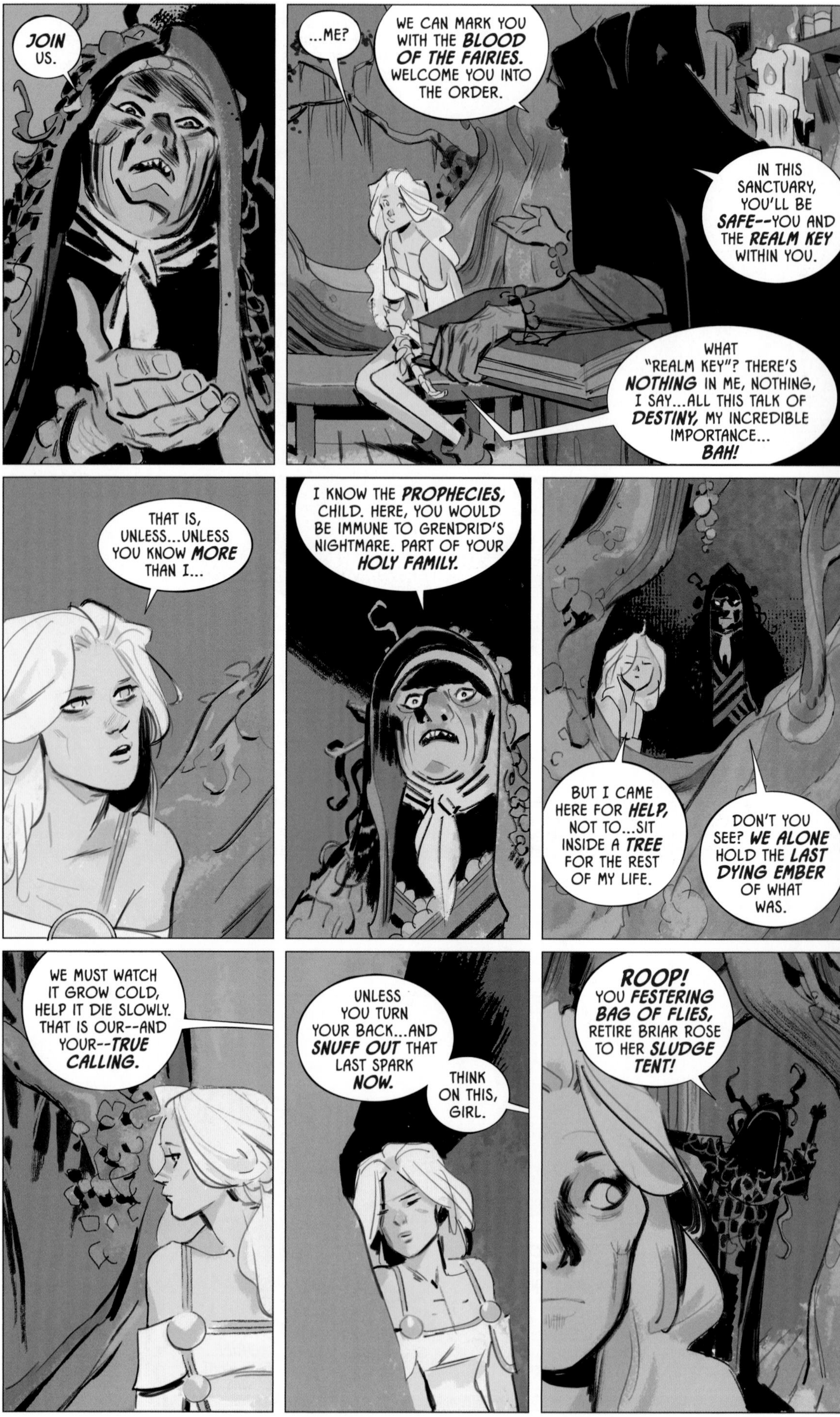
JOIN US.
...ME?
WE CAN MARK YOU WITH THE BLOOD OF THE FAIRIES. WELCOME YOU INTO THE ORDER.
IN THIS SANCTUARY, YOU'LL BE SAFE--YOU AND THE REALM KEY WITHIN YOU.
WHAT "REALM KEY"? THERE'S NOTHING IN ME, NOTHING, I SAY...ALL THIS TALK OF DESTINY, MY INCREDIBLE IMPORTANCE... BAH!
THAT IS, UNLESS...UNLESS YOU KNOW MORE THAN I...
I KNOW THE PROPHECIES, CHILD. HERE, YOU WOULD BE IMMUNE TO GRENDRID'S NIGHTMARE. PART OF YOUR HOLY FAMILY.
BUT I CAME HERE FOR HELP, NOT TO...SIT INSIDE A TREE FOR THE REST OF MY LIFE.
DON'T YOU SEE? WE ALONE HOLD THE LAST DYING EMBER OF WHAT WAS.
WE MUST WATCH IT GROW COLD, HELP IT DIE SLOWLY. THAT IS OUR--AND YOUR--TRUE CALLING.
UNLESS YOU TURN YOUR BACK...AND SNUFF OUT THAT LAST SPARK NOW.
THINK ON THIS, GIRL.
ROOP! YOU FESTERING BAG OF FLIES, RETIRE BRIAR ROSE TO HER SLUDGE TENT!

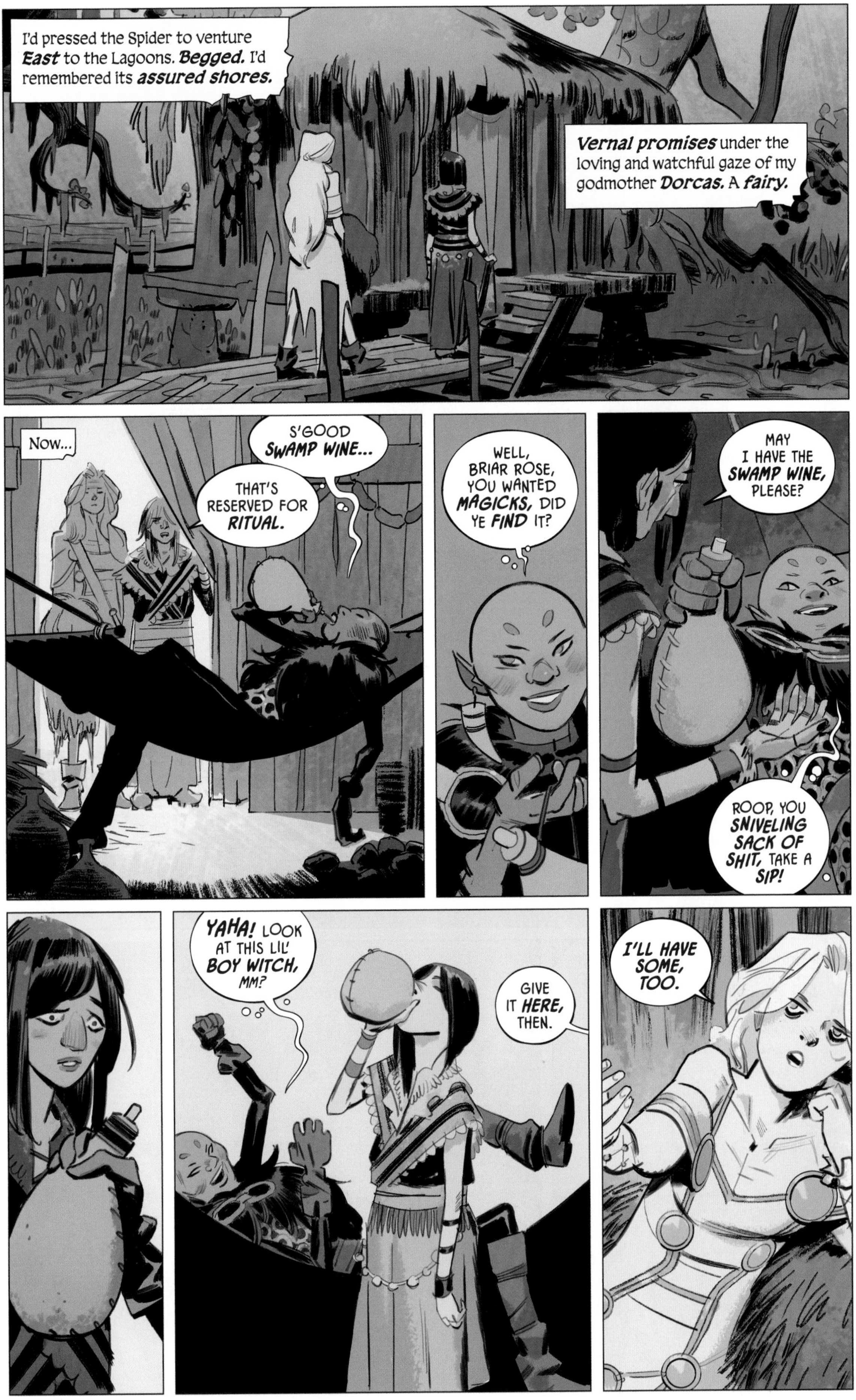
I'd pressed the Spider to venture East to the Lagoons. Begged. I'd remembered its assured shores.
Vernal promises under the loving and watchful gaze of my godmother Dorcas. A fairy.
Now...
S'GOOD SWAMP WINE...
THAT'S RESERVED FOR RITUAL.
WELL, BRIAR ROSE, YOU WANTED MAGICKS, DID YE FIND IT?
MAY I HAVE THE SWAMP WINE, PLEASE?
ROOP, YOU SNIVELING SACK OF SHIT, TAKE A SIP!
YAHA! LOOK AT THIS LIL' BOY WITCH, MM?
GIVE IT HERE, THEN.
I'LL HAVE SOME, TOO.

"WHY DO THEY *HATE* YOU SO, ROOP?"

WE RIDE *EAST,* AND PRAY THE *DREAM MARK* GUIDES US MORE *CLEARLY* THERE.

"DON'T KNOW. I'M NOT...*LIKE* THEM, FOR ONE. THOUGH I *WISH* TO BE...IN *SOME* WAYS.

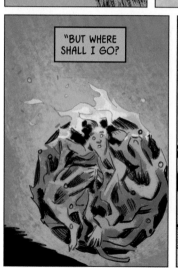

"BUT WHERE SHALL I GO?"

"INTO THE *REAL CRUELNESS* OF THE OUTER REALM?"

"AN ALIENATING PLACE WITH *NO MEANING AT ALL?*"

BUT THEY TREAT YOU LIKE *OUTHOUSE SLUDGE* HERE.

WELL, I...I HAD A *PET TOAD.* CALLED HIM *"FROG."* LITTLE JOKE TO M'SELF.

ANYWAY, HE *DIED.* I, *UM,* TRIED TO *DO* SOMETHING ABOUT IT. WITH *MAGICKS.*

MAGICKS? YOU *USED* SOME? OR-- *DID* SOME, RATHER...?

RIGHT, YES... HAVE YOU HEARD OF *NECROMANCY?*

NO.

NO.

RAISING-DEAD KIND OF SPELLS.

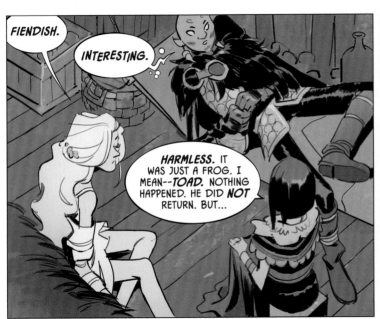

FIENDISH.

INTERESTING.

HARMLESS. IT WAS JUST A FROG. I MEAN--*TOAD.* NOTHING HAPPENED. HE DID *NOT* RETURN. BUT...

...*ELDER KROVE* DISCOVERED MY DOINGS. SHE *BEAT* ME ENDLESSLY...

PRO'LLY 'CAUSE YOU WERE TRYING TO BE A *RIGHT WARLOCK* INSTEAD OF MOPING ABOUT LIKE A *NIHILIST--*

I'M NO *WARLOCK. NO.* I'M A *WITCH.* A *BOG WITCH. JUST* AS THE OTHERS.

OF COURSE... *SORRY...*

NO *HARM.* BUT YES, A WITCH SHOULD *WITCH.* A WITCH WHICH *WITCHES NOT* IS *NO WITCH* AT ALL.

WHY WITCH WHEN THERE'S NO POINT? WHEN THIS *GRENDRID--*

SHHH! DON'T SAY HER NAME! KROVE SAID--

FUCK KROVE! FUCK ORDERS, RULES, RITUALS, AN'...COVENS AN' CASTLES AN'...

Y'KNOW, I WAS ONCE *HONOR-BOUND,* TOO--*ALLEGIANT.* IN THE *NORTH...*

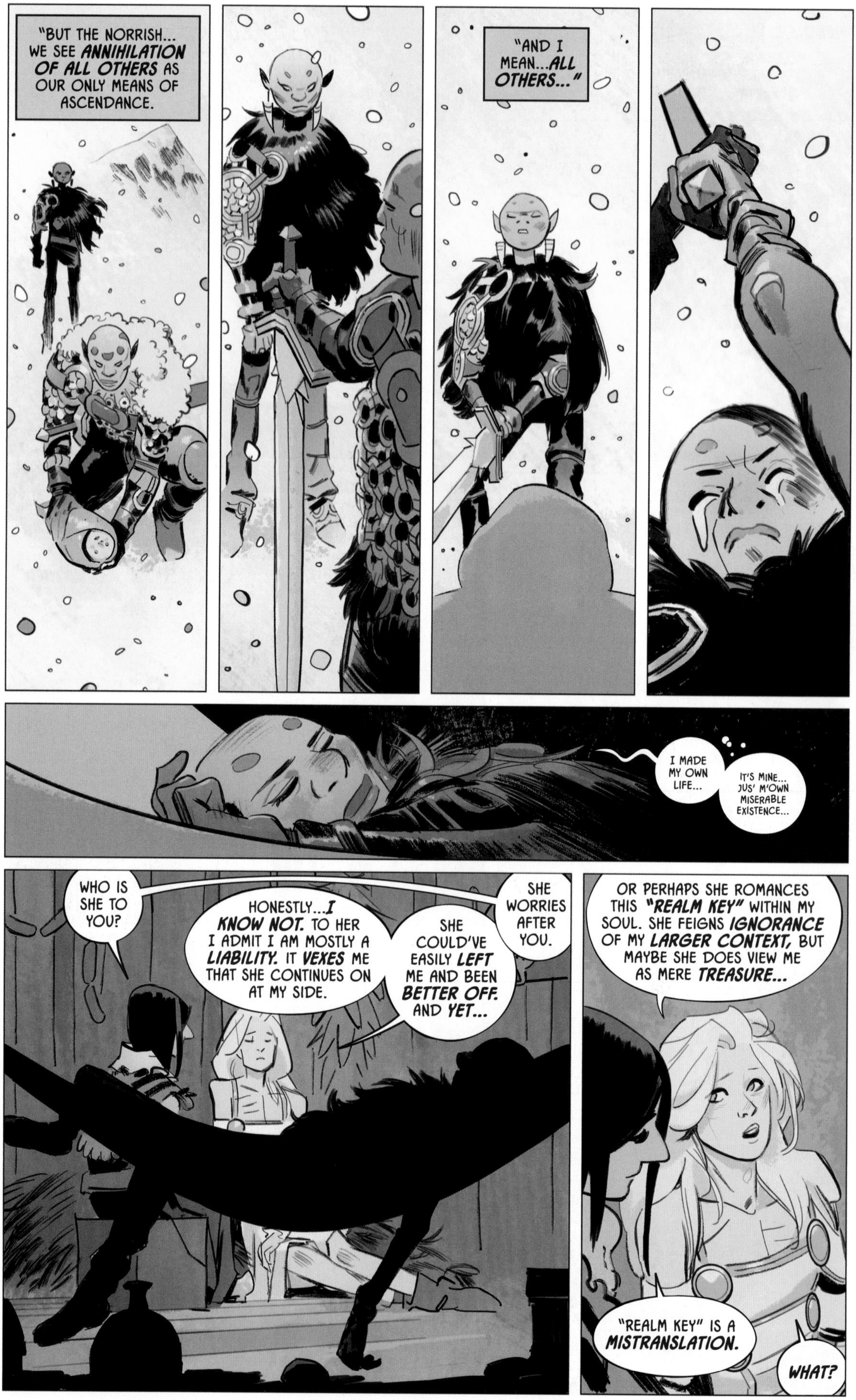
"BUT THE NORRISH... WE SEE ANNIHILATION OF ALL OTHERS AS OUR ONLY MEANS OF ASCENDANCE.
"AND I MEAN...ALL OTHERS..."
I MADE MY OWN LIFE...
IT'S MINE... JUS' M'OWN MISERABLE EXISTENCE...
WHO IS SHE TO YOU?
HONESTLY...I KNOW NOT. TO HER I ADMIT I AM MOSTLY A LIABILITY. IT VEXES ME THAT SHE CONTINUES ON AT MY SIDE.
SHE WORRIES AFTER YOU.
SHE COULD'VE EASILY LEFT ME AND BEEN BETTER OFF. AND YET...
OR PERHAPS SHE ROMANCES THIS "REALM KEY" WITHIN MY SOUL. SHE FEIGNS IGNORANCE OF MY LARGER CONTEXT, BUT MAYBE SHE DOES VIEW ME AS MERE TREASURE...
"REALM KEY" IS A MISTRANSLATION.
WHAT?

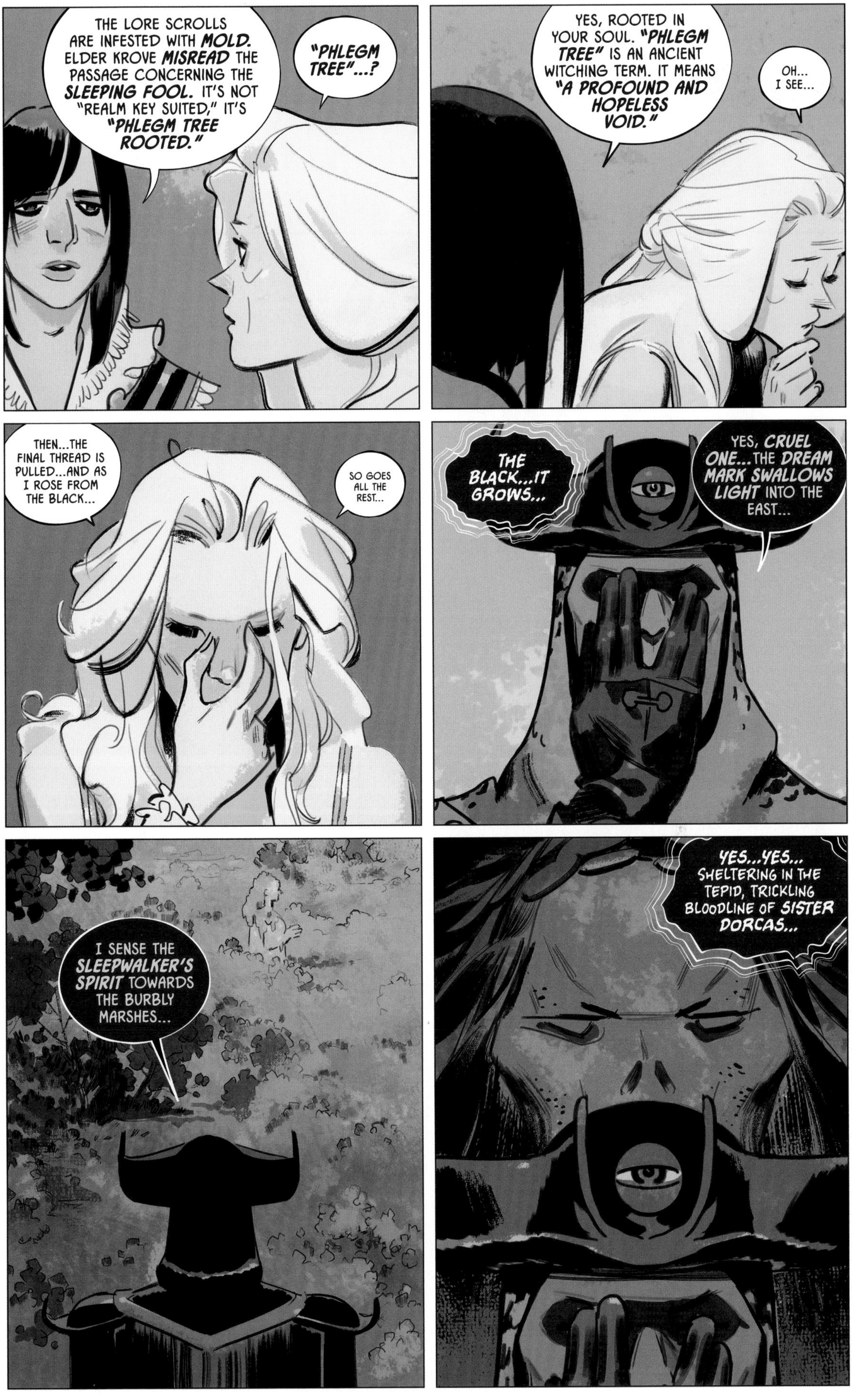
THE LORE SCROLLS ARE INFESTED WITH MOLD. ELDER KROVE MISREAD THE PASSAGE CONCERNING THE SLEEPING FOOL. IT'S NOT "REALM KEY SUITED," IT'S "PHLEGM TREE ROOTED."
"PHLEGM TREE"...?
YES, ROOTED IN YOUR SOUL. "PHLEGM TREE" IS AN ANCIENT WITCHING TERM. IT MEANS "A PROFOUND AND HOPELESS VOID."
OH... I SEE...
THEN...THE FINAL THREAD IS PULLED...AND AS I ROSE FROM THE BLACK...
SO GOES ALL THE REST...
THE BLACK...IT GROWS...
YES, CRUEL ONE...THE DREAM MARK SWALLOWS LIGHT INTO THE EAST...
I SENSE THE SLEEPWALKER'S SPIRIT TOWARDS THE BURBLY MARSHES...
YES...YES... SHELTERING IN THE TEPID, TRICKLING BLOODLINE OF SISTER DORCAS...

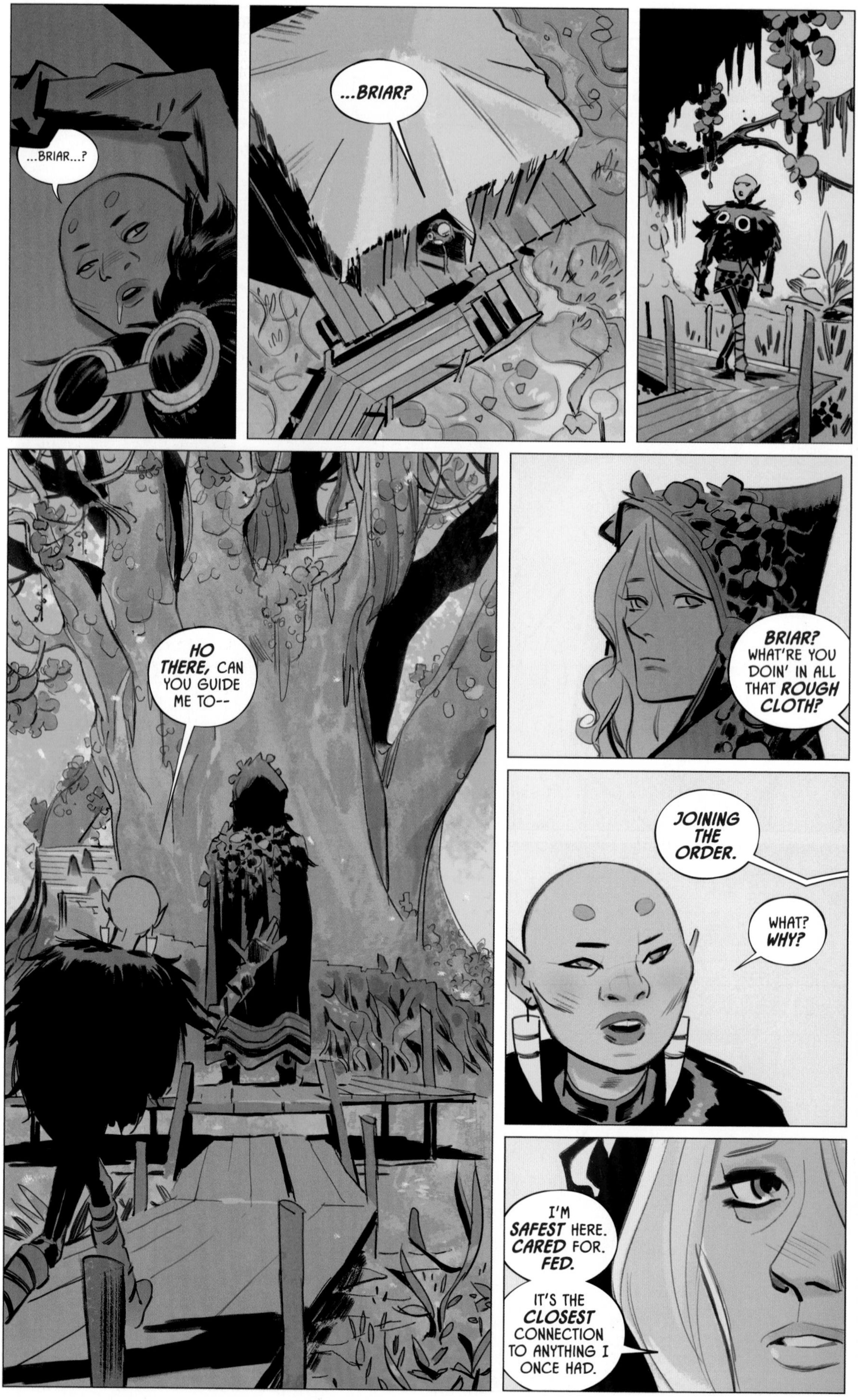
...BRIAR...?
...BRIAR?
HO THERE, CAN YOU GUIDE ME TO--
BRIAR? WHAT'RE YOU DOIN' IN ALL THAT ROUGH CLOTH?
JOINING THE ORDER.
WHAT? WHY?
I'M SAFEST HERE. CARED FOR. FED.
IT'S THE CLOSEST CONNECTION TO ANYTHING I ONCE HAD.

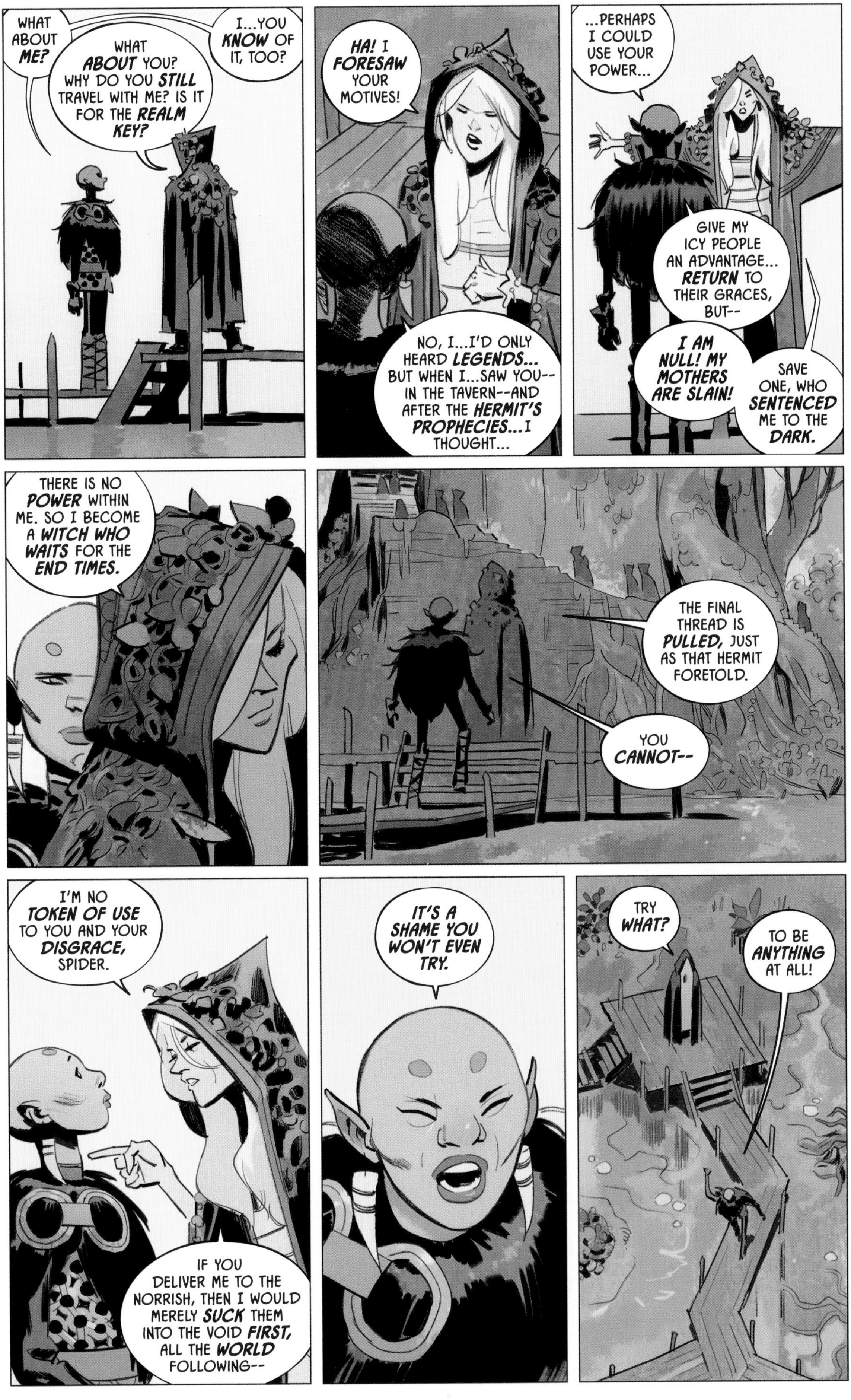
WHAT ABOUT ME?
WHAT ABOUT YOU? WHY DO YOU STILL TRAVEL WITH ME? IS IT FOR THE REALM KEY?
I...YOU KNOW OF IT, TOO?
HA! I FORESAW YOUR MOTIVES!
NO, I...I'D ONLY HEARD LEGENDS... BUT WHEN I...SAW YOU--IN THE TAVERN--AND AFTER THE HERMIT'S PROPHECIES...I THOUGHT...
...PERHAPS I COULD USE YOUR POWER...
GIVE MY ICY PEOPLE AN ADVANTAGE... RETURN TO THEIR GRACES, BUT--
I AM NULL! MY MOTHERS ARE SLAIN!
SAVE ONE, WHO SENTENCED ME TO THE DARK.
THERE IS NO POWER WITHIN ME. SO I BECOME A WITCH WHO WAITS FOR THE END TIMES.
THE FINAL THREAD IS PULLED, JUST AS THAT HERMIT FORETOLD.
YOU CANNOT--
I'M NO TOKEN OF USE TO YOU AND YOUR DISGRACE, SPIDER.
IF YOU DELIVER ME TO THE NORRISH, THEN I WOULD MERELY SUCK THEM INTO THE VOID FIRST, ALL THE WORLD FOLLOWING--
IT'S A SHAME YOU WON'T EVEN TRY.
TRY WHAT?
TO BE ANYTHING AT ALL!

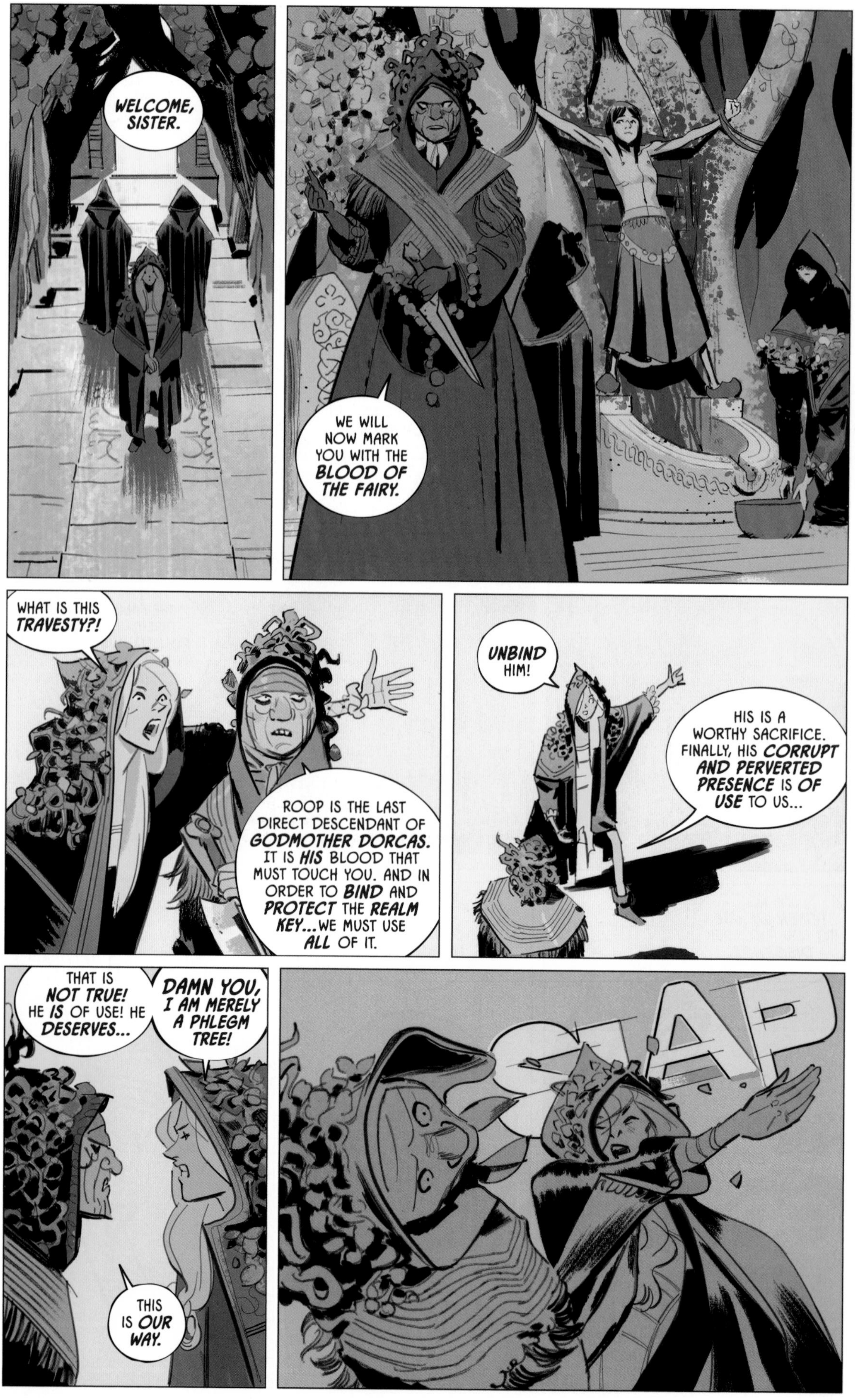
WELCOME, SISTER.
WE WILL NOW MARK YOU WITH THE BLOOD OF THE FAIRY.
WHAT IS THIS TRAVESTY?!
ROOP IS THE LAST DIRECT DESCENDANT OF GODMOTHER DORCAS. IT IS HIS BLOOD THAT MUST TOUCH YOU. AND IN ORDER TO BIND AND PROTECT THE REALM KEY...WE MUST USE ALL OF IT.
UNBIND HIM!
HIS IS A WORTHY SACRIFICE. FINALLY, HIS CORRUPT AND PERVERTED PRESENCE IS OF USE TO US...
THAT IS NOT TRUE! HE IS OF USE! HE DESERVES...
DAMN YOU, I AM MERELY A PHLEGM TREE!
THIS IS OUR WAY.
SLAP

THEN **FUCK** YOUR WAY.

YOU **BETRAY** US HERE, IN THE **SHADOW OF DORCAS?**

DORCAS IS **DEAD.**

SHE IS ONE **DEAD DORCAS.**

AN' YOU ALL 'RE FREE TO **JOIN HER** IF YOU TRY T'HURT **MY FRIENDS** UP THERE.

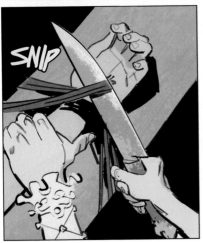

SNIP

WHAT NOW...?

UH... **YOU COME WITH US.**

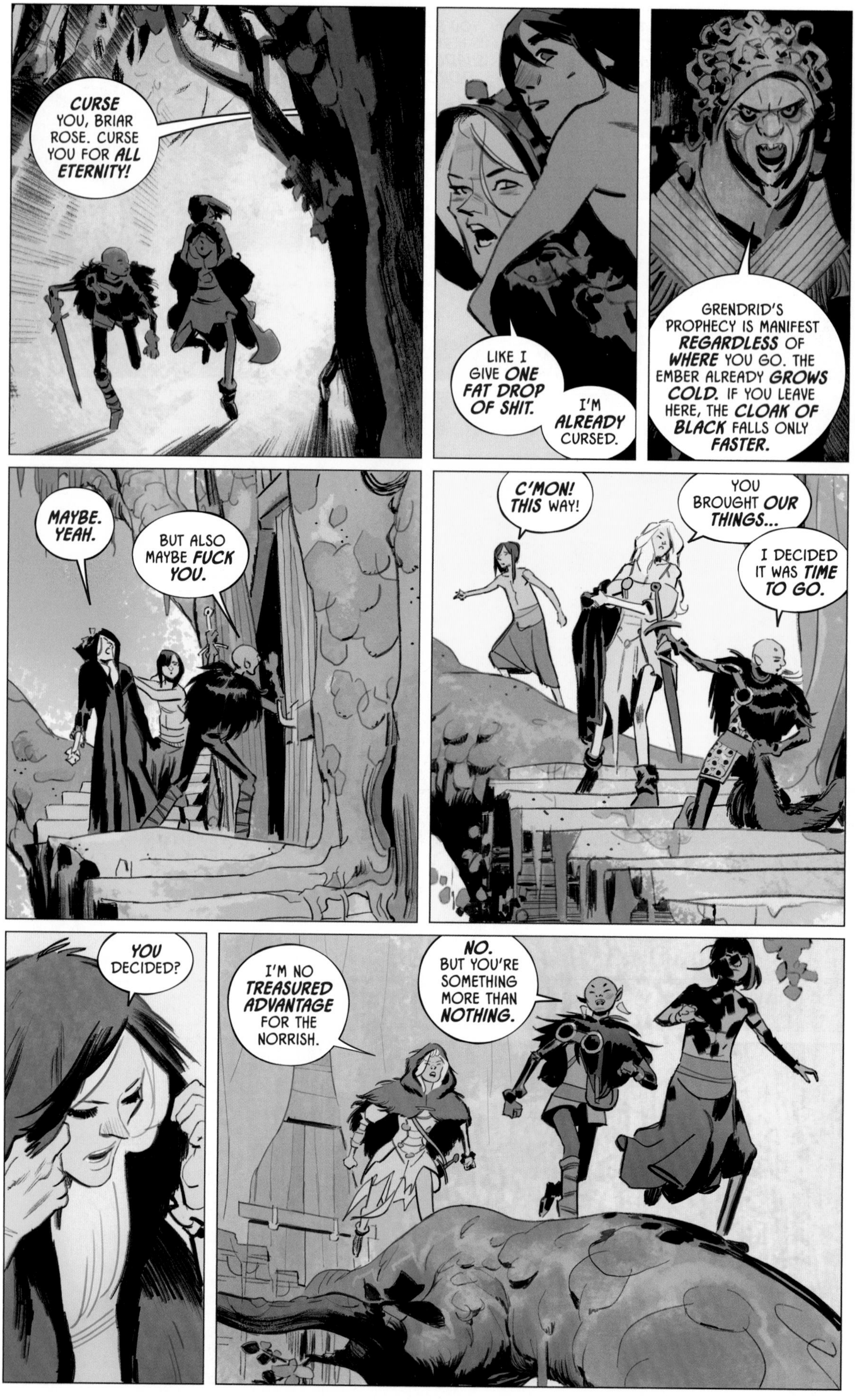
CURSE YOU, BRIAR ROSE. CURSE YOU FOR ALL ETERNITY!
LIKE I GIVE ONE FAT DROP OF SHIT.
I'M ALREADY CURSED.
GRENDRID'S PROPHECY IS MANIFEST REGARDLESS OF WHERE YOU GO. THE EMBER ALREADY GROWS COLD. IF YOU LEAVE HERE, THE CLOAK OF BLACK FALLS ONLY FASTER.
MAYBE. YEAH.
BUT ALSO MAYBE FUCK YOU.
C'MON! THIS WAY!
YOU BROUGHT OUR THINGS...
I DECIDED IT WAS TIME TO GO.
YOU DECIDED?
I'M NO TREASURED ADVANTAGE FOR THE NORRISH.
NO. BUT YOU'RE SOMETHING MORE THAN NOTHING.

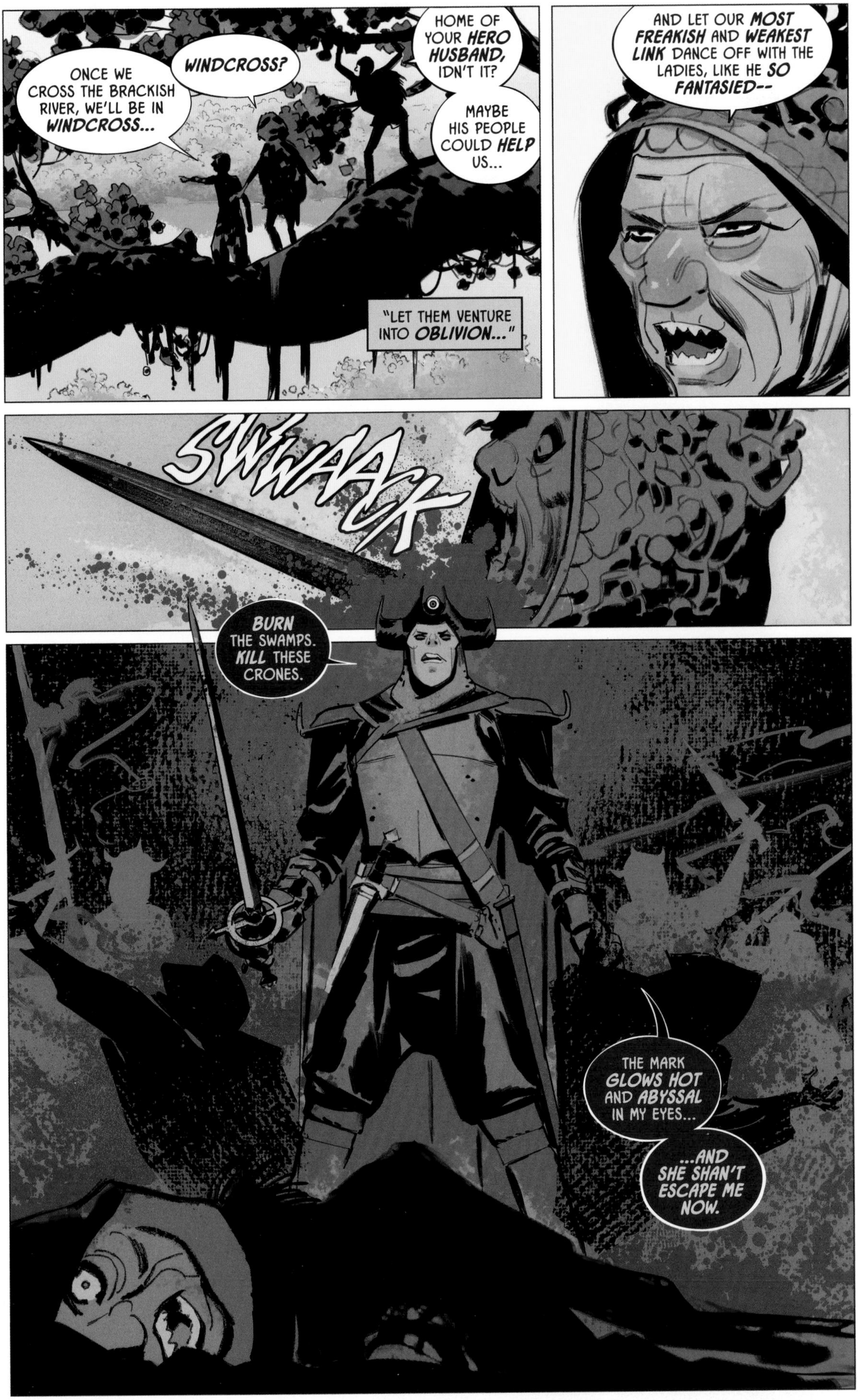
ONCE WE CROSS THE BRACKISH RIVER, WE'LL BE IN WINDCROSS...
WINDCROSS?
HOME OF YOUR HERO HUSBAND, IDN'T IT?
MAYBE HIS PEOPLE COULD HELP US...
"LET THEM VENTURE INTO OBLIVION..."
AND LET OUR MOST FREAKISH AND WEAKEST LINK DANCE OFF WITH THE LADIES, LIKE HE SO FANTASIED--
SWWAAACK
BURN THE SWAMPS. KILL THESE CRONES.
THE MARK GLOWS HOT AND ABYSSAL IN MY EYES...
...AND SHE SHAN'T ESCAPE ME NOW.

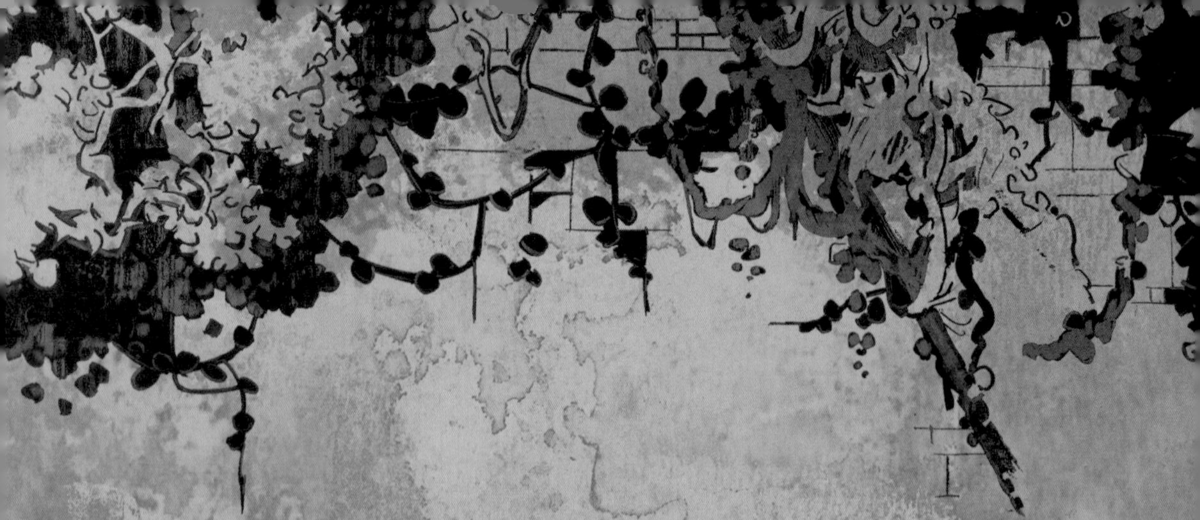

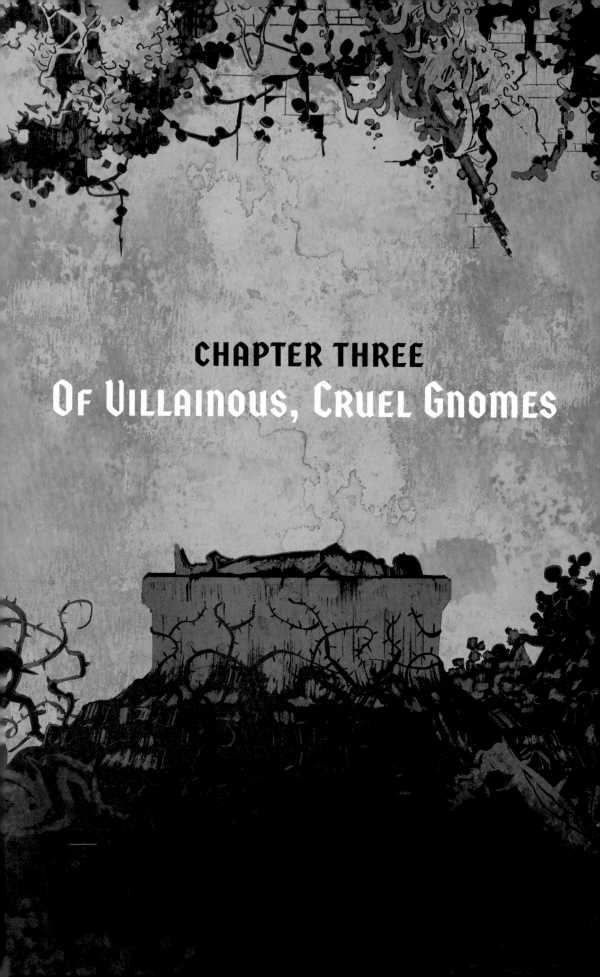

CHAPTER THREE
Of Villainous, Cruel Gnomes

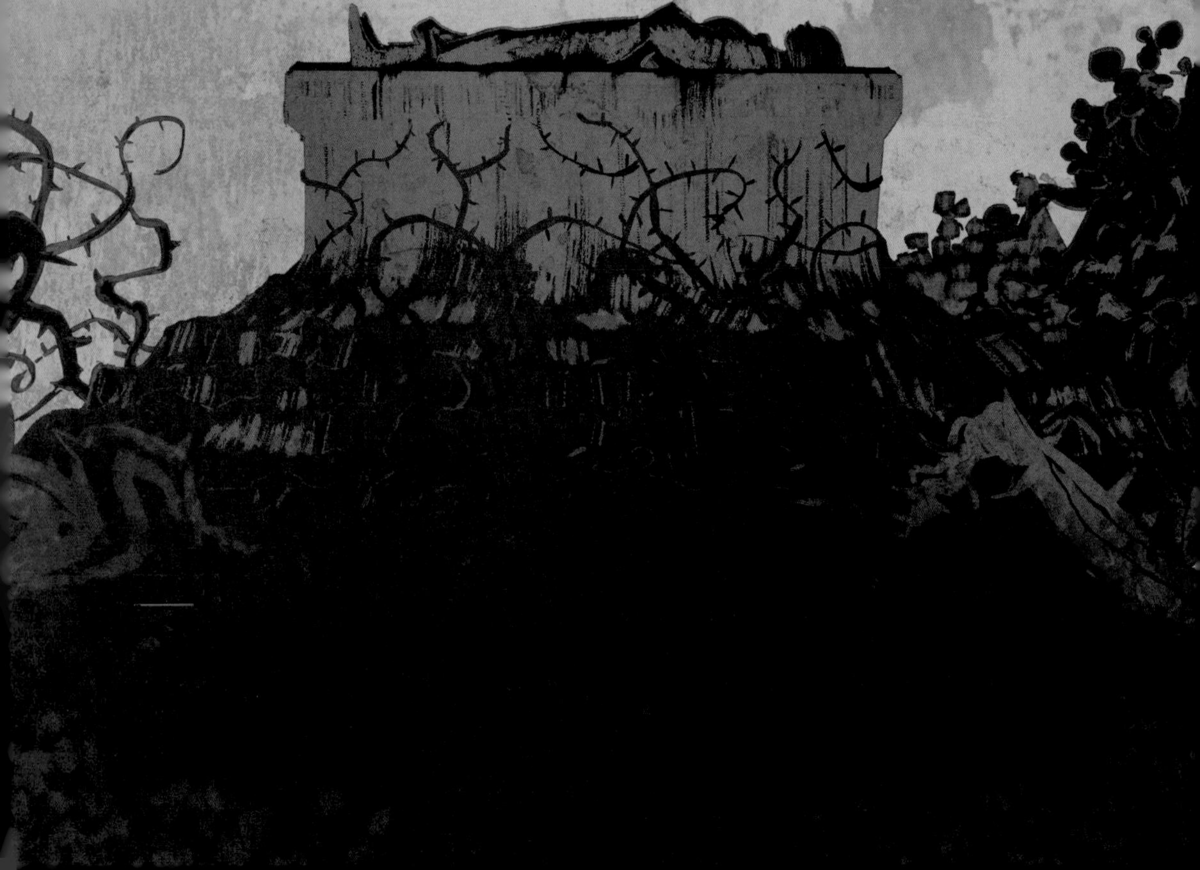

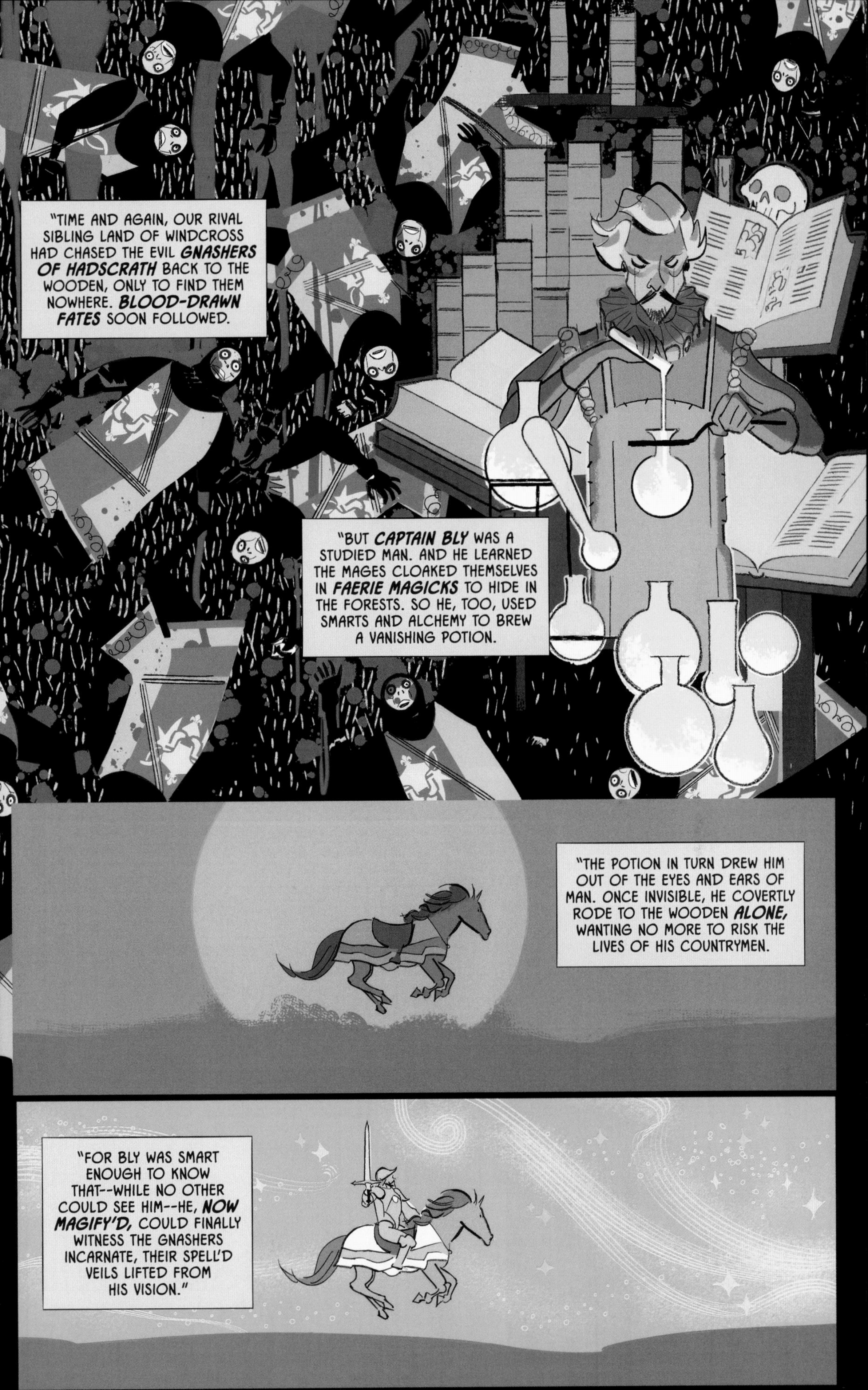
"TIME AND AGAIN, OUR RIVAL SIBLING LAND OF WINDCROSS HAD CHASED THE EVIL GNASHERS OF HADSCRATH BACK TO THE WOODEN, ONLY TO FIND THEM NOWHERE. BLOOD-DRAWN FATES SOON FOLLOWED.
"BUT CAPTAIN BLY WAS A STUDIED MAN. AND HE LEARNED THE MAGES CLOAKED THEMSELVES IN FAERIE MAGICKS TO HIDE IN THE FORESTS. SO HE, TOO, USED SMARTS AND ALCHEMY TO BREW A VANISHING POTION.
"THE POTION IN TURN DREW HIM OUT OF THE EYES AND EARS OF MAN. ONCE INVISIBLE, HE COVERTLY RODE TO THE WOODEN ALONE, WANTING NO MORE TO RISK THE LIVES OF HIS COUNTRYMEN.
"FOR BLY WAS SMART ENOUGH TO KNOW THAT--WHILE NO OTHER COULD SEE HIM--HE, NOW MAGIFY'D, COULD FINALLY WITNESS THE GNASHERS INCARNATE, THEIR SPELL'D VEILS LIFTED FROM HIS VISION."

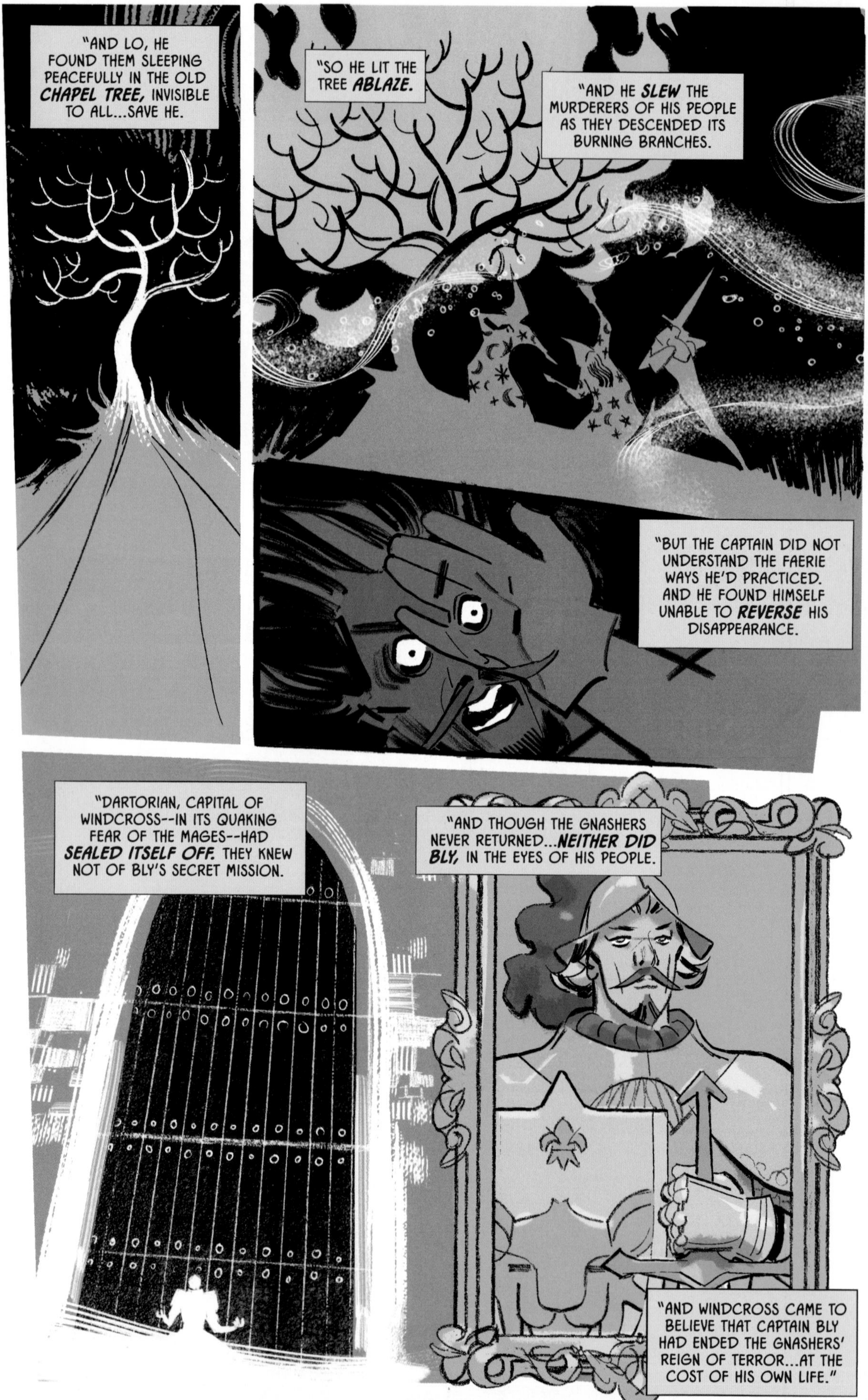
"AND LO, HE FOUND THEM SLEEPING PEACEFULLY IN THE OLD **CHAPEL TREE,** INVISIBLE TO ALL...SAVE HE.
"SO HE LIT THE TREE **ABLAZE.**
"AND HE **SLEW** THE MURDERERS OF HIS PEOPLE AS THEY DESCENDED ITS BURNING BRANCHES.
"BUT THE CAPTAIN DID NOT UNDERSTAND THE FAERIE WAYS HE'D PRACTICED. AND HE FOUND HIMSELF UNABLE TO **REVERSE** HIS DISAPPEARANCE.
"DARTORIAN, CAPITAL OF WINDCROSS--IN ITS QUAKING FEAR OF THE MAGES--HAD **SEALED ITSELF OFF.** THEY KNEW NOT OF BLY'S SECRET MISSION.
"AND THOUGH THE GNASHERS NEVER RETURNED...**NEITHER DID BLY,** IN THE EYES OF HIS PEOPLE.
"AND WINDCROSS CAME TO BELIEVE THAT CAPTAIN BLY HAD ENDED THE GNASHERS' REIGN OF TERROR...AT THE COST OF HIS OWN LIFE."

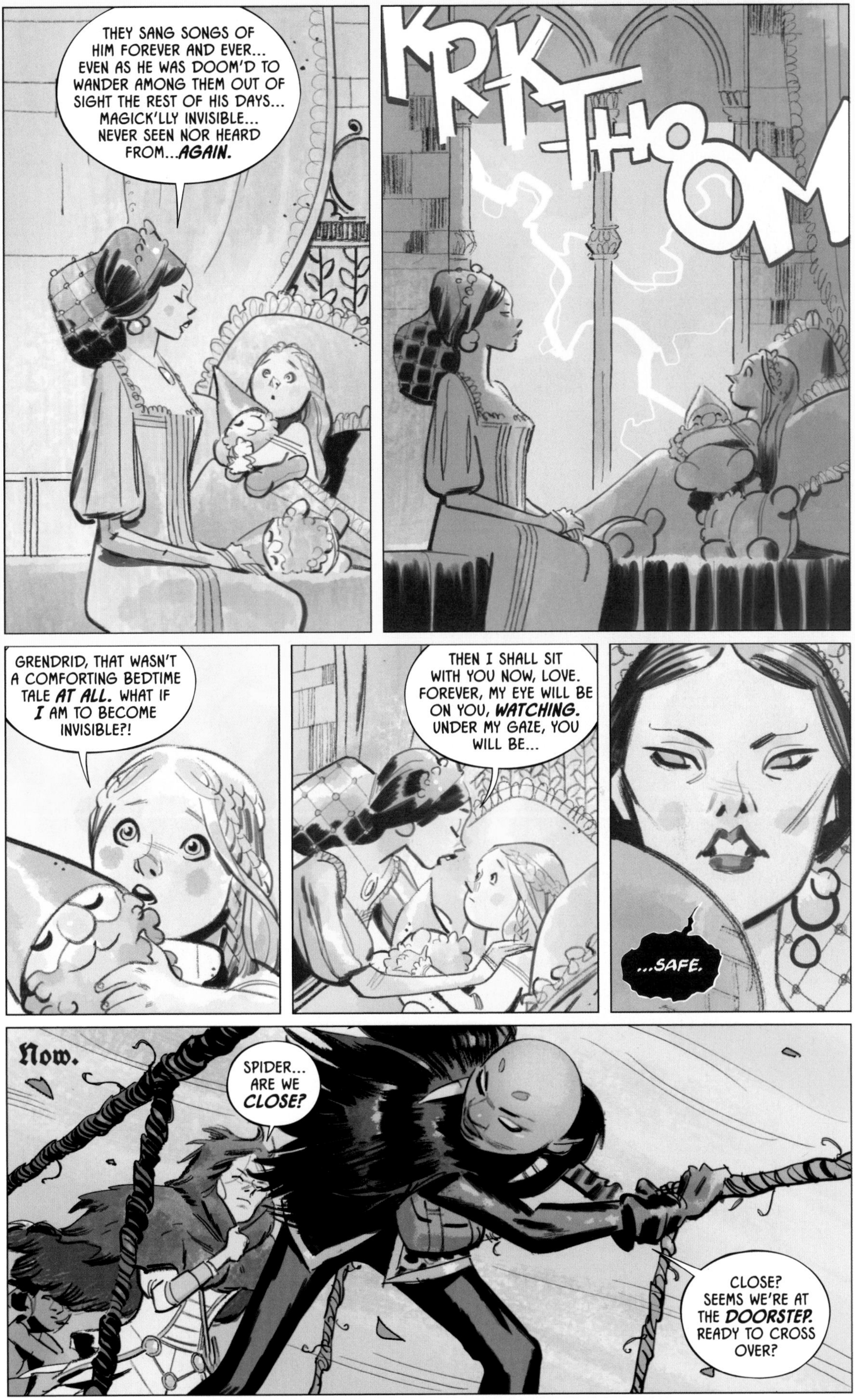

THEY SANG SONGS OF HIM FOREVER AND EVER... EVEN AS HE WAS DOOM'D TO WANDER AMONG THEM OUT OF SIGHT THE REST OF HIS DAYS... MAGICK'LLY INVISIBLE... NEVER SEEN NOR HEARD FROM...AGAIN.
KRK-THOOM
GRENDRID, THAT WASN'T A COMFORTING BEDTIME TALE AT ALL. WHAT IF I AM TO BECOME INVISIBLE?!
THEN I SHALL SIT WITH YOU NOW, LOVE. FOREVER, MY EYE WILL BE ON YOU, WATCHING. UNDER MY GAZE, YOU WILL BE...
...SAFE.
Now.
SPIDER... ARE WE CLOSE?
CLOSE? SEEMS WE'RE AT THE DOORSTEP. READY TO CROSS OVER?

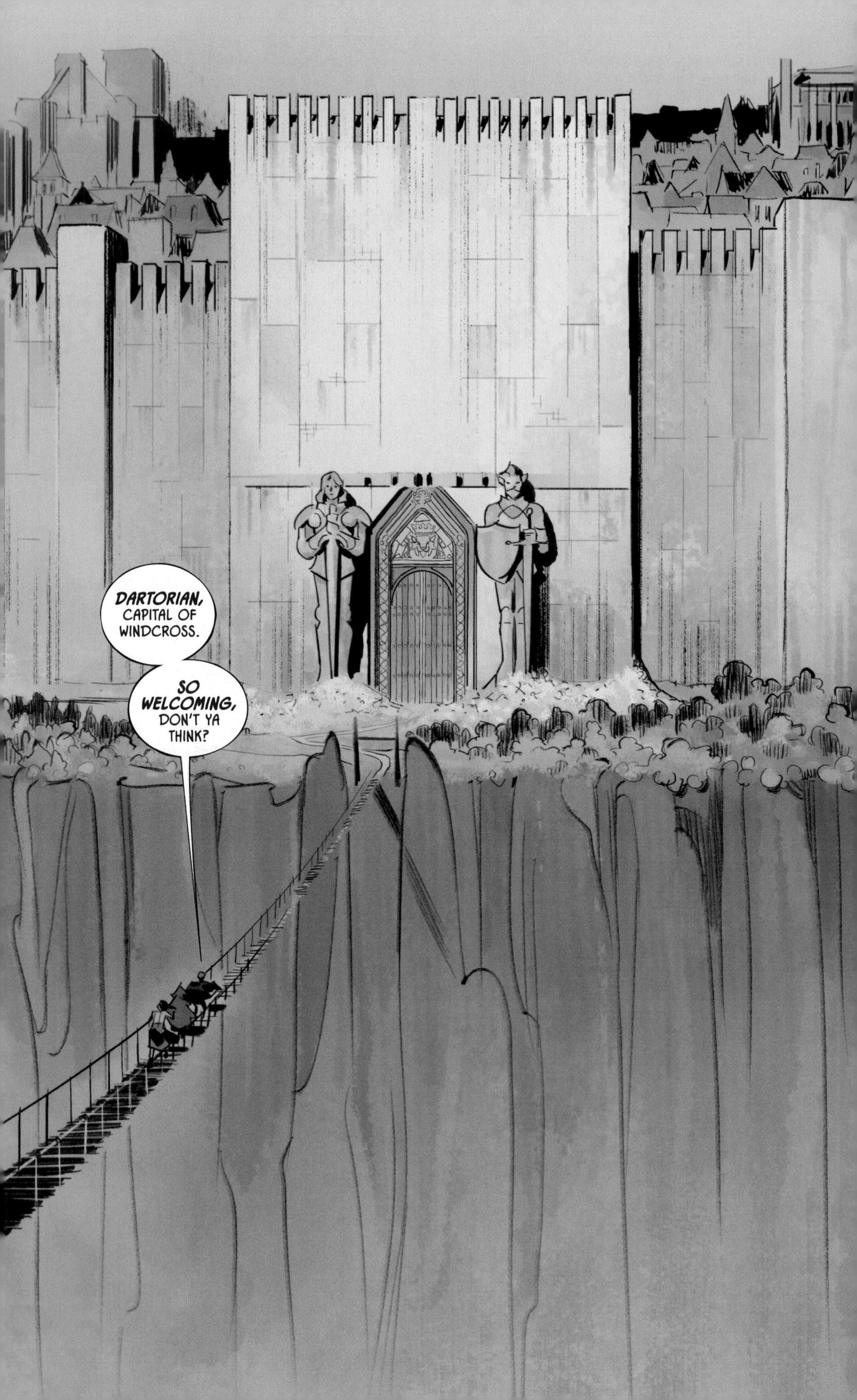
DARTORIAN, CAPITAL OF WINDCROSS.
SO WELCOMING, DON'T YA THINK?

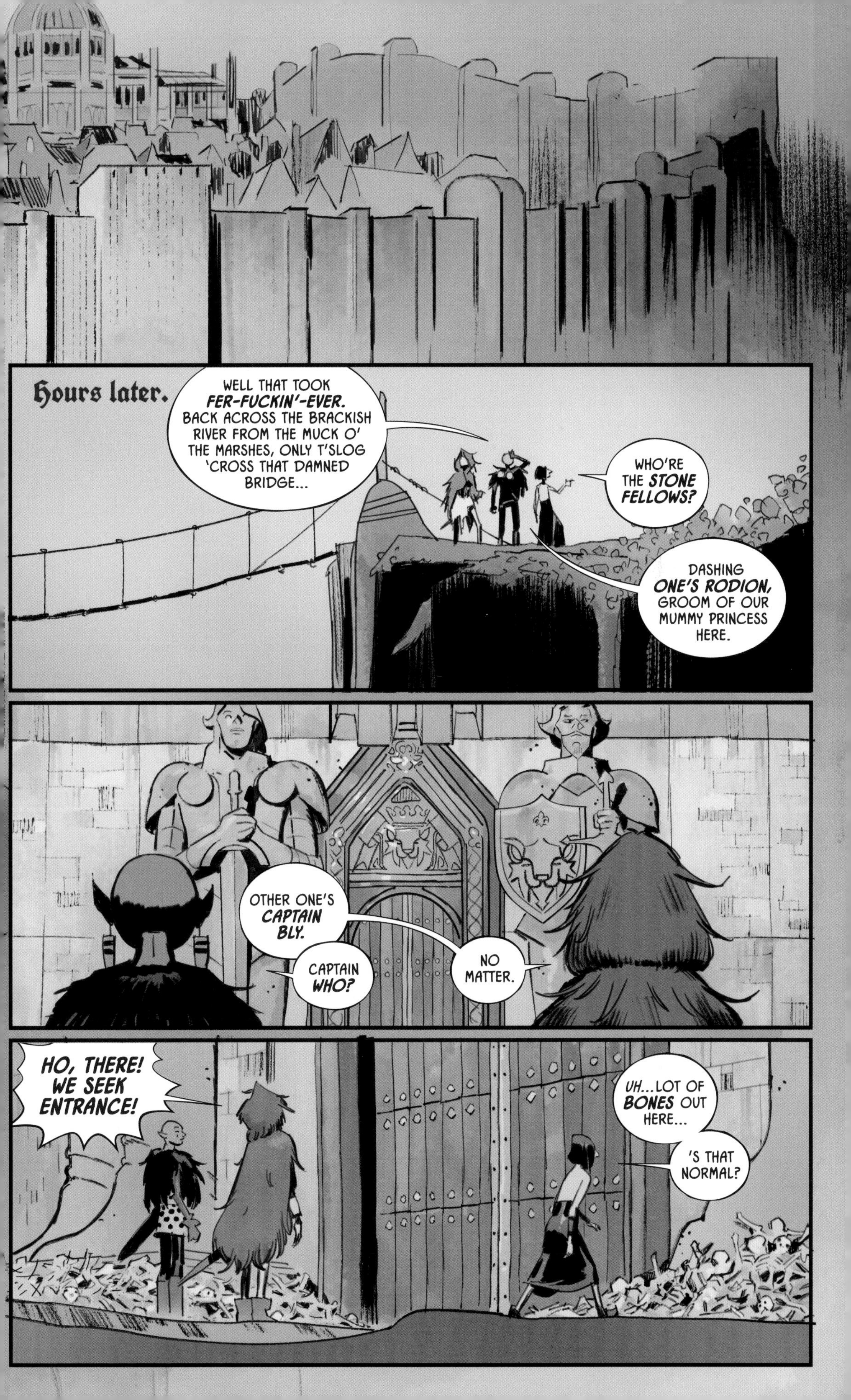
Hours later.
WELL THAT TOOK FER-FUCKIN'-EVER. BACK ACROSS THE BRACKISH RIVER FROM THE MUCK O' THE MARSHES, ONLY T'SLOG 'CROSS THAT DAMNED BRIDGE...
WHO'RE THE STONE FELLOWS?
DASHING ONE'S RODION, GROOM OF OUR MUMMY PRINCESS HERE.
OTHER ONE'S CAPTAIN BLY.
CAPTAIN WHO?
NO MATTER.
HO, THERE! WE SEEK ENTRANCE!
UH...LOT OF BONES OUT HERE...
'S THAT NORMAL?

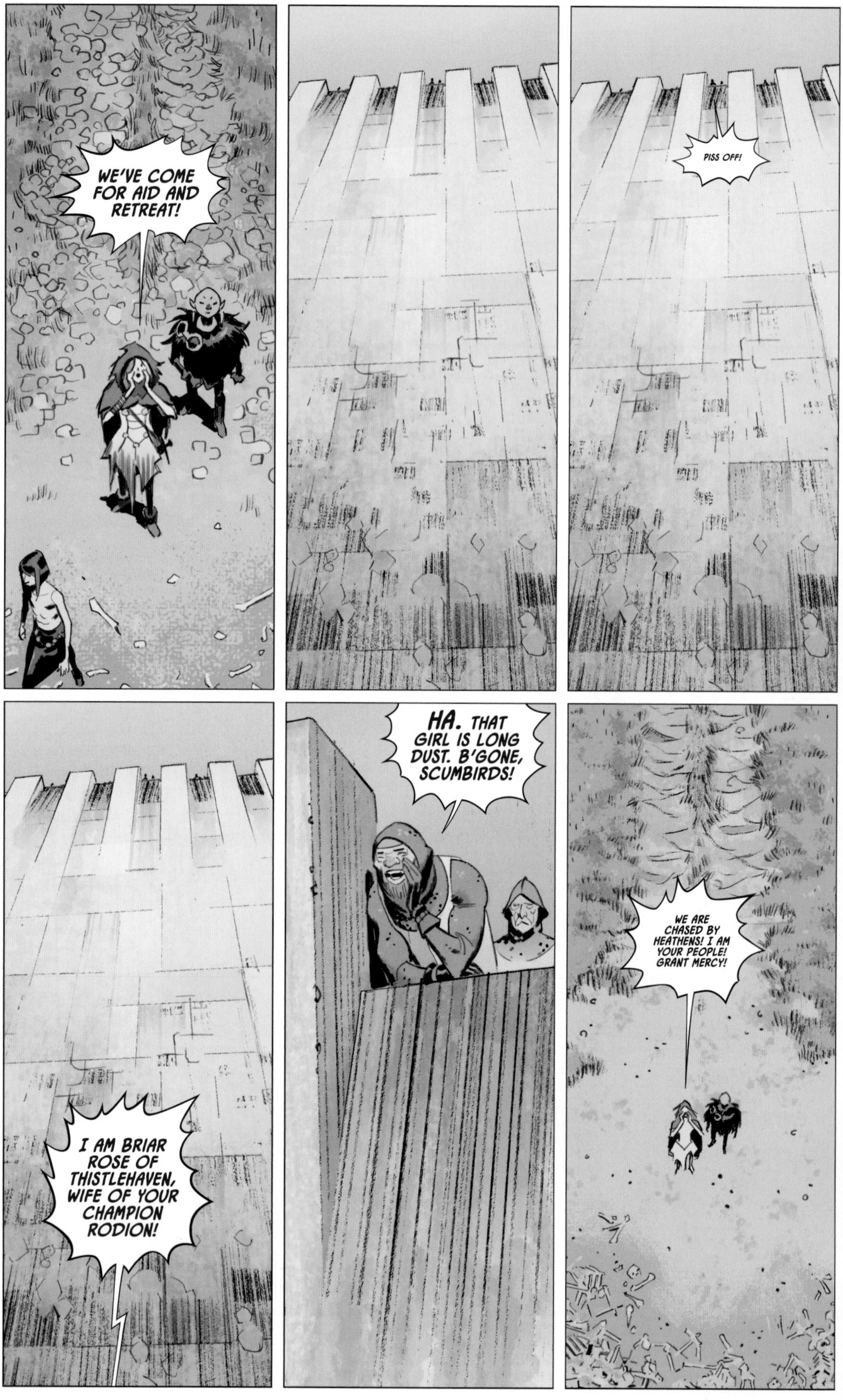
WE'VE COME FOR AID AND RETREAT!
PISS OFF!
I AM BRIAR ROSE OF THISTLEHAVEN, WIFE OF YOUR CHAMPION RODION!
HA. THAT GIRL IS LONG DUST. B'GONE, SCUMBIRDS!
WE ARE CHASED BY HEATHENS! I AM YOUR PEOPLE! GRANT MERCY!

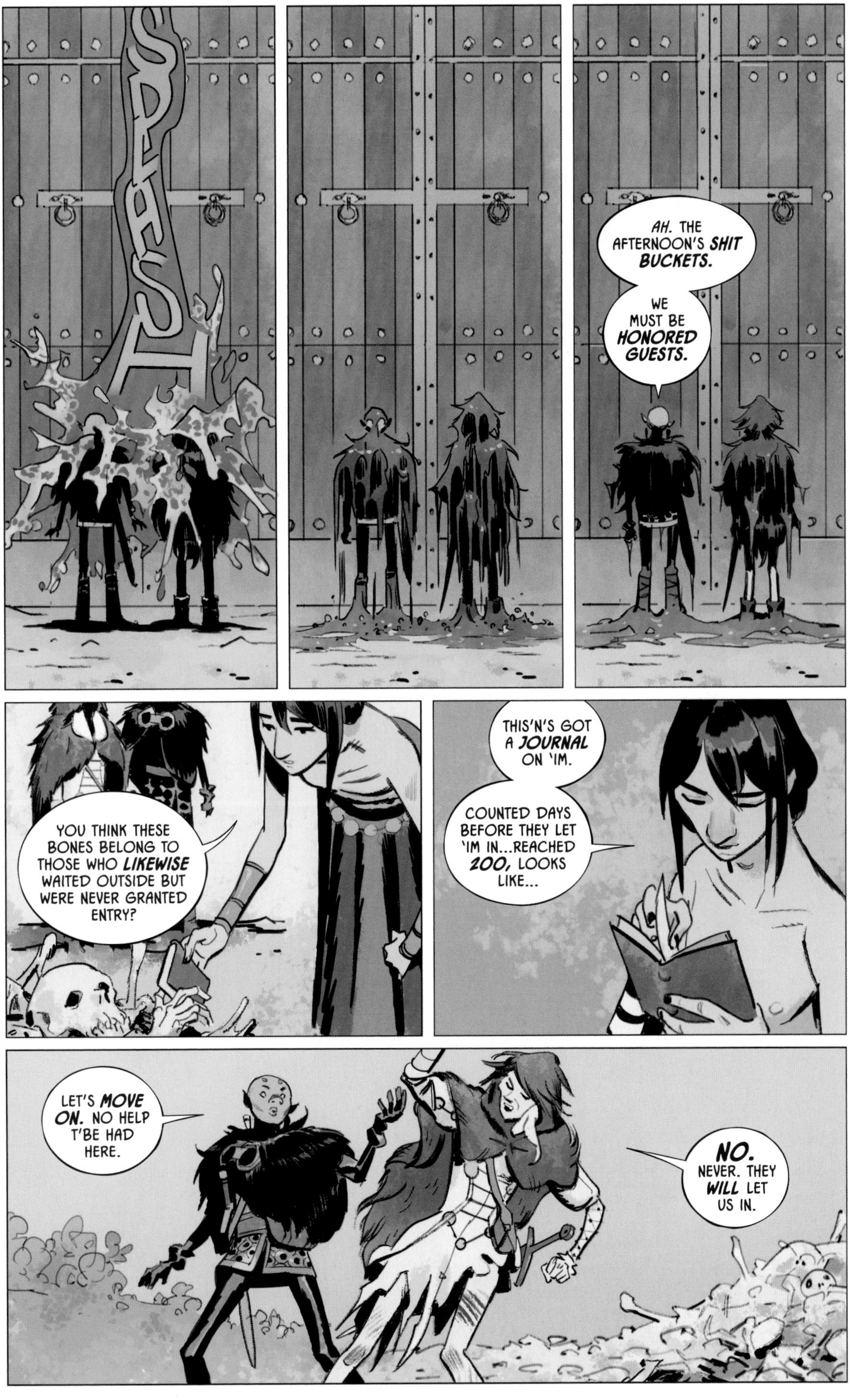
SPLASH
AH. THE AFTERNOON'S SHIT BUCKETS.
WE MUST BE HONORED GUESTS.
YOU THINK THESE BONES BELONG TO THOSE WHO LIKEWISE WAITED OUTSIDE BUT WERE NEVER GRANTED ENTRY?
THIS'N'S GOT A JOURNAL ON 'IM.
COUNTED DAYS BEFORE THEY LET 'IM IN...REACHED 200, LOOKS LIKE...
LET'S MOVE ON. NO HELP T'BE HAD HERE.
NO. NEVER. THEY WILL LET US IN.

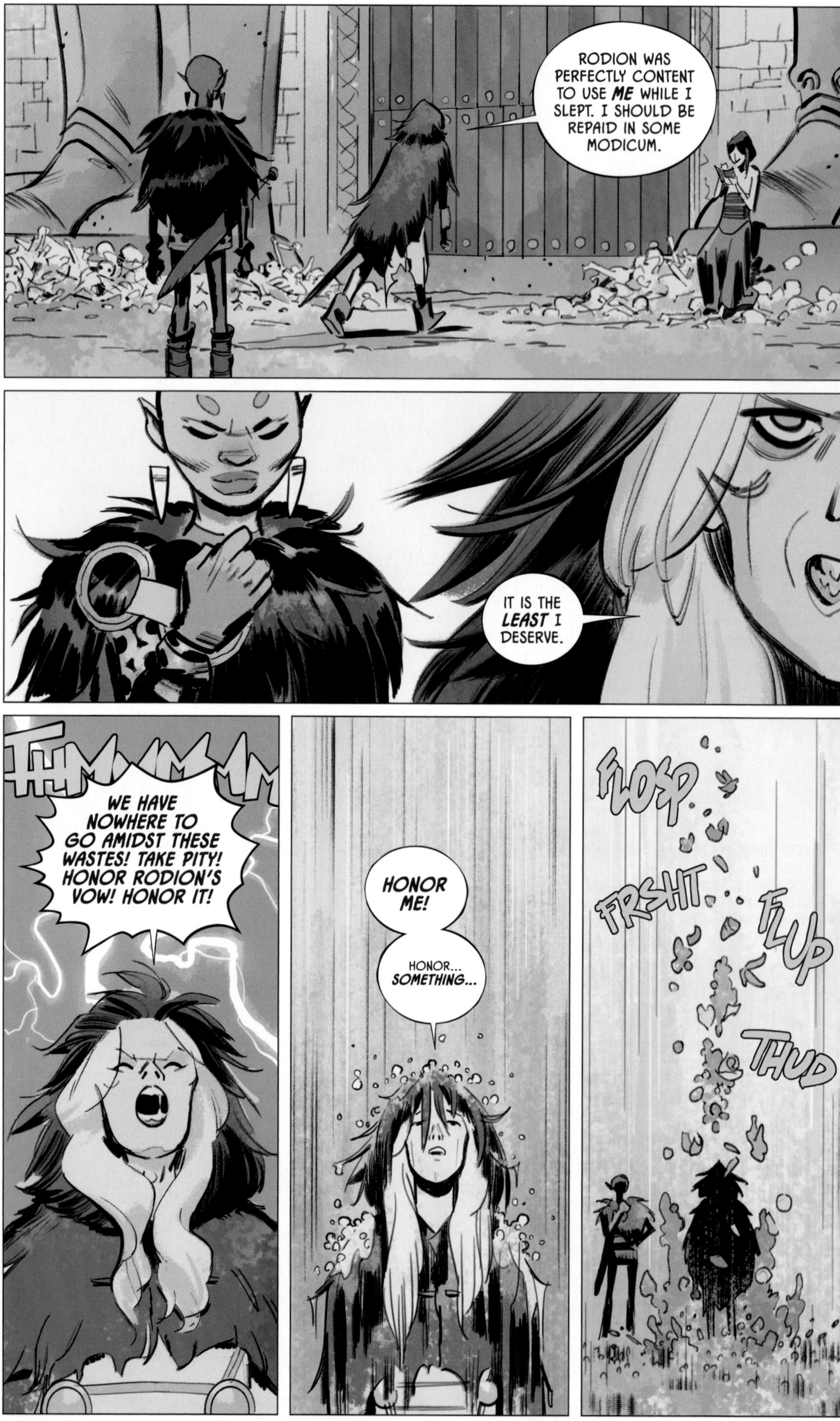
RODION WAS PERFECTLY CONTENT TO USE ME WHILE I SLEPT. I SHOULD BE REPAID IN SOME MODICUM.
IT IS THE LEAST I DESERVE.
THMMMMM
WE HAVE NOWHERE TO GO AMIDST THESE WASTES! TAKE PITY! HONOR RODION'S VOW! HONOR IT!
HONOR ME!
HONOR... SOMETHING...
FLOSP
FRSHT
FLUP
THUD

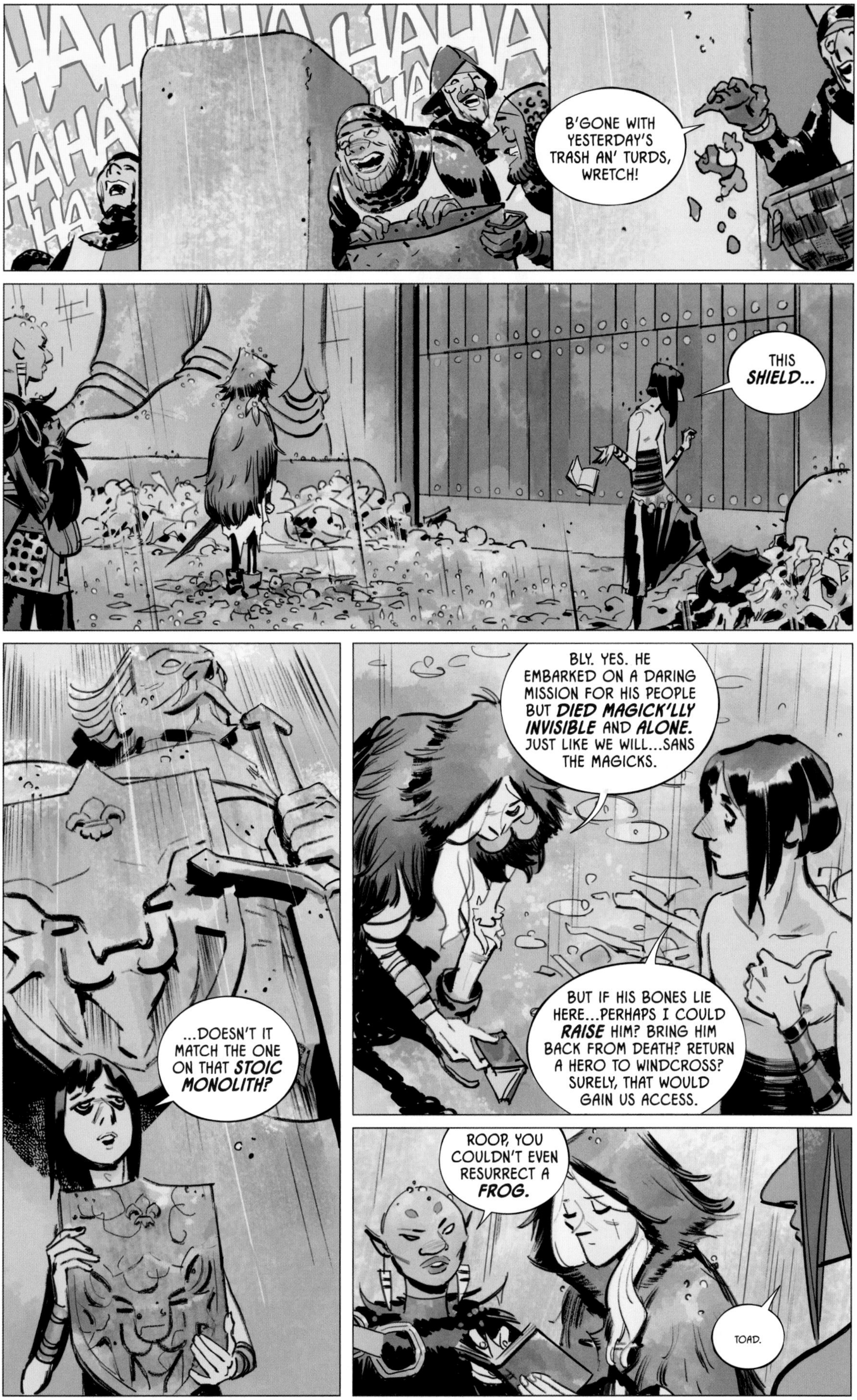
HAHAHAHA HAHAHA HAHA
B'GONE WITH YESTERDAY'S TRASH AN' TURDS, WRETCH!
THIS SHIELD...
...DOESN'T IT MATCH THE ONE ON THAT STOIC MONOLITH?
BLY. YES. HE EMBARKED ON A DARING MISSION FOR HIS PEOPLE BUT DIED MAGICK'LLY INVISIBLE AND ALONE. JUST LIKE WE WILL...SANS THE MAGICKS.
BUT IF HIS BONES LIE HERE...PERHAPS I COULD RAISE HIM? BRING HIM BACK FROM DEATH? RETURN A HERO TO WINDCROSS? SURELY, THAT WOULD GAIN US ACCESS.
ROOP, YOU COULDN'T EVEN RESURRECT A FROG.
TOAD.

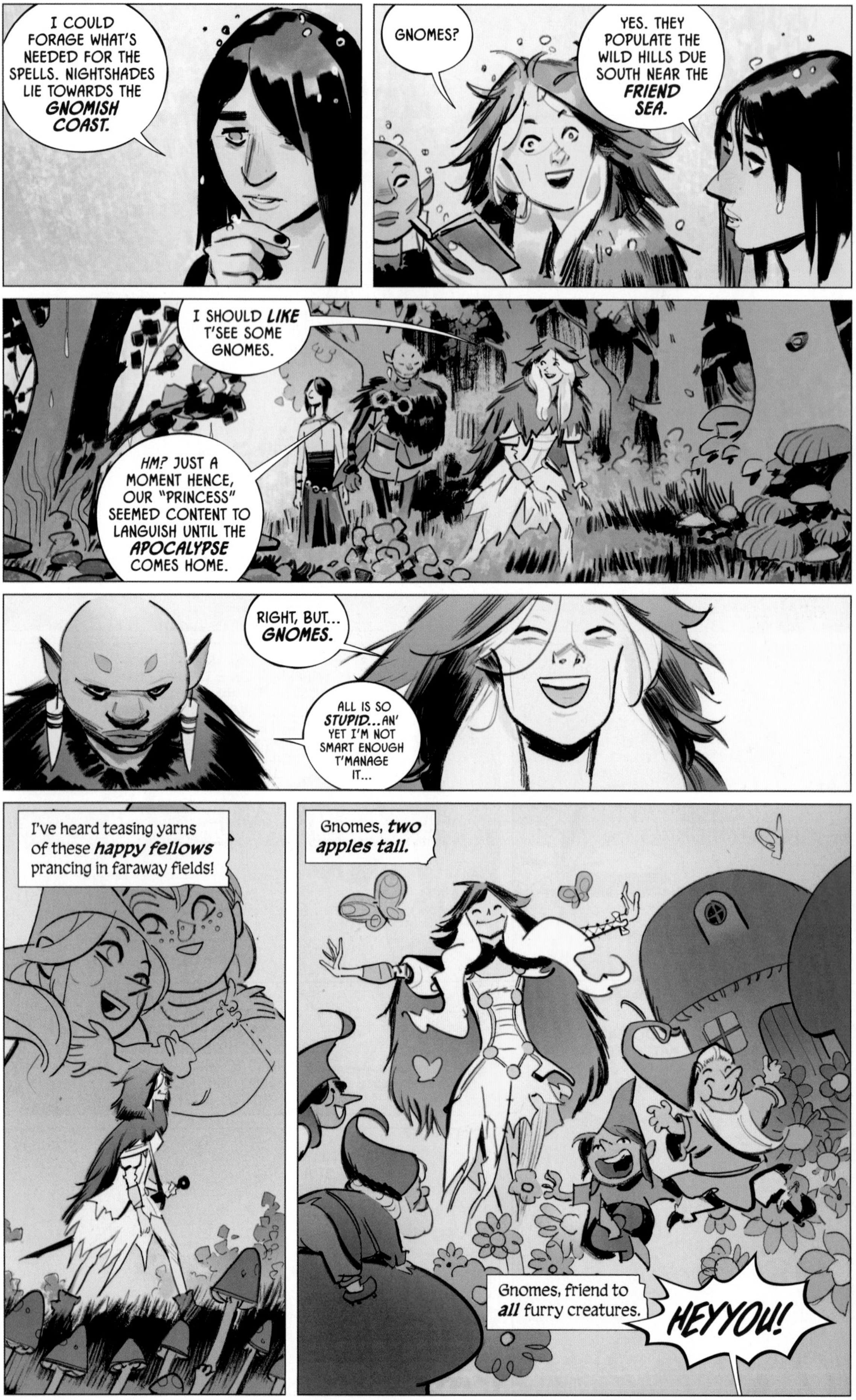
I COULD FORAGE WHAT'S NEEDED FOR THE SPELLS. NIGHTSHADES LIE TOWARDS THE ***GNOMISH COAST.***
GNOMES?
YES. THEY POPULATE THE WILD HILLS DUE SOUTH NEAR THE ***FRIEND SEA.***
I SHOULD ***LIKE*** T'SEE SOME GNOMES.
HM? JUST A MOMENT HENCE, OUR "PRINCESS" SEEMED CONTENT TO LANGUISH UNTIL THE ***APOCALYPSE*** COMES HOME.
RIGHT, BUT... ***GNOMES.***
ALL IS SO ***STUPID...*** AN' YET I'M NOT SMART ENOUGH T'MANAGE IT...
I've heard teasing yarns of these ***happy fellows*** prancing in faraway fields!
Gnomes, ***two apples tall.***
Gnomes, friend to ***all*** furry creatures.
HEYYOU!

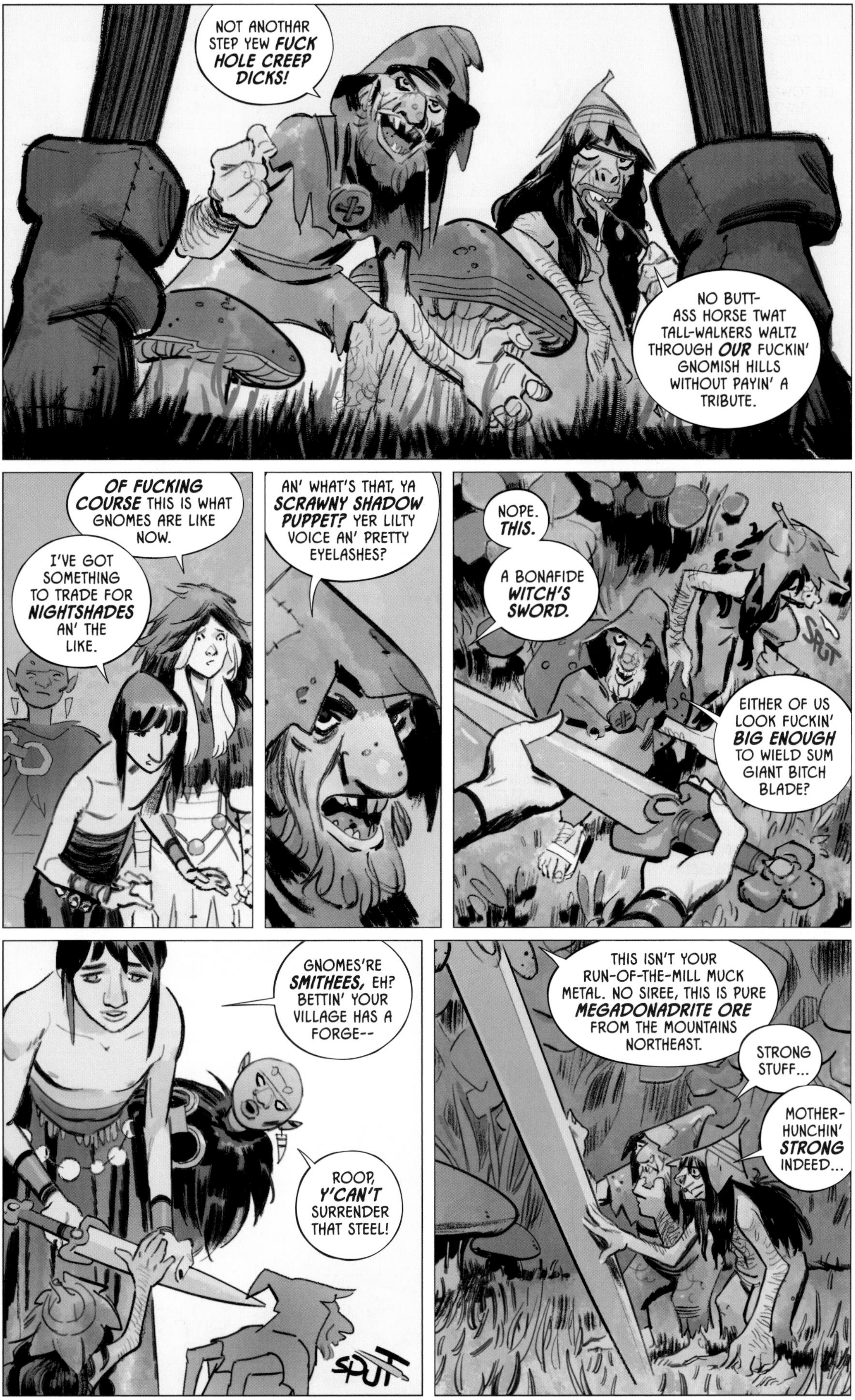
NOT ANOTHAR STEP YEW FUCK HOLE CREEP DICKS!
NO BUTT-ASS HORSE TWAT TALL-WALKERS WALTZ THROUGH OUR FUCKIN' GNOMISH HILLS WITHOUT PAYIN' A TRIBUTE.
OF FUCKING COURSE THIS IS WHAT GNOMES ARE LIKE NOW.
I'VE GOT SOMETHING TO TRADE FOR NIGHTSHADES AN' THE LIKE.
AN' WHAT'S THAT, YA SCRAWNY SHADOW PUPPET? YER LILTY VOICE AN' PRETTY EYELASHES?
NOPE. THIS.
A BONAFIDE WITCH'S SWORD.
SPUT
EITHER OF US LOOK FUCKIN' BIG ENOUGH TO WIELD SUM GIANT BITCH BLADE?
GNOMES'RE SMITHEES, EH? BETTIN' YOUR VILLAGE HAS A FORGE--
ROOP, Y'CAN'T SURRENDER THAT STEEL!
SPUT
THIS ISN'T YOUR RUN-OF-THE-MILL MUCK METAL. NO SIREE, THIS IS PURE MEGADONADRITE ORE FROM THE MOUNTAINS NORTHEAST.
STRONG STUFF...
MOTHER-HUNCHIN' STRONG INDEED...

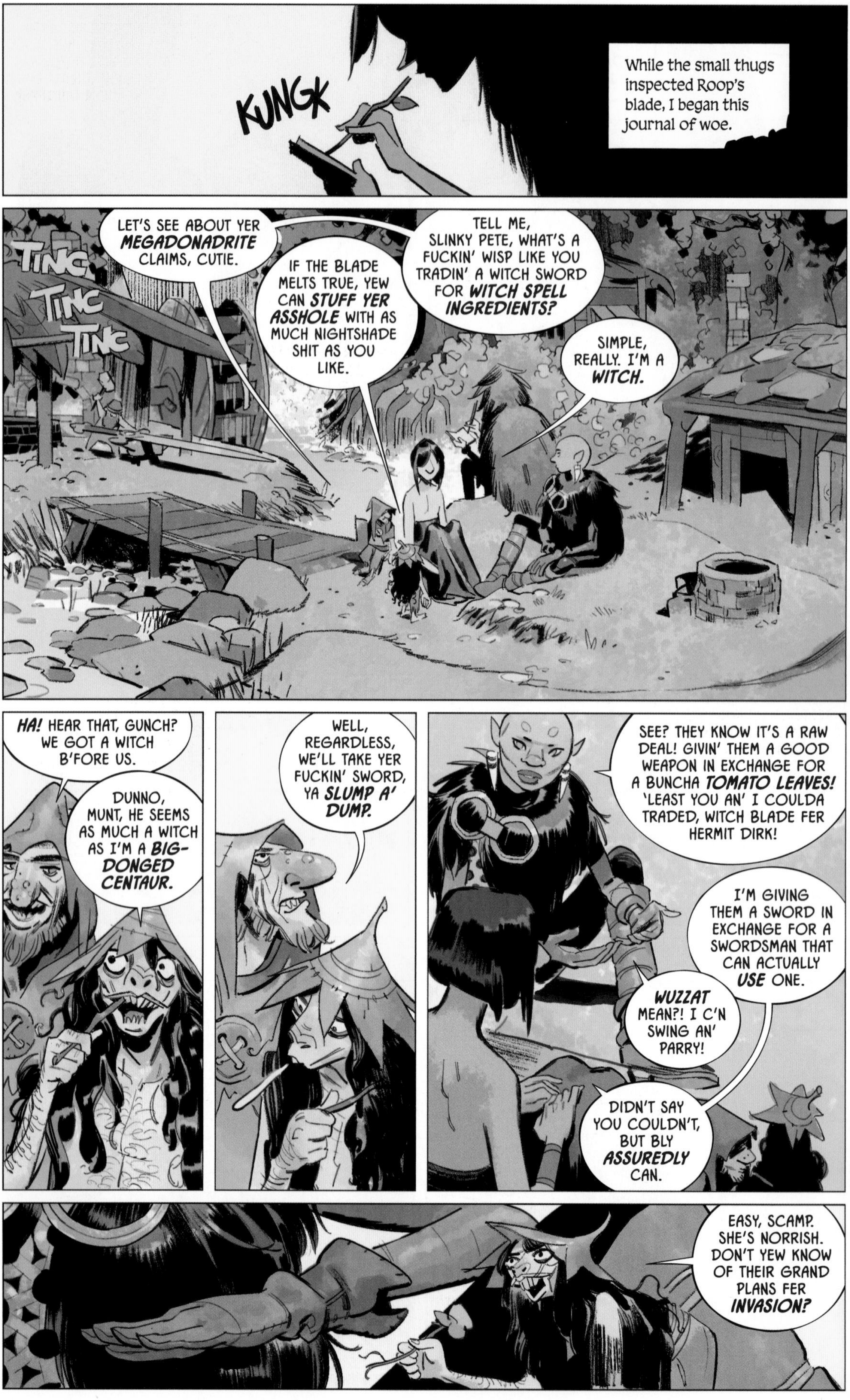
While the small thugs inspected Roop's blade, I began this journal of woe.
KUNGK
TINC
TINC
TINC
LET'S SEE ABOUT YER MEGADONADRITE CLAIMS, CUTIE.
IF THE BLADE MELTS TRUE, YEW CAN STUFF YER ASSHOLE WITH AS MUCH NIGHTSHADE SHIT AS YOU LIKE.
TELL ME, SLINKY PETE, WHAT'S A FUCKIN' WISP LIKE YOU TRADIN' A WITCH SWORD FOR WITCH SPELL INGREDIENTS?
SIMPLE, REALLY. I'M A WITCH.
HA! HEAR THAT, GUNCH? WE GOT A WITCH B'FORE US.
DUNNO, MUNT, HE SEEMS AS MUCH A WITCH AS I'M A BIG-DONGED CENTAUR.
WELL, REGARDLESS, WE'LL TAKE YER FUCKIN' SWORD, YA SLUMP A' DUMP.
SEE? THEY KNOW IT'S A RAW DEAL! GIVIN' THEM A GOOD WEAPON IN EXCHANGE FOR A BUNCHA TOMATO LEAVES! 'LEAST YOU AN' I COULDA TRADED, WITCH BLADE FER HERMIT DIRK!
I'M GIVING THEM A SWORD IN EXCHANGE FOR A SWORDSMAN THAT CAN ACTUALLY USE ONE.
WUZZAT MEAN?! I C'N SWING AN' PARRY!
DIDN'T SAY YOU COULDN'T, BUT BLY ASSUREDLY CAN.
EASY, SCAMP. SHE'S NORRISH. DON'T YEW KNOW OF THEIR GRAND PLANS FER INVASION?

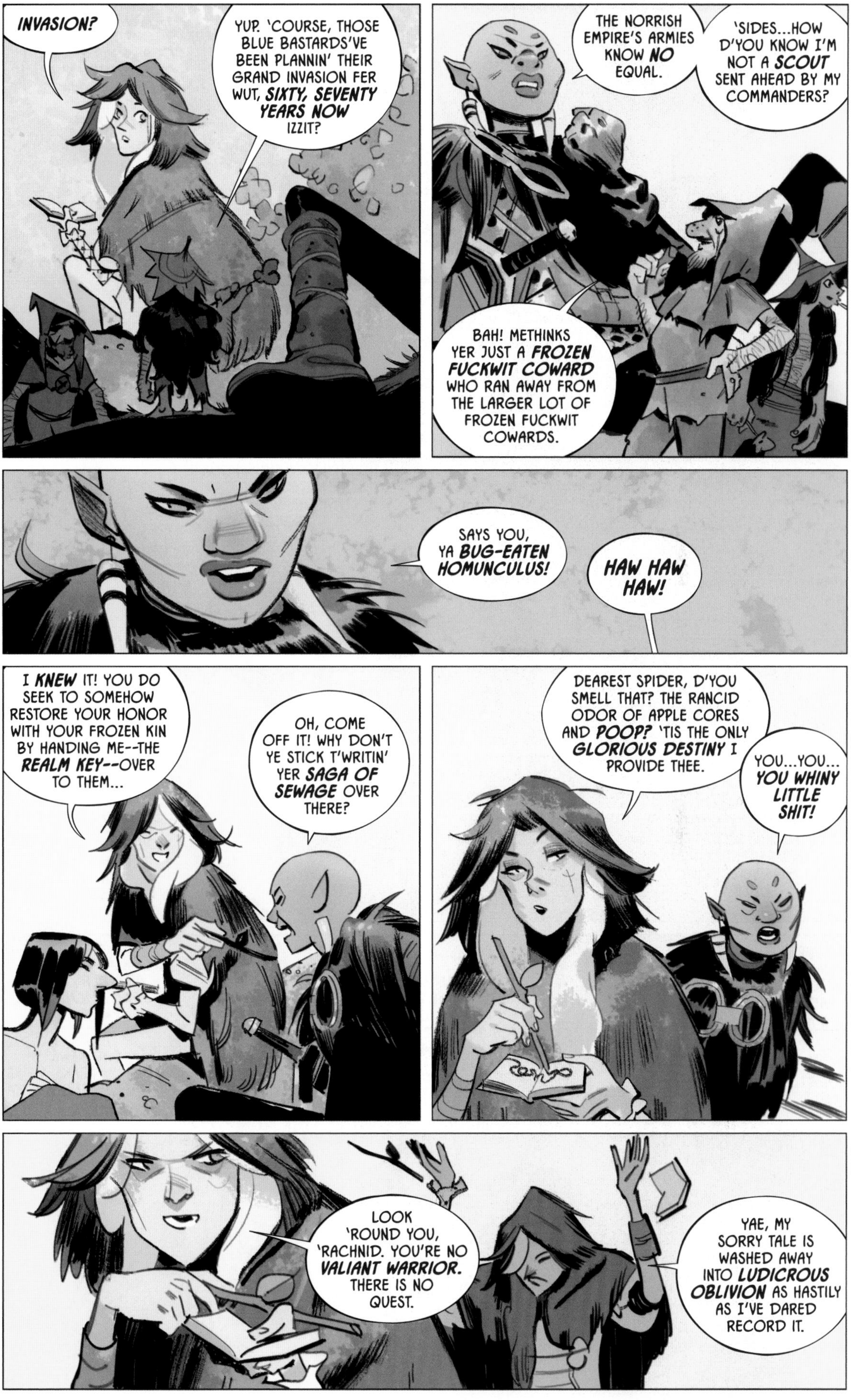
INVASION?
YUP. 'COURSE, THOSE BLUE BASTARDS'VE BEEN PLANNIN' THEIR GRAND INVASION FER WUT, SIXTY, SEVENTY YEARS NOW IZZIT?
THE NORRISH EMPIRE'S ARMIES KNOW NO EQUAL.
'SIDES...HOW D'YOU KNOW I'M NOT A SCOUT SENT AHEAD BY MY COMMANDERS?
BAH! METHINKS YER JUST A FROZEN FUCKWIT COWARD WHO RAN AWAY FROM THE LARGER LOT OF FROZEN FUCKWIT COWARDS.
SAYS YOU, YA BUG-EATEN HOMUNCULUS!
HAW HAW HAW!
I KNEW IT! YOU DO SEEK TO SOMEHOW RESTORE YOUR HONOR WITH YOUR FROZEN KIN BY HANDING ME--THE REALM KEY--OVER TO THEM...
OH, COME OFF IT! WHY DON'T YE STICK T'WRITIN' YER SAGA OF SEWAGE OVER THERE?
DEAREST SPIDER, D'YOU SMELL THAT? THE RANCID ODOR OF APPLE CORES AND POOP? 'TIS THE ONLY GLORIOUS DESTINY I PROVIDE THEE.
YOU...YOU... YOU WHINY LITTLE SHIT!
LOOK 'ROUND YOU, 'RACHNID. YOU'RE NO VALIANT WARRIOR. THERE IS NO QUEST.
YAE, MY SORRY TALE IS WASHED AWAY INTO LUDICROUS OBLIVION AS HASTILY AS I'VE DARED RECORD IT.

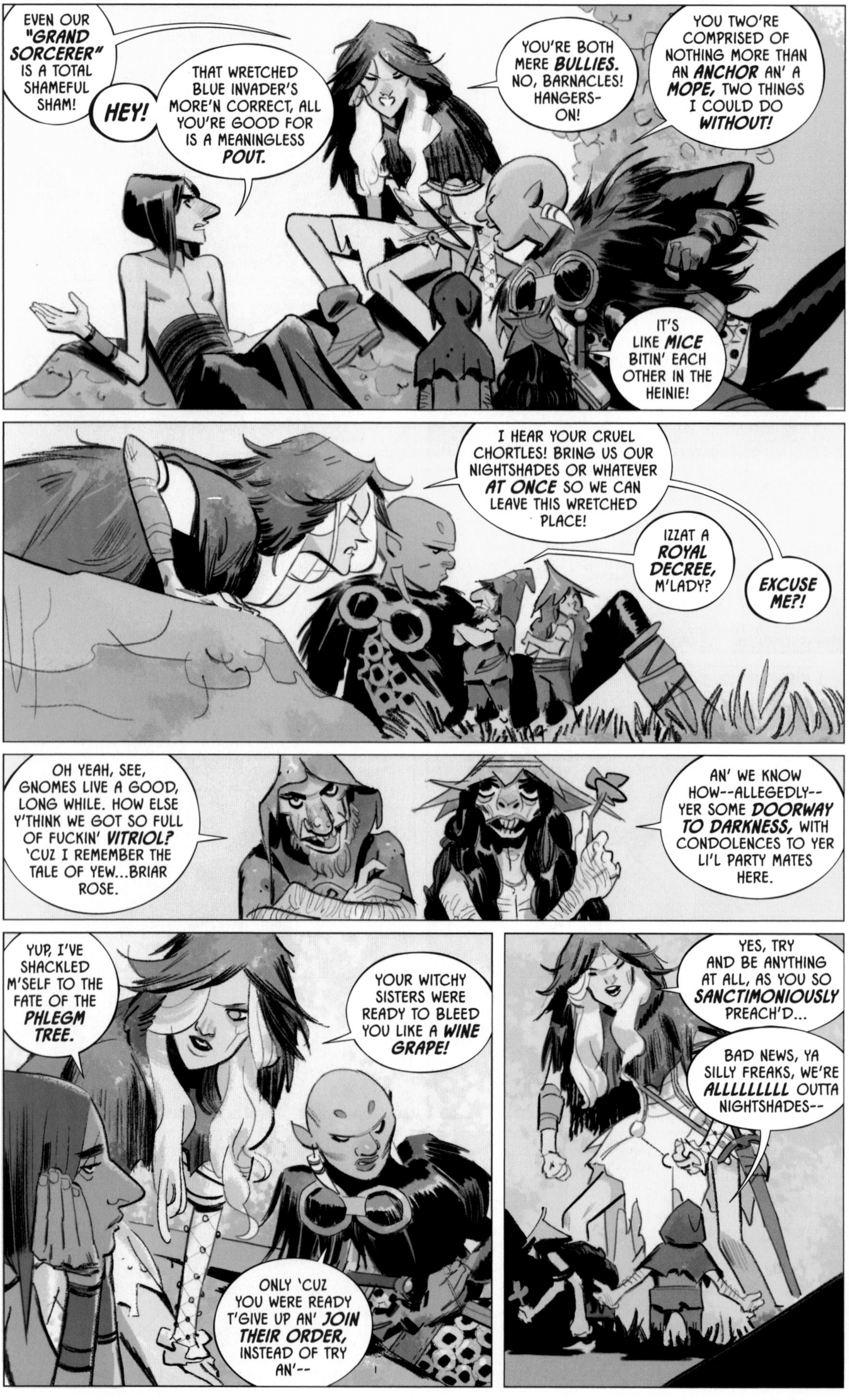

EVEN OUR "GRAND SORCERER" IS A TOTAL SHAMEFUL SHAM!
HEY!
THAT WRETCHED BLUE INVADER'S MORE'N CORRECT, ALL YOU'RE GOOD FOR IS A MEANINGLESS POUT.
YOU'RE BOTH MERE BULLIES. NO, BARNACLES! HANGERS-ON!
YOU TWO'RE COMPRISED OF NOTHING MORE THAN AN ANCHOR AN' A MOPE, TWO THINGS I COULD DO WITHOUT!
IT'S LIKE MICE BITIN' EACH OTHER IN THE HEINIE!
I HEAR YOUR CRUEL CHORTLES! BRING US OUR NIGHTSHADES OR WHATEVER AT ONCE SO WE CAN LEAVE THIS WRETCHED PLACE!
IZZAT A ROYAL DECREE, M'LADY?
EXCUSE ME?!
OH YEAH, SEE, GNOMES LIVE A GOOD, LONG WHILE. HOW ELSE Y'THINK WE GOT SO FULL OF FUCKIN' VITRIOL? 'CUZ I REMEMBER THE TALE OF YEW...BRIAR ROSE.
AN' WE KNOW HOW--ALLEGEDLY--YER SOME DOORWAY TO DARKNESS, WITH CONDOLENCES TO YER LI'L PARTY MATES HERE.
YUP, I'VE SHACKLED M'SELF TO THE FATE OF THE PHLEGM TREE.
YOUR WITCHY SISTERS WERE READY TO BLEED YOU LIKE A WINE GRAPE!
ONLY 'CUZ YOU WERE READY T'GIVE UP AN' JOIN THEIR ORDER, INSTEAD OF TRY AN'--
YES, TRY AND BE ANYTHING AT ALL, AS YOU SO SANCTIMONIOUSLY PREACH'D...
BAD NEWS, YA SILLY FREAKS, WE'RE ALLLLLLLLL OUTTA NIGHTSHADES--

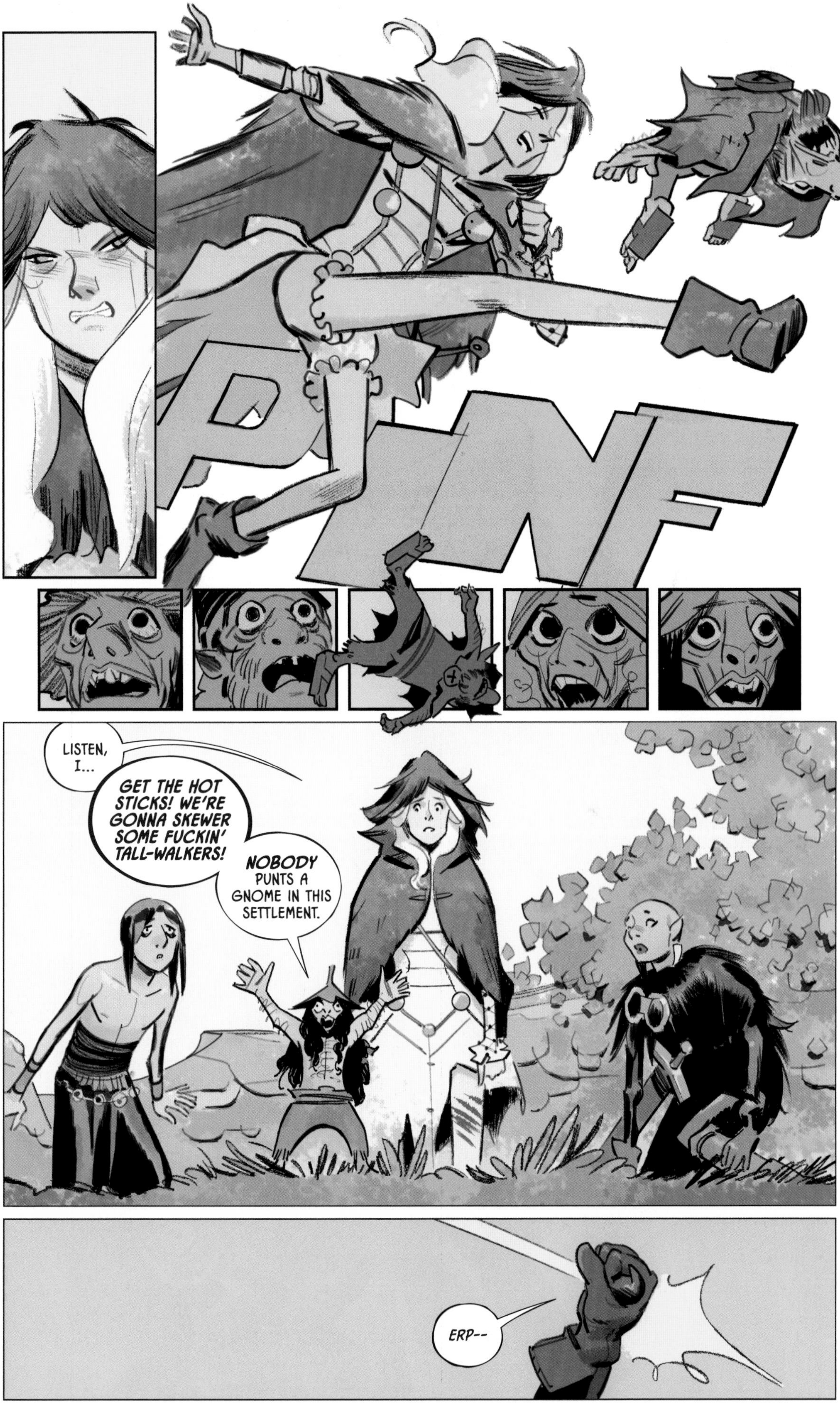
PUNF
LISTEN, I...
GET THE HOT STICKS! WE'RE GONNA SKEWER SOME FUCKIN' TALL-WALKERS!
NOBODY PUNTS A GNOME IN THIS SETTLEMENT.
ERP--

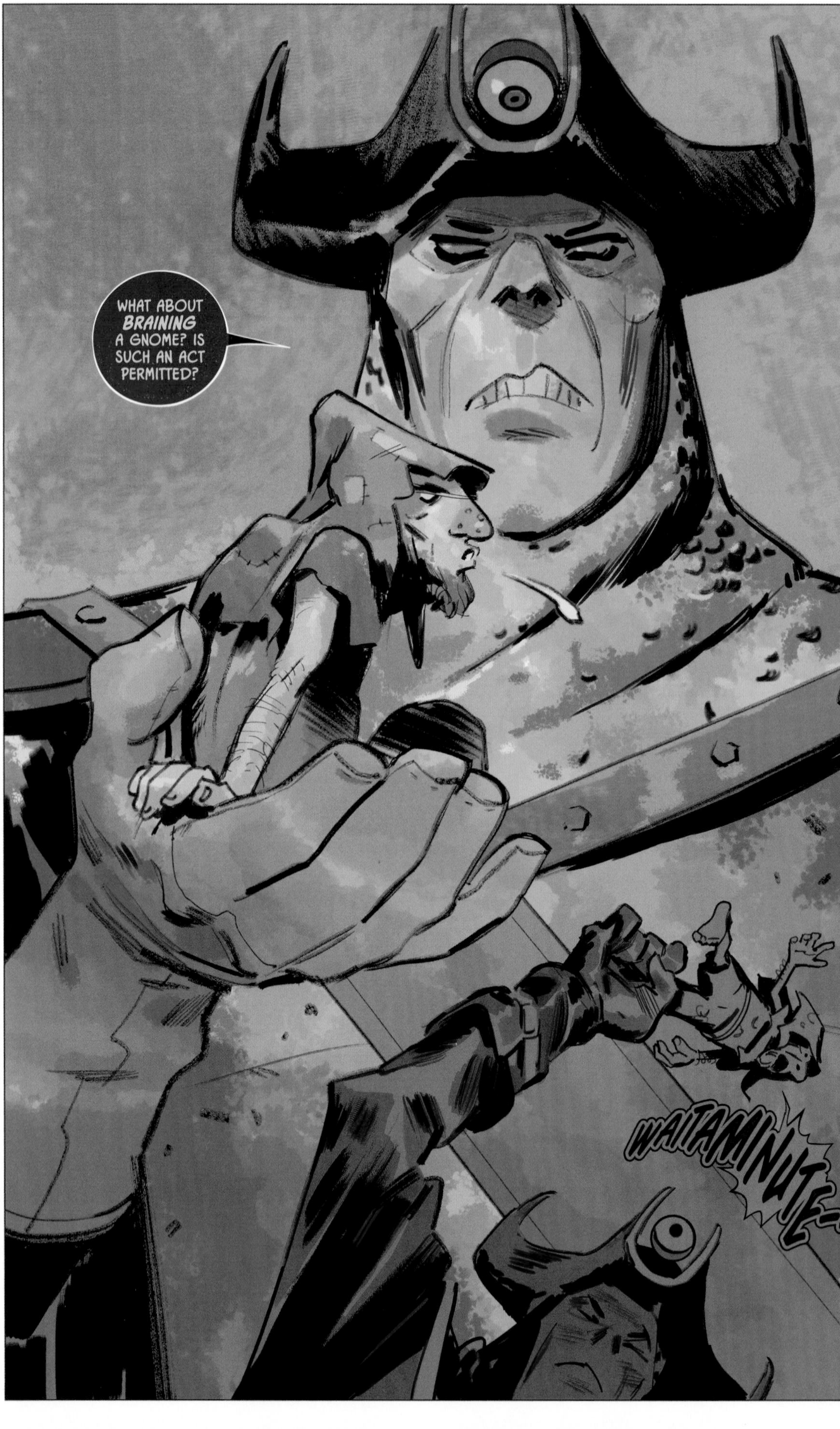
WHAT ABOUT *BRAINING* A GNOME? IS SUCH AN ACT PERMITTED?
WAITAMINUTE--

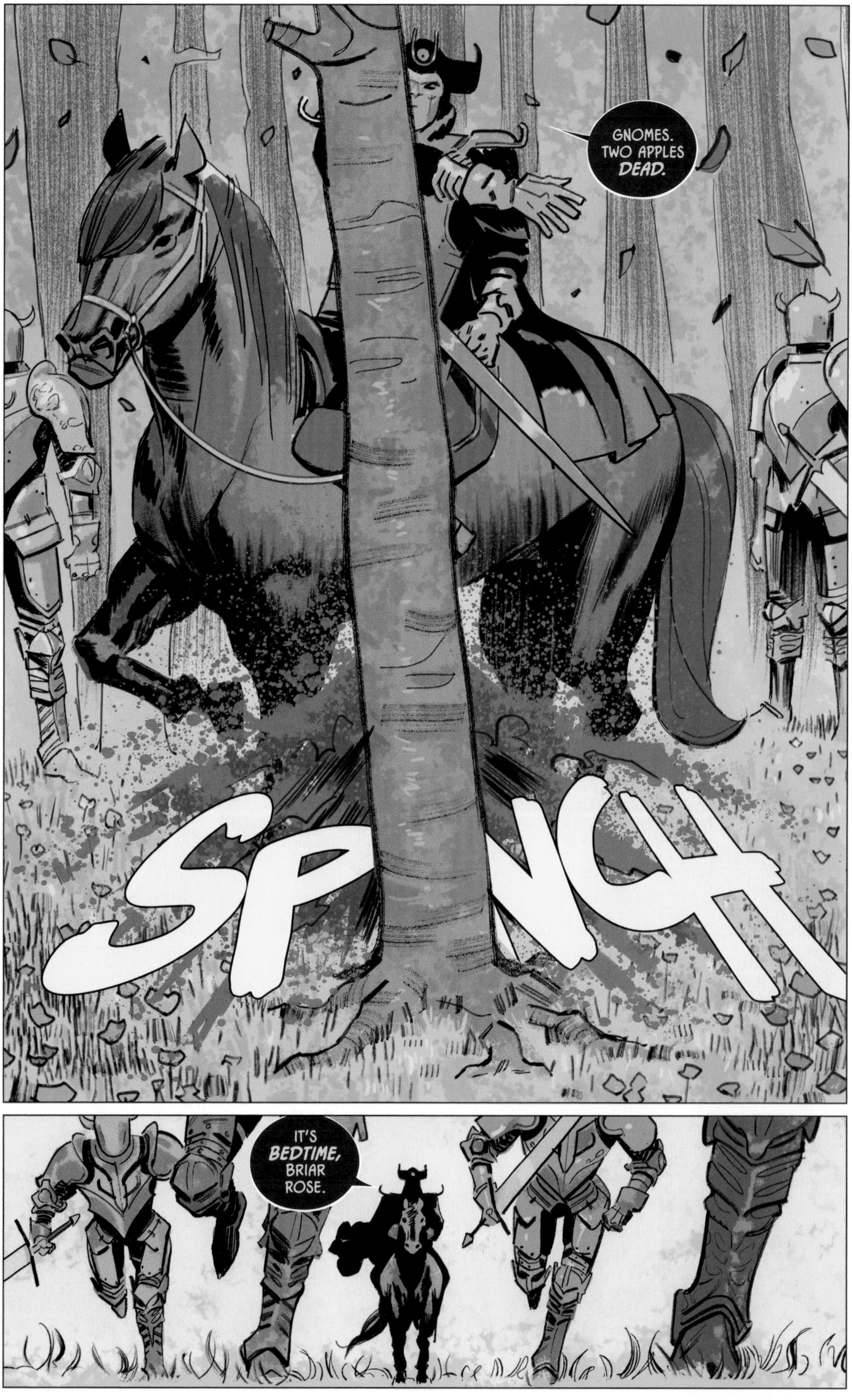
GNOMES. TWO APPLES DEAD.
IT'S BEDTIME, BRIAR ROSE.

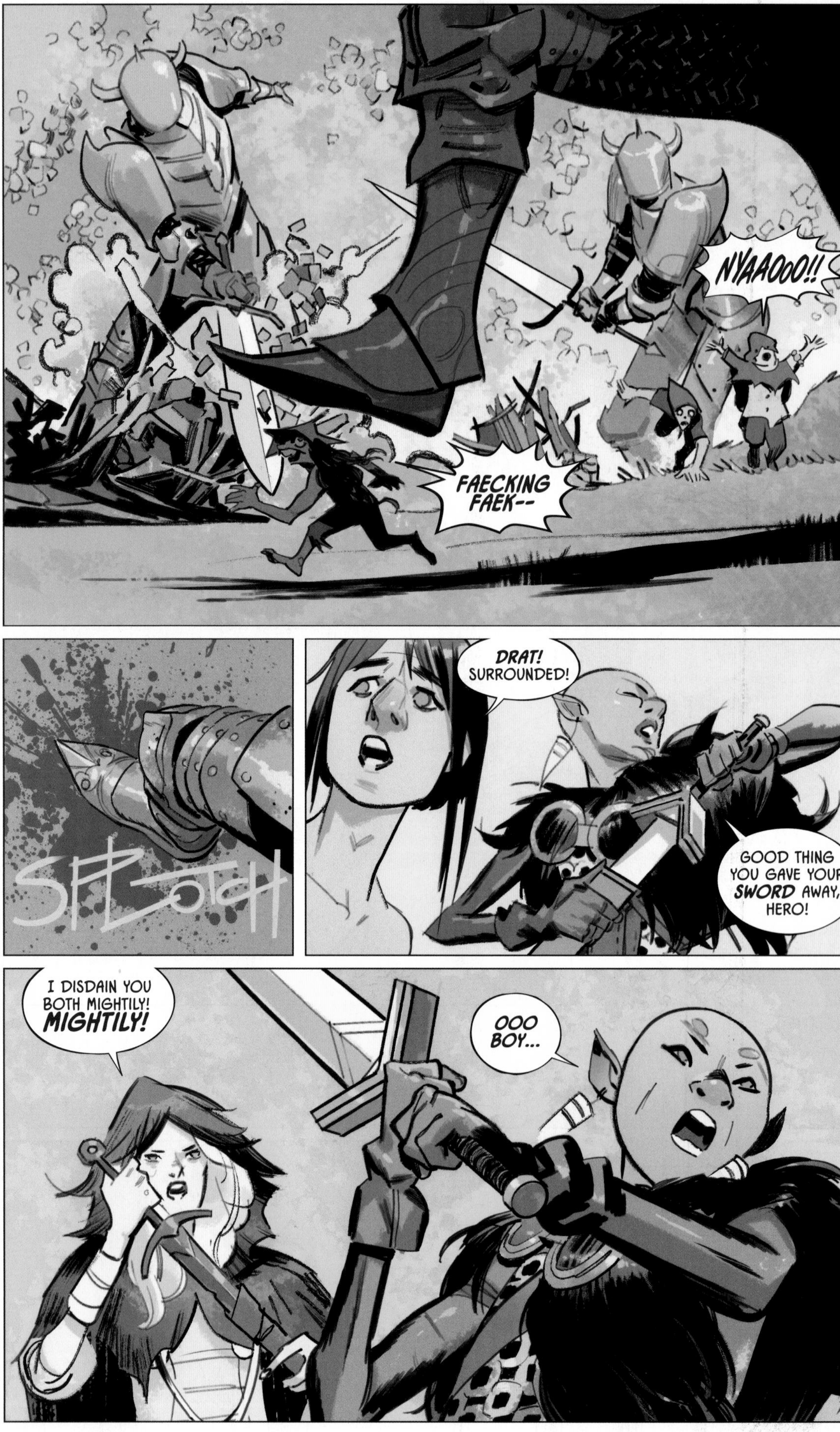
NYAAOOO!!
FAECKING FAEK--
SPLOTCH
DRAT! SURROUNDED!
GOOD THING YOU GAVE YOUR SWORD AWAY, HERO!
I DISDAIN YOU BOTH MIGHTILY! MIGHTILY!
OOO BOY...

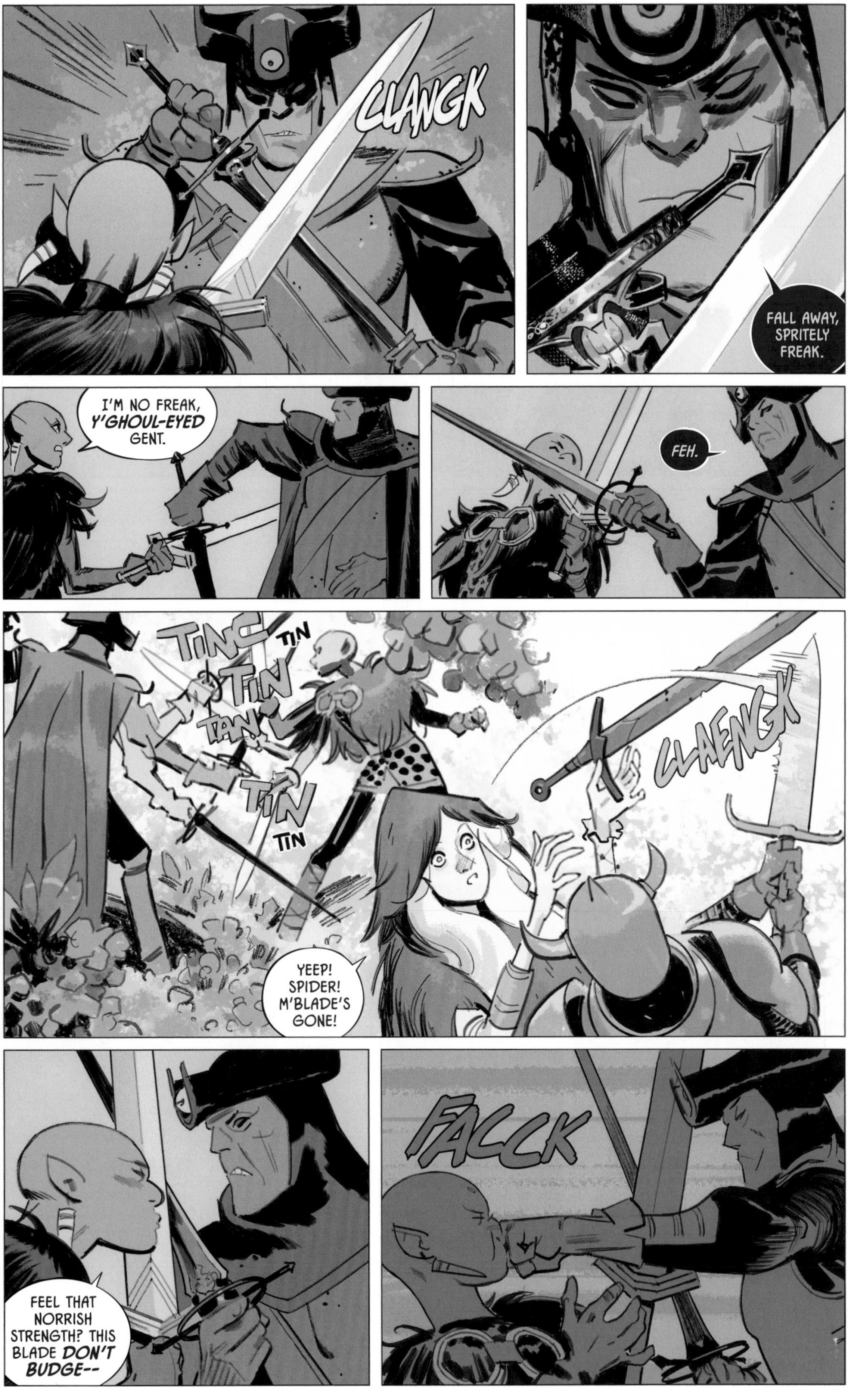
CLANGK
FALL AWAY, SPRITELY FREAK.
I'M NO FREAK, Y'GHOUL-EYED GENT.
FEH.
TINC
TIN
TIN
TAN
TIN
TIN
CLAENGK
YEEP! SPIDER! M'BLADE'S GONE!
FEEL THAT NORRISH STRENGTH? THIS BLADE DON'T BUDGE--
FACCK

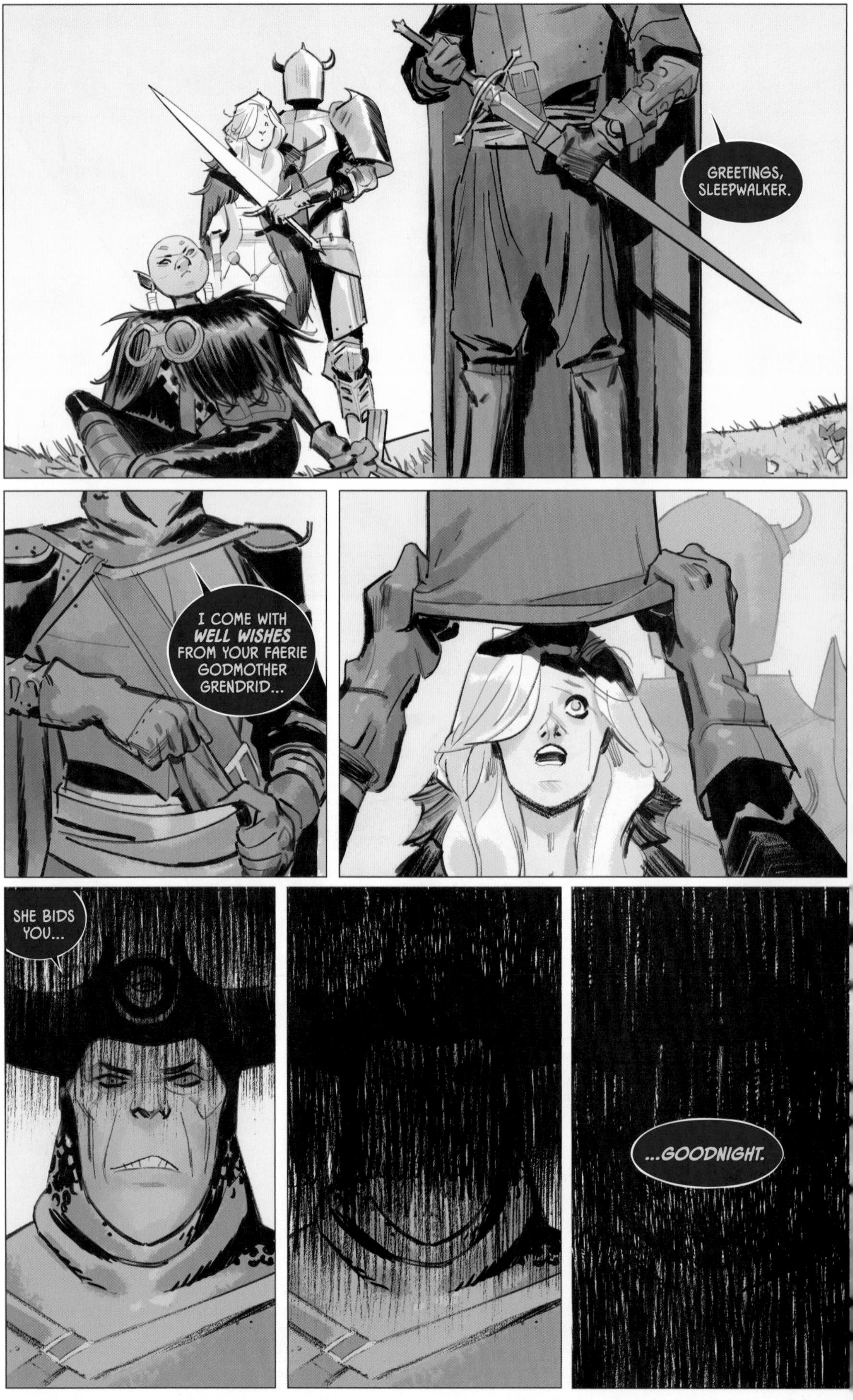
GREETINGS, SLEEPWALKER.
I COME WITH WELL WISHES FROM YOUR FAERIE GODMOTHER GRENDRID...
SHE BIDS YOU...
...GOODNIGHT.

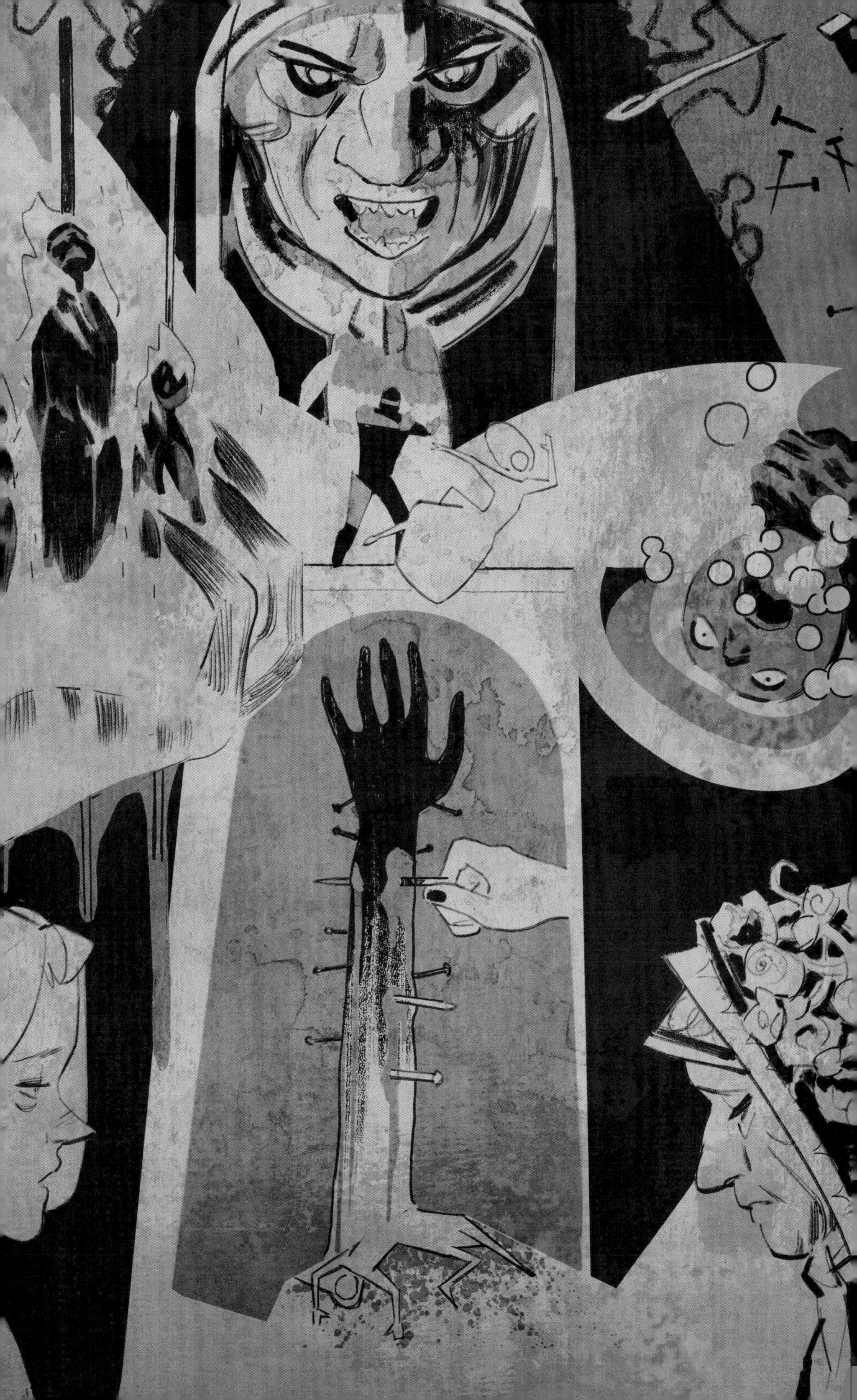

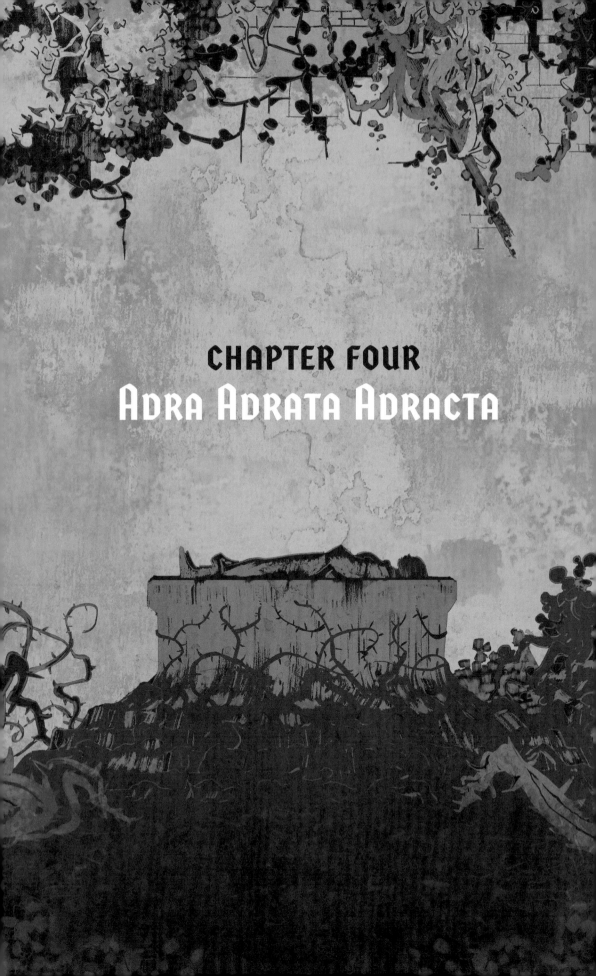

CHAPTER FOUR
Adra Adrata Adracta

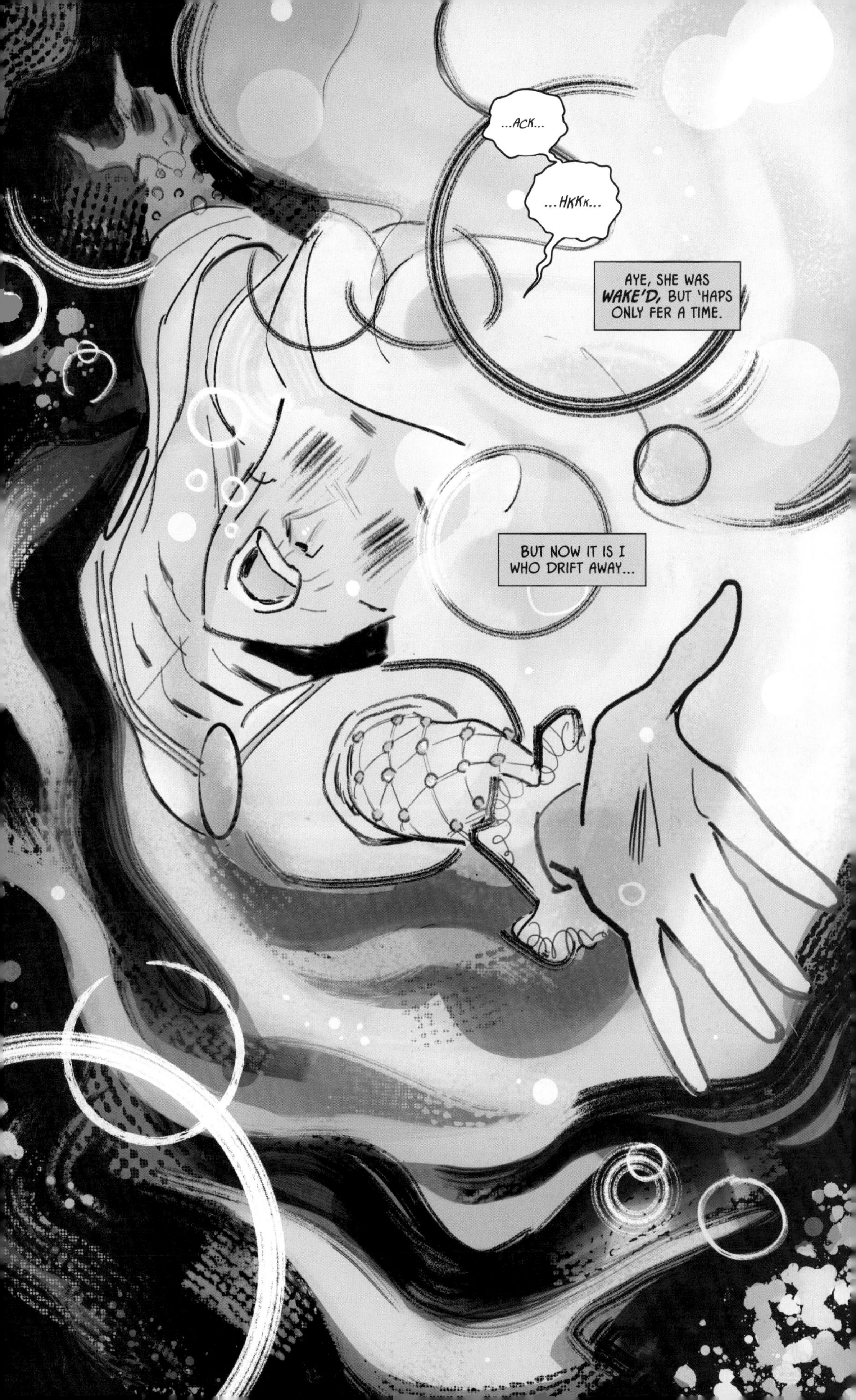
...ACK...
...HKKK...
AYE, SHE WAS WAKE'D, BUT 'HAPS ONLY FER A TIME.
BUT NOW IT IS I WHO DRIFT AWAY...

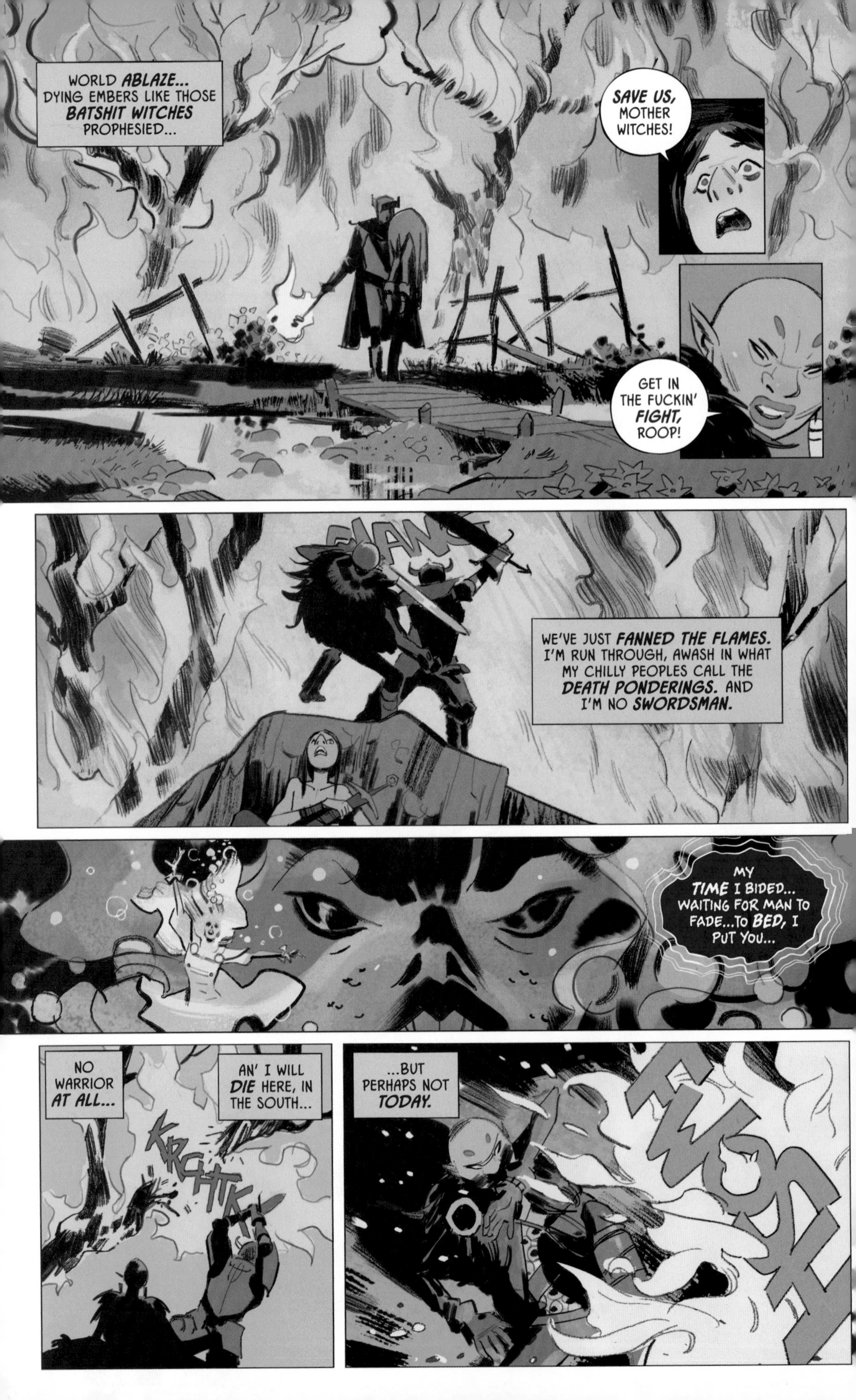
WORLD ABLAZE... DYING EMBERS LIKE THOSE BATSHIT WITCHES PROPHESIED...
SAVE US, MOTHER WITCHES!
GET IN THE FUCKIN' FIGHT, ROOP!
WE'VE JUST FANNED THE FLAMES. I'M RUN THROUGH, AWASH IN WHAT MY CHILLY PEOPLES CALL THE DEATH PONDERINGS. AND I'M NO SWORDSMAN.
MY TIME I BIDED... WAITING FOR MAN TO FADE...TO BED, I PUT YOU...
NO WARRIOR AT ALL...
AN' I WILL DIE HERE, IN THE SOUTH...
KRCHTK
...BUT PERHAPS NOT TODAY.
FWOOSH

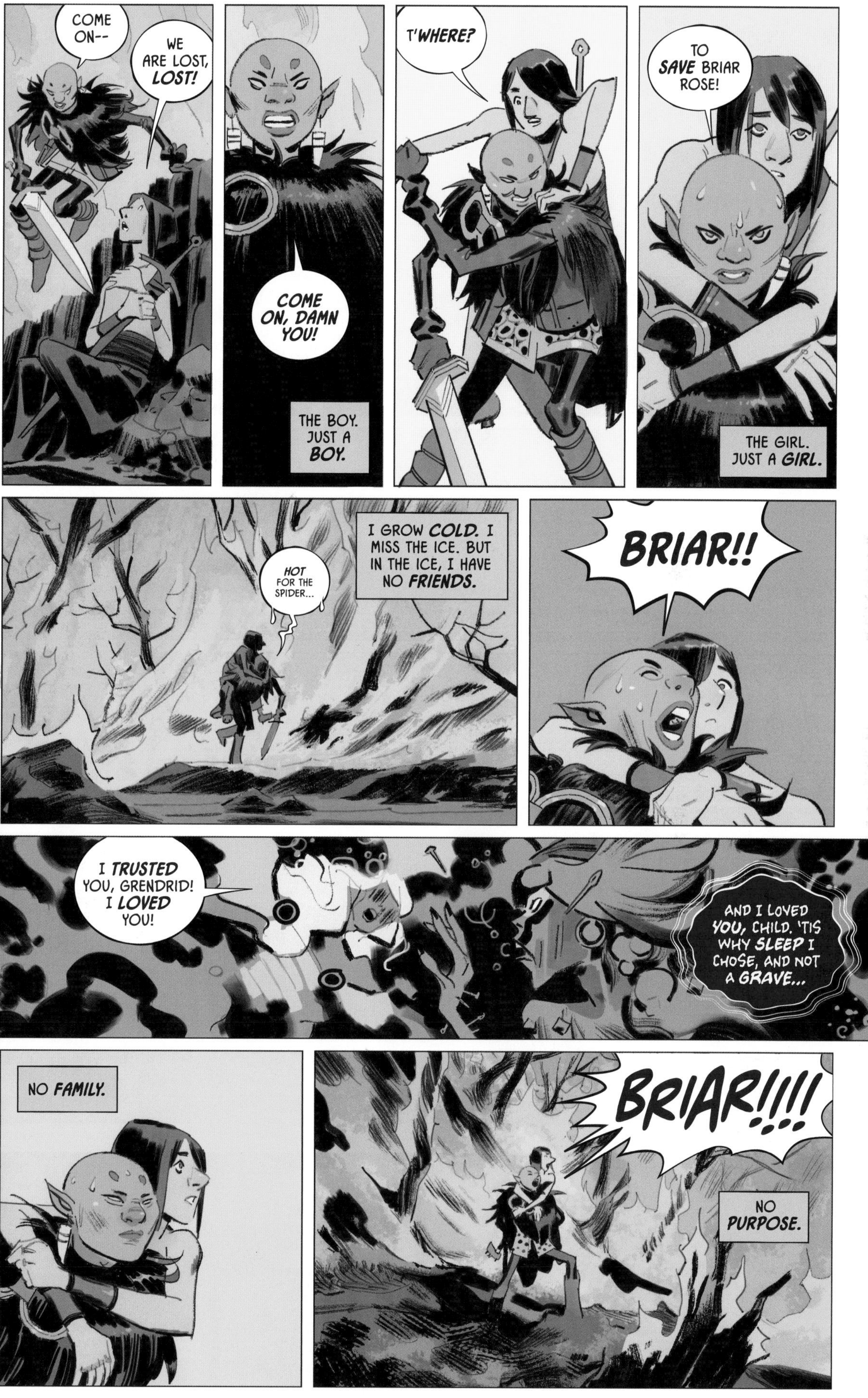
COME ON--
WE ARE LOST, LOST!
COME ON, DAMN YOU!
THE BOY. JUST A BOY.
T'WHERE?
TO SAVE BRIAR ROSE!
THE GIRL. JUST A GIRL.
HOT FOR THE SPIDER...
I GROW COLD. I MISS THE ICE. BUT IN THE ICE, I HAVE NO FRIENDS.
BRIAR!!
I TRUSTED YOU, GRENDRID! I LOVED YOU!
AND I LOVED YOU, CHILD. 'TIS WHY SLEEP I CHOSE, AND NOT A GRAVE...
NO FAMILY.
BRIAR!!!!
NO PURPOSE.

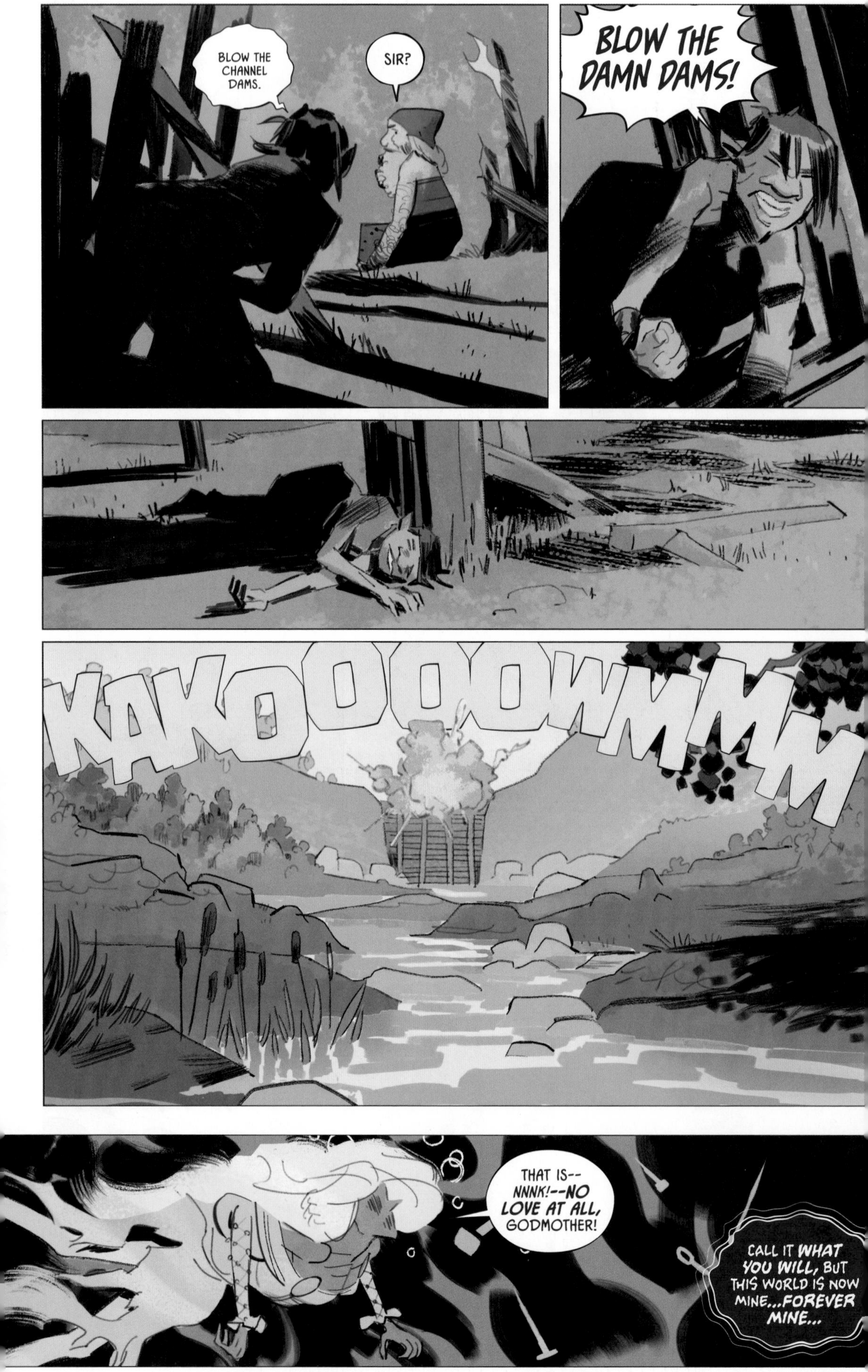
BLOW THE CHANNEL DAMS.
SIR?
BLOW THE DAMN DAMS!
KAKOOOOWMMM
THAT IS-- NNNK!--NO LOVE AT ALL, GODMOTHER!
CALL IT WHAT YOU WILL, BUT THIS WORLD IS NOW MINE...FOREVER MINE...

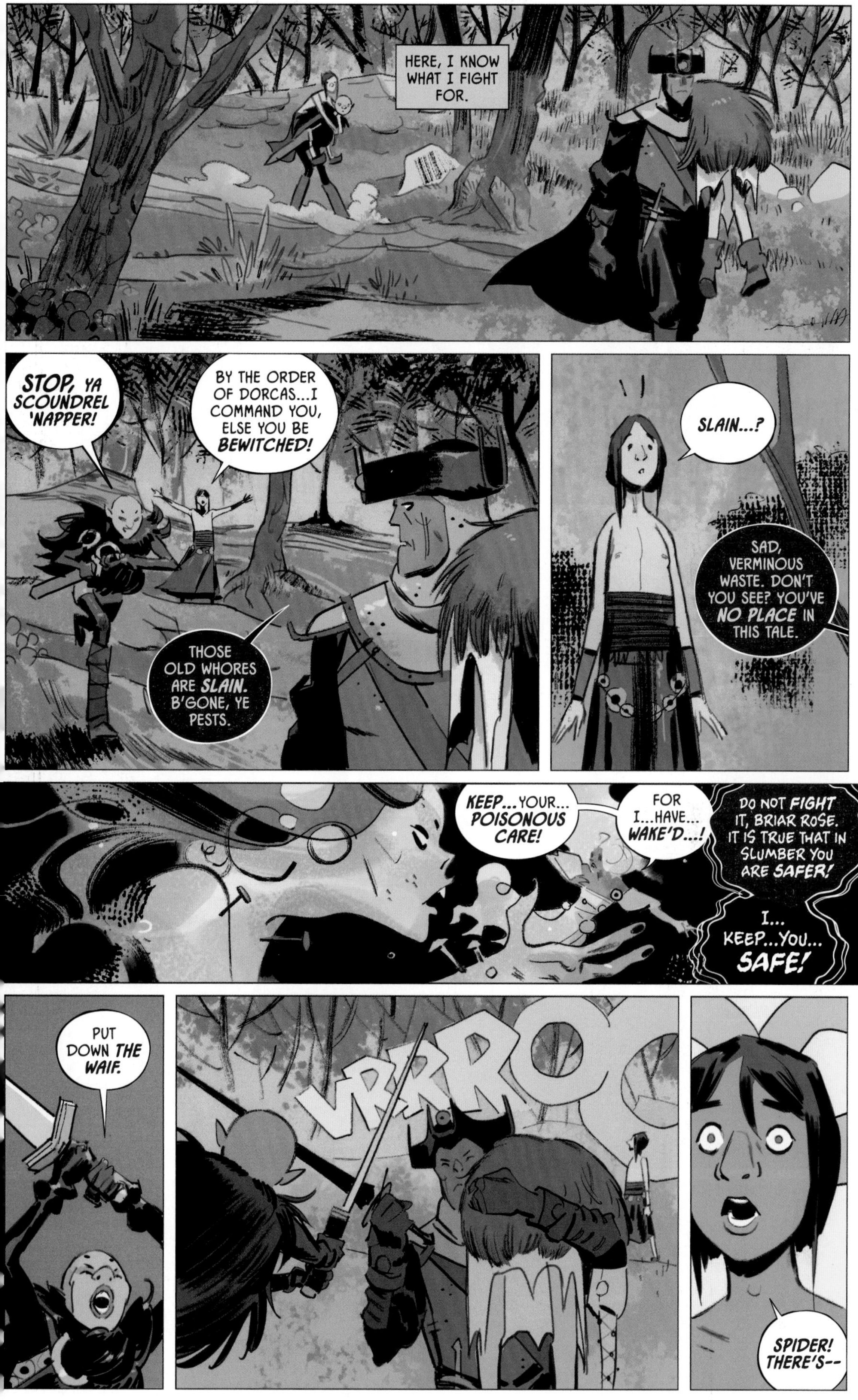
HERE, I KNOW WHAT I FIGHT FOR.
STOP, YA SCOUNDREL 'NAPPER!
BY THE ORDER OF DORCAS...I COMMAND YOU, ELSE YOU BE BEWITCHED!
THOSE OLD WHORES ARE SLAIN. B'GONE, YE PESTS.
SLAIN...?
SAD, VERMINOUS WASTE. DON'T YOU SEE? YOU'VE NO PLACE IN THIS TALE.
KEEP...YOUR... POISONOUS CARE!
FOR I...HAVE... WAKE'D...!
DO NOT FIGHT IT, BRIAR ROSE. IT IS TRUE THAT IN SLUMBER YOU ARE SAFER!
I... KEEP...YOU... SAFE!
PUT DOWN THE WAIF.
VRRRO
SPIDER! THERE'S--

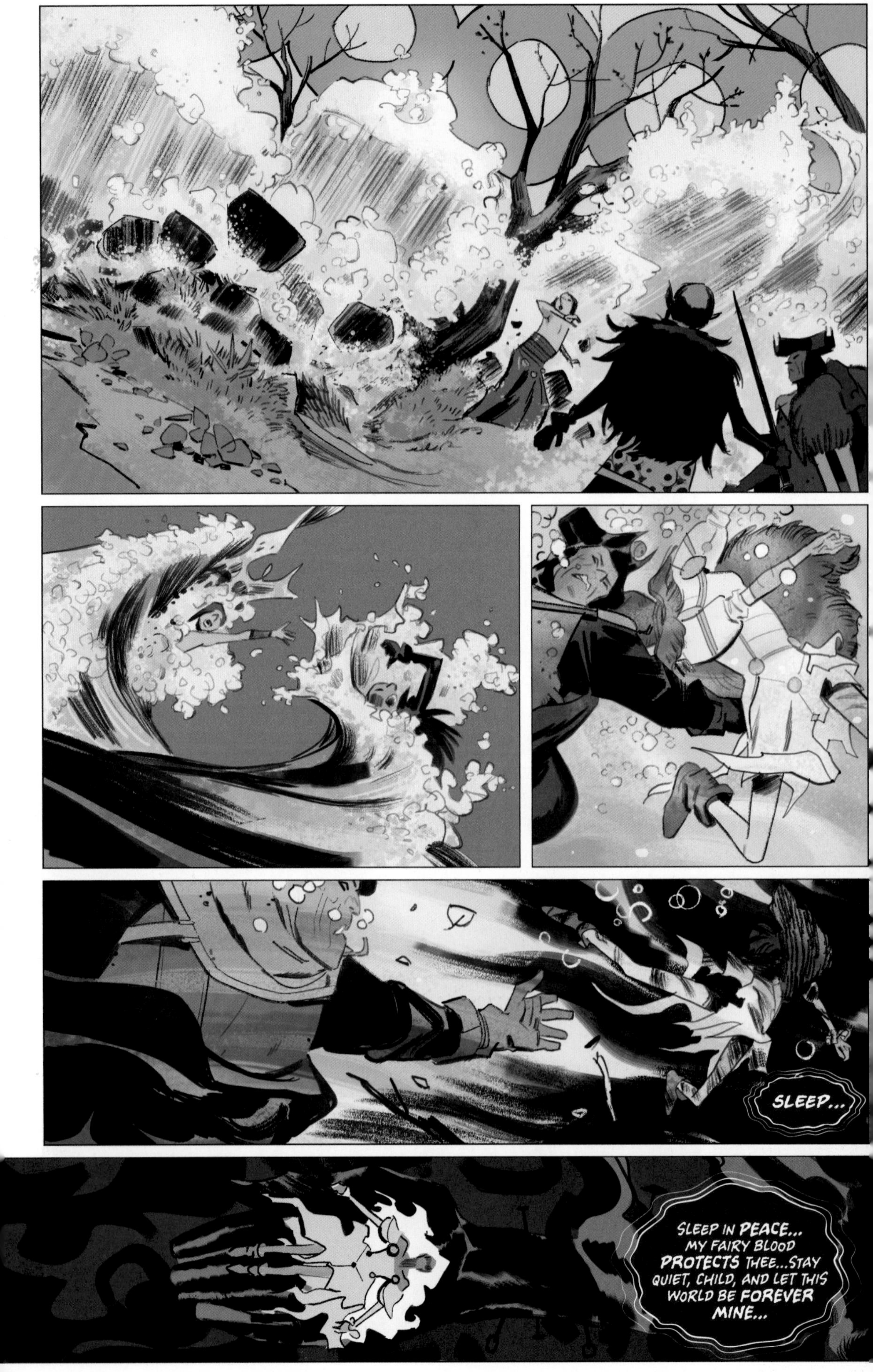
SLEEP...
SLEEP IN PEACE... MY FAIRY BLOOD PROTECTS THEE...STAY QUIET, CHILD, AND LET THIS WORLD BE FOREVER MINE...

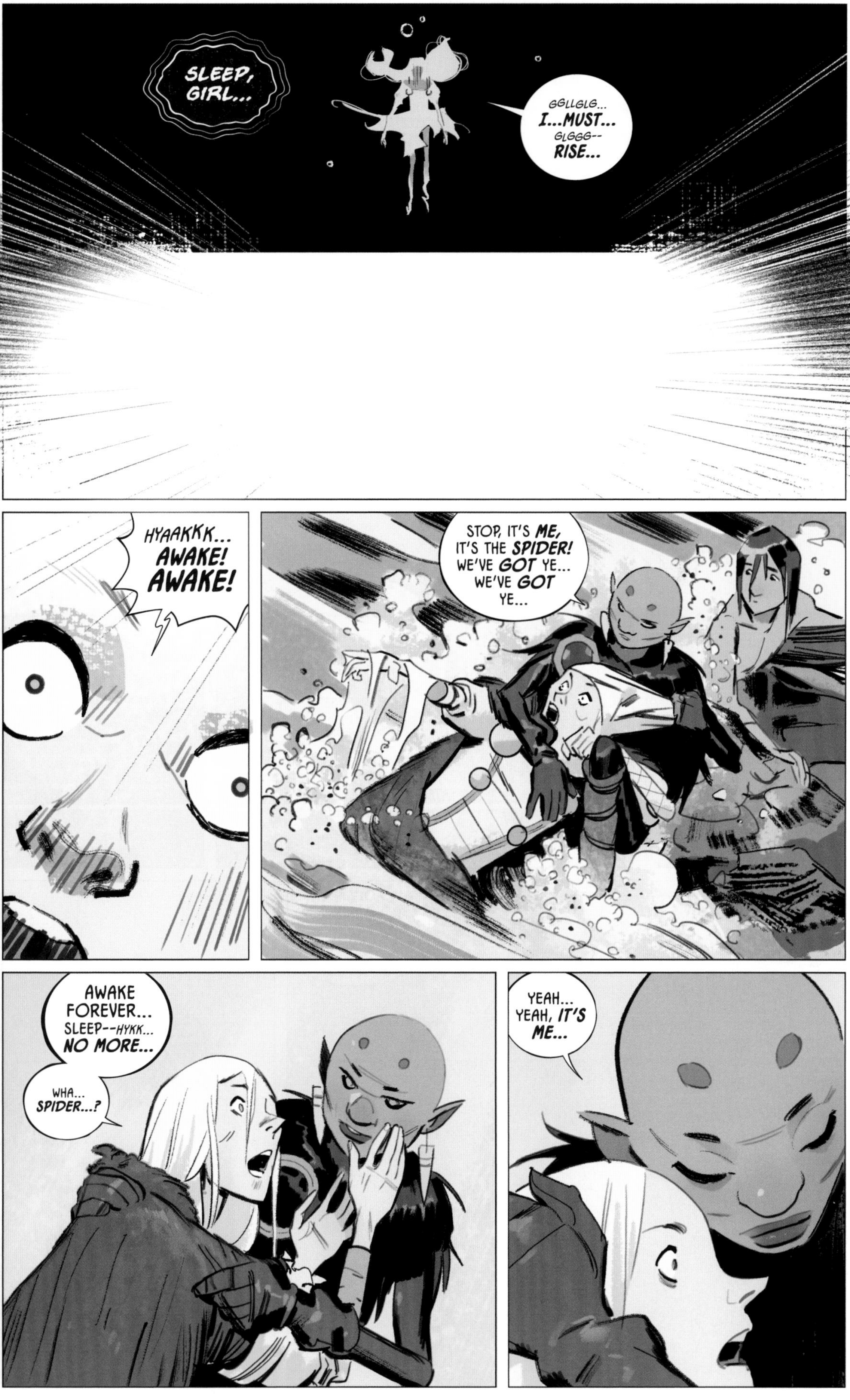
SLEEP, GIRL...
GGLLGLG... I...MUST... GLGGG-- RISE...
HYAAKKK... AWAKE! AWAKE!
STOP, IT'S ME, IT'S THE SPIDER! WE'VE GOT YE... WE'VE GOT YE...
AWAKE FOREVER... SLEEP--HYKK... NO MORE...
WHA... SPIDER...?
YEAH... YEAH, IT'S ME...

GRENDRID'S TWISTED *HENCH-FUCK* SEEMS T'HAVE WASHED AWAYS...

FACK ME, THIS IS WINDCROSS... WE'VE SWEPT ALL THE WAY BACK TO *DARTORIAN*...

LOOKEE! *NIGHTSHADES!* A WHOLE FLOOD OF 'EM...

AN' AGAIN OUR ONLY HOPE IS *BONES.*

AHOY! THE *FUCKWADS* HAVE RETURNED!

FOUND 'IM. AND HIS SHIELD AN' SWORD...

THEN, ROOP, IF YOU WOULDN'T MIND NECROMANCING OUR *GRAND SKELETAL SAVIOR* BACK TO LIFE, PLEASE...

CAREFUL. THAT *GNOME-KILLER'S* LIABLE TO SHOW AT ANY MOMENT...

IF HE DOES...I'VE A *MESSAGE* FOR HIM...

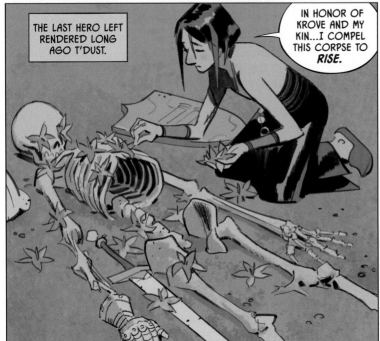

THE LAST HERO LEFT RENDERED LONG AGO T'DUST.

IN HONOR OF KROVE AND MY KIN...I COMPEL THIS CORPSE TO *RISE.*

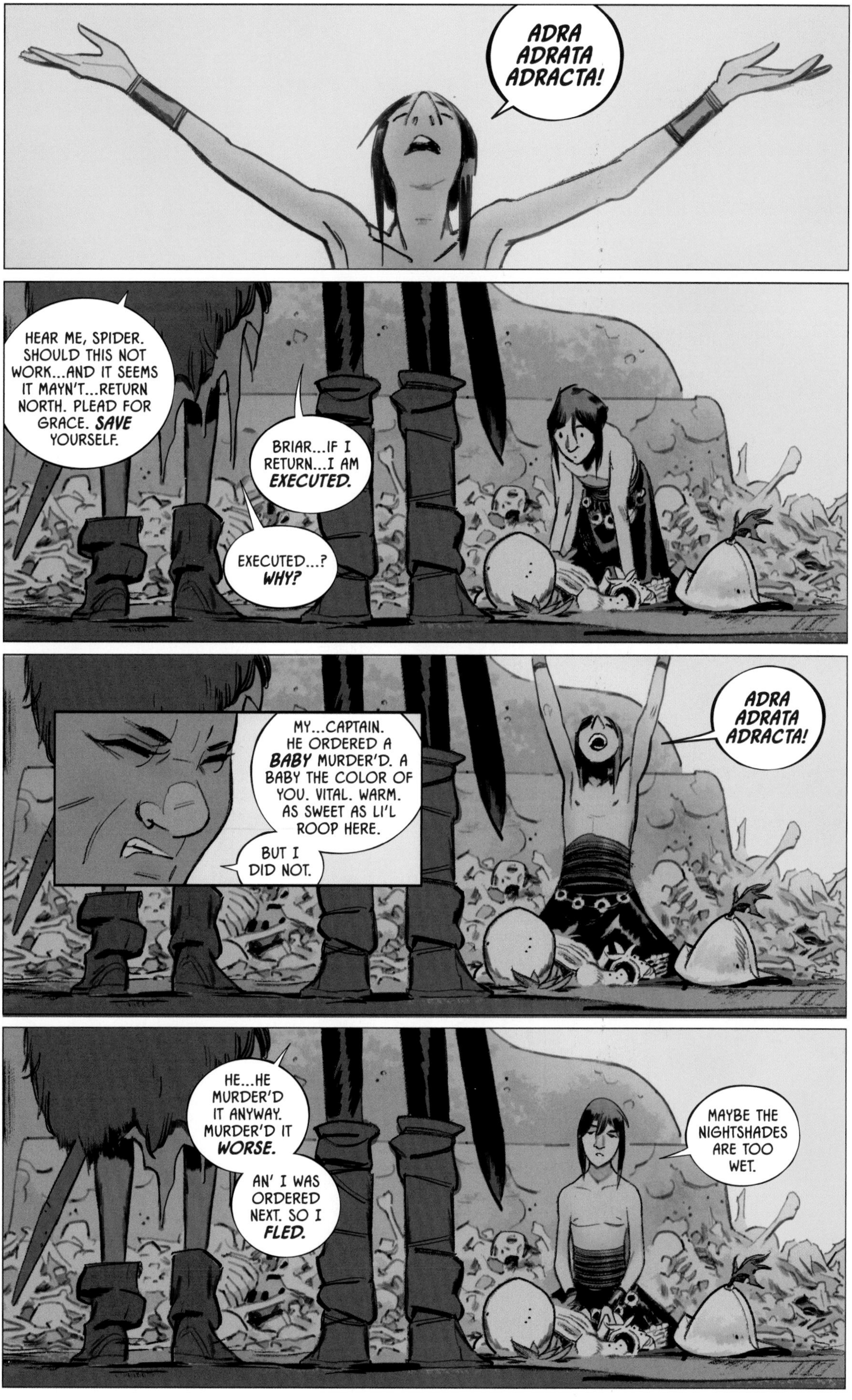
ADRA ADRATA ADRACTA!
HEAR ME, SPIDER. SHOULD THIS NOT WORK...AND IT SEEMS IT MAYN'T...RETURN NORTH. PLEAD FOR GRACE. SAVE YOURSELF.
BRIAR...IF I RETURN...I AM EXECUTED.
EXECUTED...? WHY?
MY...CAPTAIN. HE ORDERED A BABY MURDER'D. A BABY THE COLOR OF YOU. VITAL. WARM. AS SWEET AS LI'L ROOP HERE.
BUT I DID NOT.
ADRA ADRATA ADRACTA!
HE...HE MURDER'D IT ANYWAY. MURDER'D IT WORSE.
AN' I WAS ORDERED NEXT. SO I FLED.
MAYBE THE NIGHTSHADES ARE TOO WET.

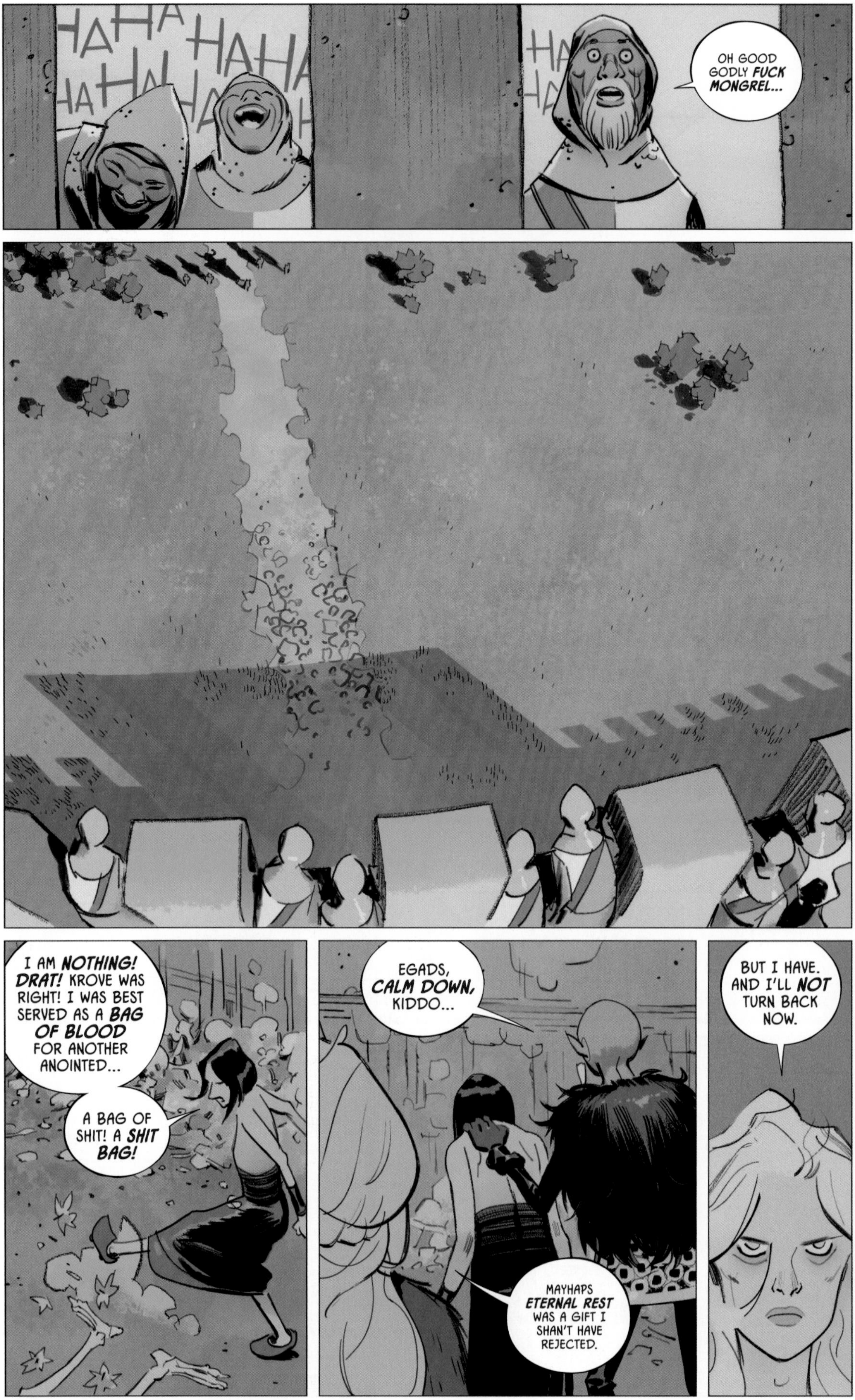
HAHAHA HAHA HAHA HA
HA HA
OH GOOD GODLY FUCK MONGREL...
I AM NOTHING! DRAT! KROVE WAS RIGHT! I WAS BEST SERVED AS A BAG OF BLOOD FOR ANOTHER ANOINTED...
A BAG OF SHIT! A SHIT BAG!
EGADS, CALM DOWN, KIDDO...
MAYHAPS ETERNAL REST WAS A GIFT I SHAN'T HAVE REJECTED.
BUT I HAVE. AND I'LL NOT TURN BACK NOW.

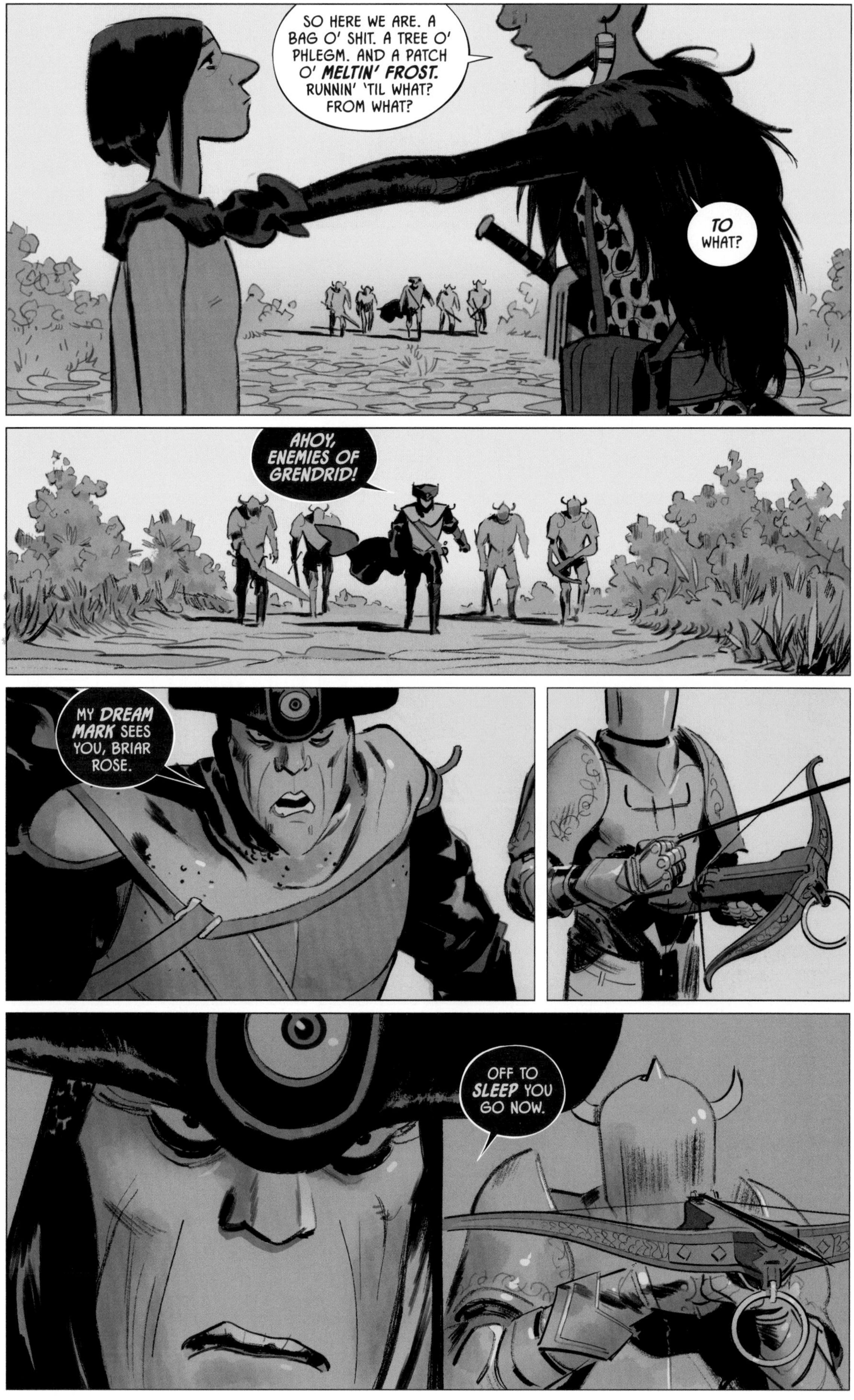
SO HERE WE ARE. A BAG O' SHIT. A TREE O' PHLEGM. AND A PATCH O' MELTIN' FROST. RUNNIN' 'TIL WHAT? FROM WHAT?
TO WHAT?
AHOY, ENEMIES OF GRENDRID!
MY DREAM MARK SEES YOU, BRIAR ROSE.
OFF TO SLEEP YOU GO NOW.

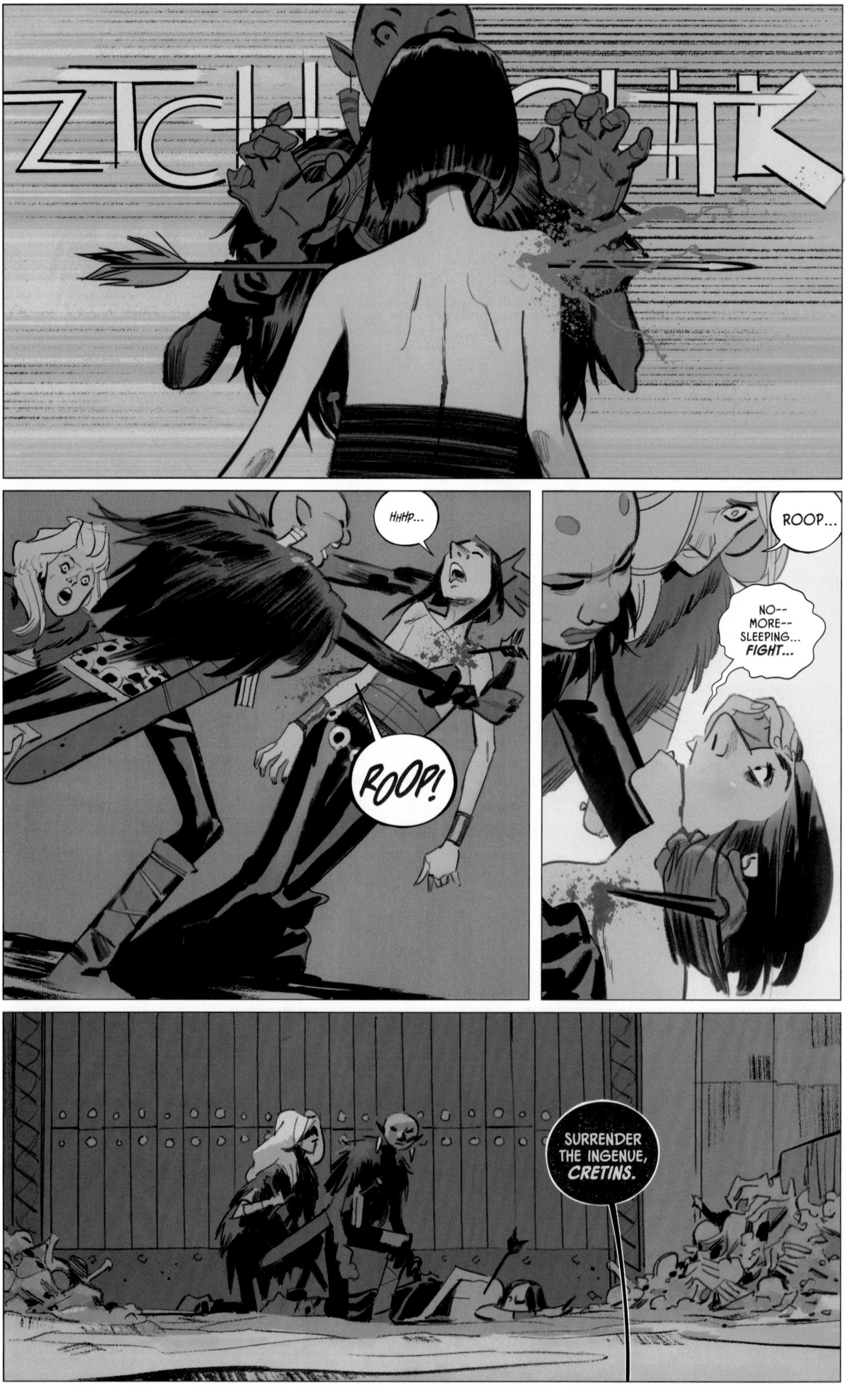
ZTCHUCHTK
HHHP...
ROOP!
ROOP...
NO-- MORE-- SLEEPING... FIGHT...
SURRENDER THE INGENUE, CRETINS.

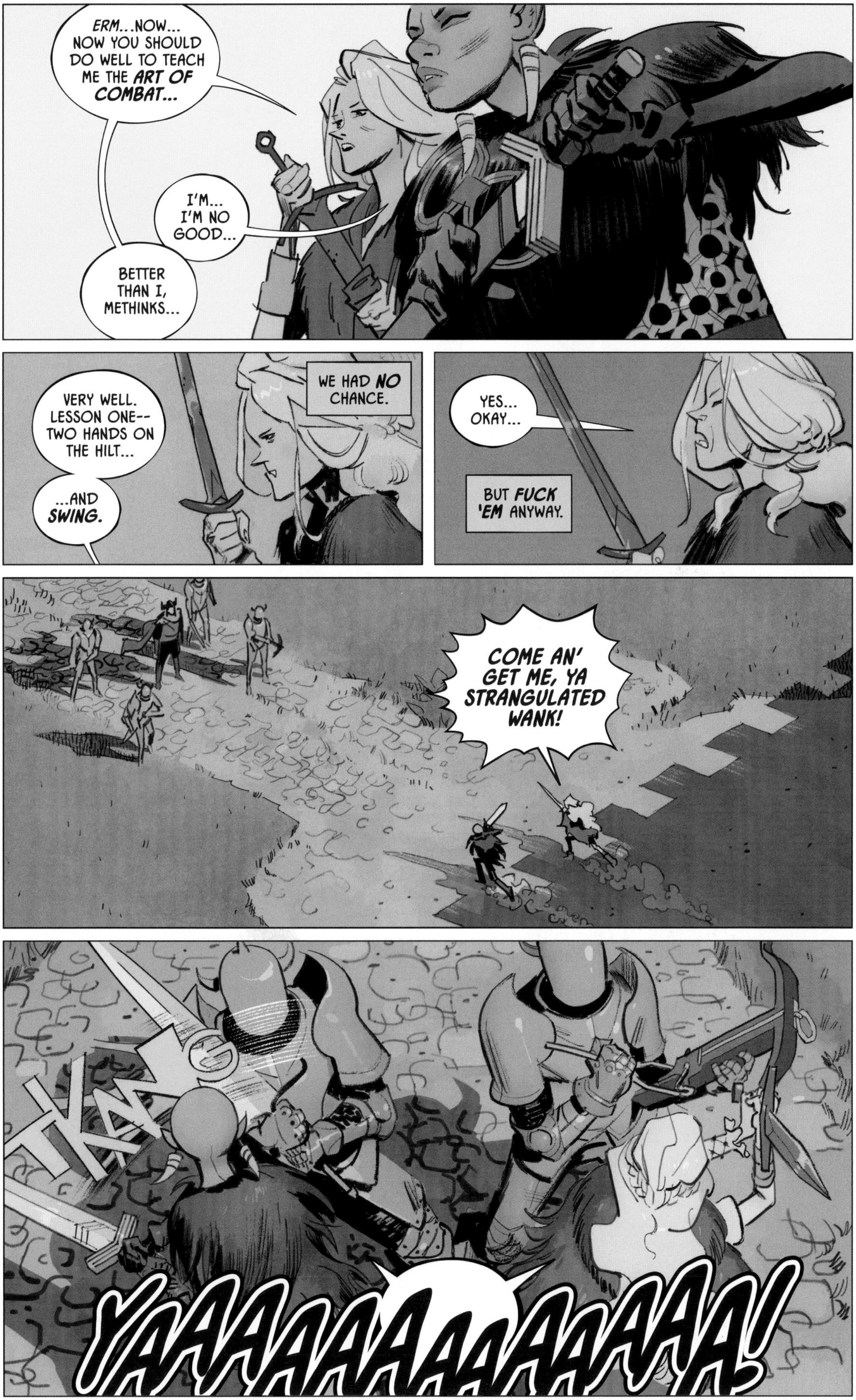
ERM...NOW... NOW YOU SHOULD DO WELL TO TEACH ME THE ART OF COMBAT...
I'M... I'M NO GOOD...
BETTER THAN I, METHINKS...
VERY WELL. LESSON ONE-- TWO HANDS ON THE HILT...
...AND SWING.
WE HAD NO CHANCE.
YES... OKAY...
BUT FUCK 'EM ANYWAY.
COME AN' GET ME, YA STRANGULATED WANK!
TKAW
YAAAAAAAAAAAAA!

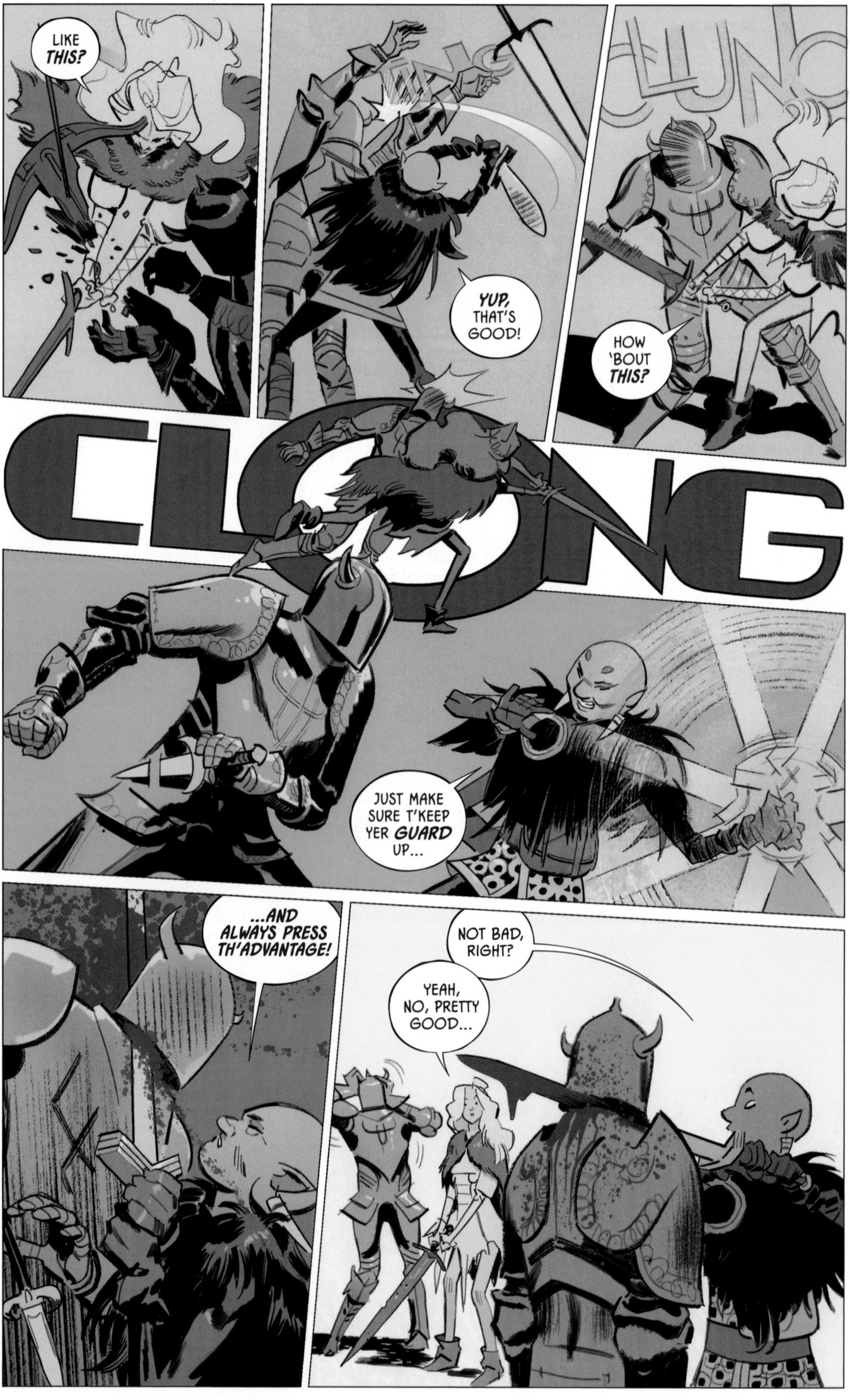
LIKE THIS?
YUP, THAT'S GOOD!
CLUNG
HOW 'BOUT THIS?
CLONG
JUST MAKE SURE T'KEEP YER GUARD UP...
...AND ALWAYS PRESS TH'ADVANTAGE!
NOT BAD, RIGHT?
YEAH, NO, PRETTY GOOD...

BUT LIKE I SAID...

...I AM *RUN THROUGH*.

NO!!

NOW IT IS *I* WHO DRIFT AWAY...LOST IN THESE DEATH PONDERINGS.

CHANGK

AN' I WILL *DIE* HERE, IN THE SOUTH...

...BUT PERHAPS NOT TODAY.

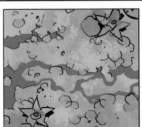

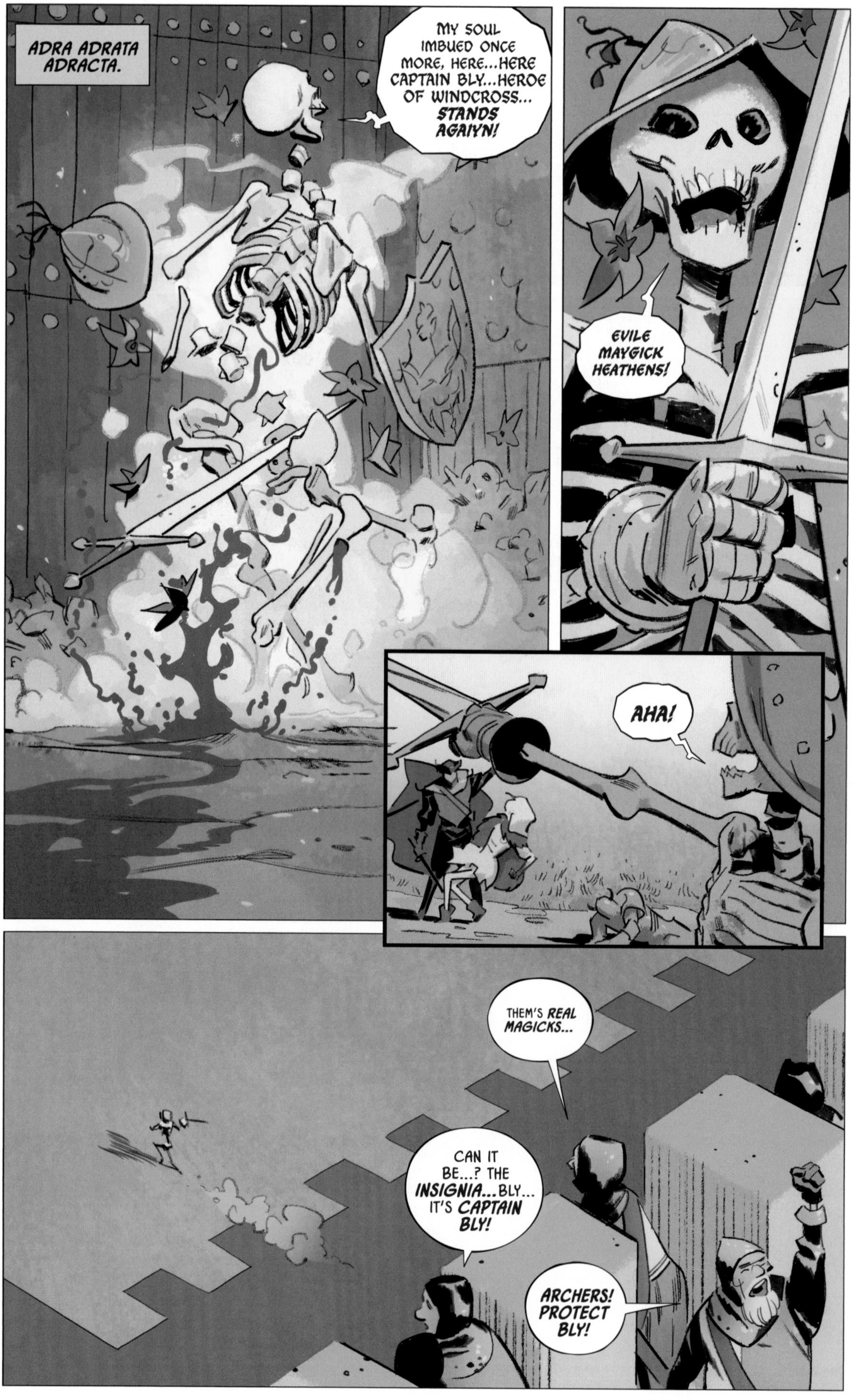
ADRA ADRATA ADRACTA.
MY SOUL IMBUED ONCE MORE, HERE...HERE CAPTAIN BLY...HEROE OF WINDCROSS... STANDS AGAIYN!
EVILE MAYGICK HEATHENS!
AHA!
THEM'S REAL MAGICKS...
CAN IT BE...? THE INSIGNIA...BLY... IT'S CAPTAIN BLY!
ARCHERS! PROTECT BLY!

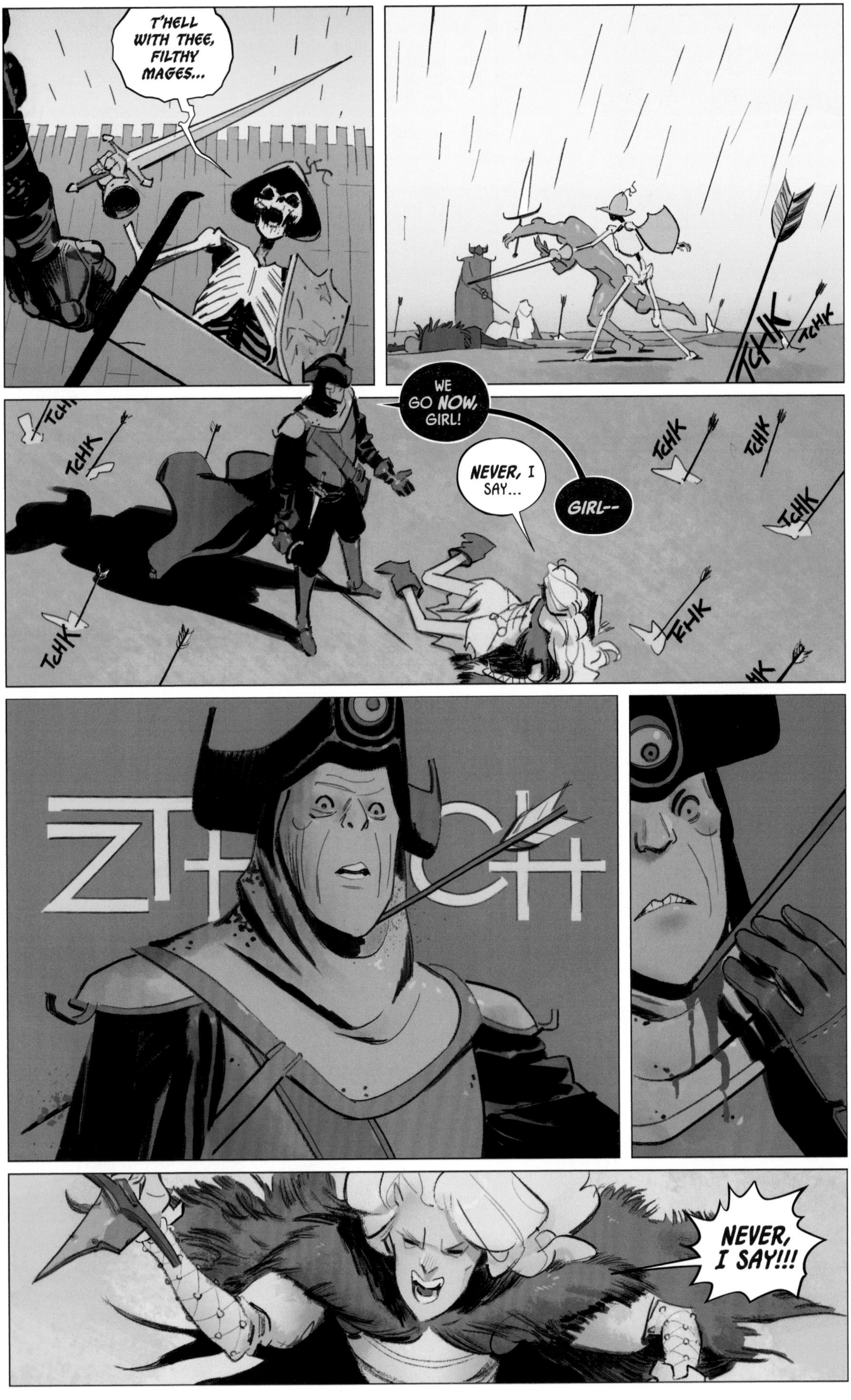
T'HELL WITH THEE, FILTHY MAGES...
TCHK
TCHK
WE GO NOW, GIRL!
NEVER, I SAY...
GIRL--
TCHK
TCHK
TCHK
TCHK
TCHK
TCHK
TCHK
ZTHOCH
NEVER, I SAY!!!

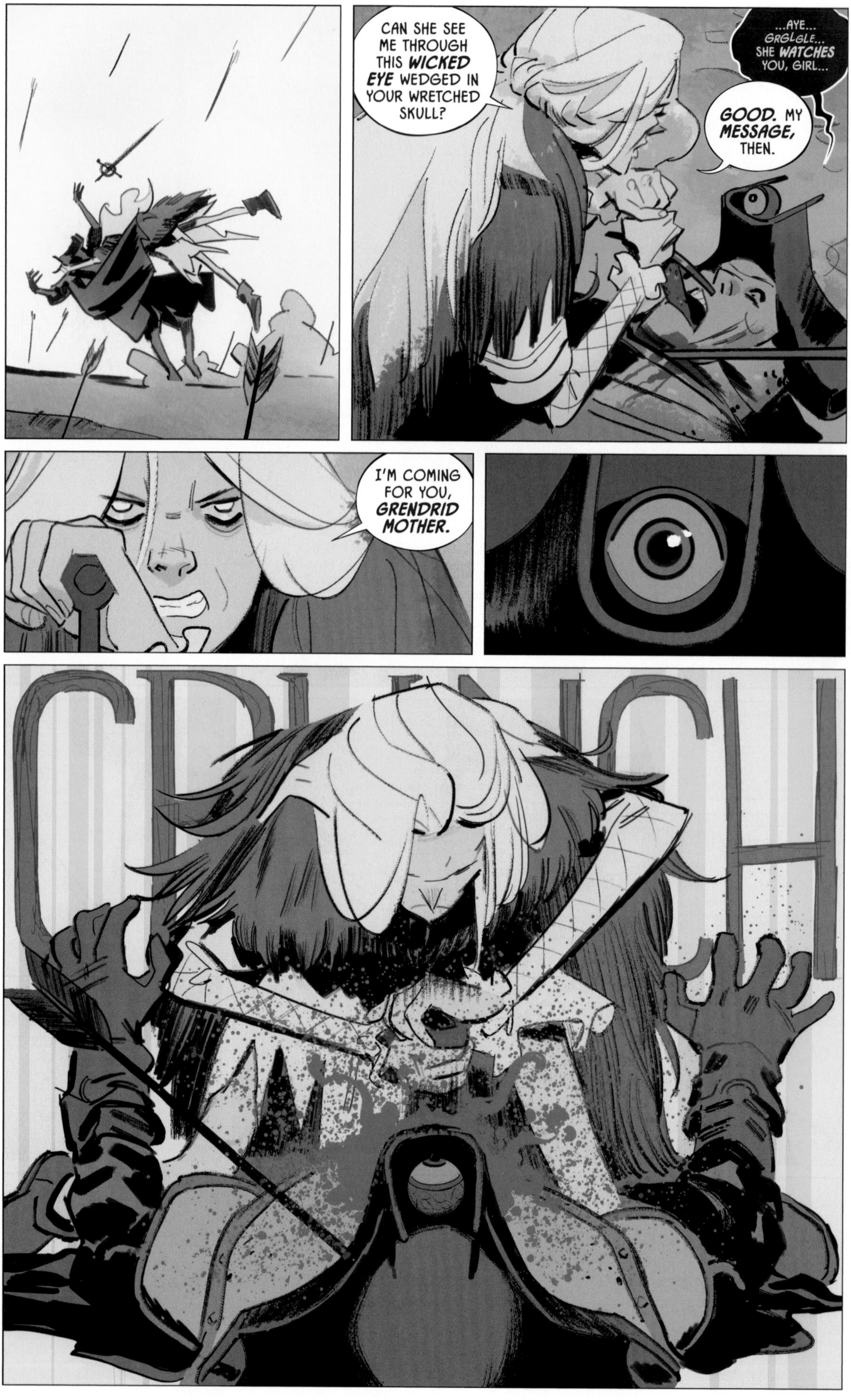
CAN SHE SEE ME THROUGH THIS WICKED EYE WEDGED IN YOUR WRETCHED SKULL?
...AYE... GRGLGLE... SHE WATCHES YOU, GIRL...
GOOD. MY MESSAGE, THEN.
I'M COMING FOR YOU, GRENDRID MOTHER.

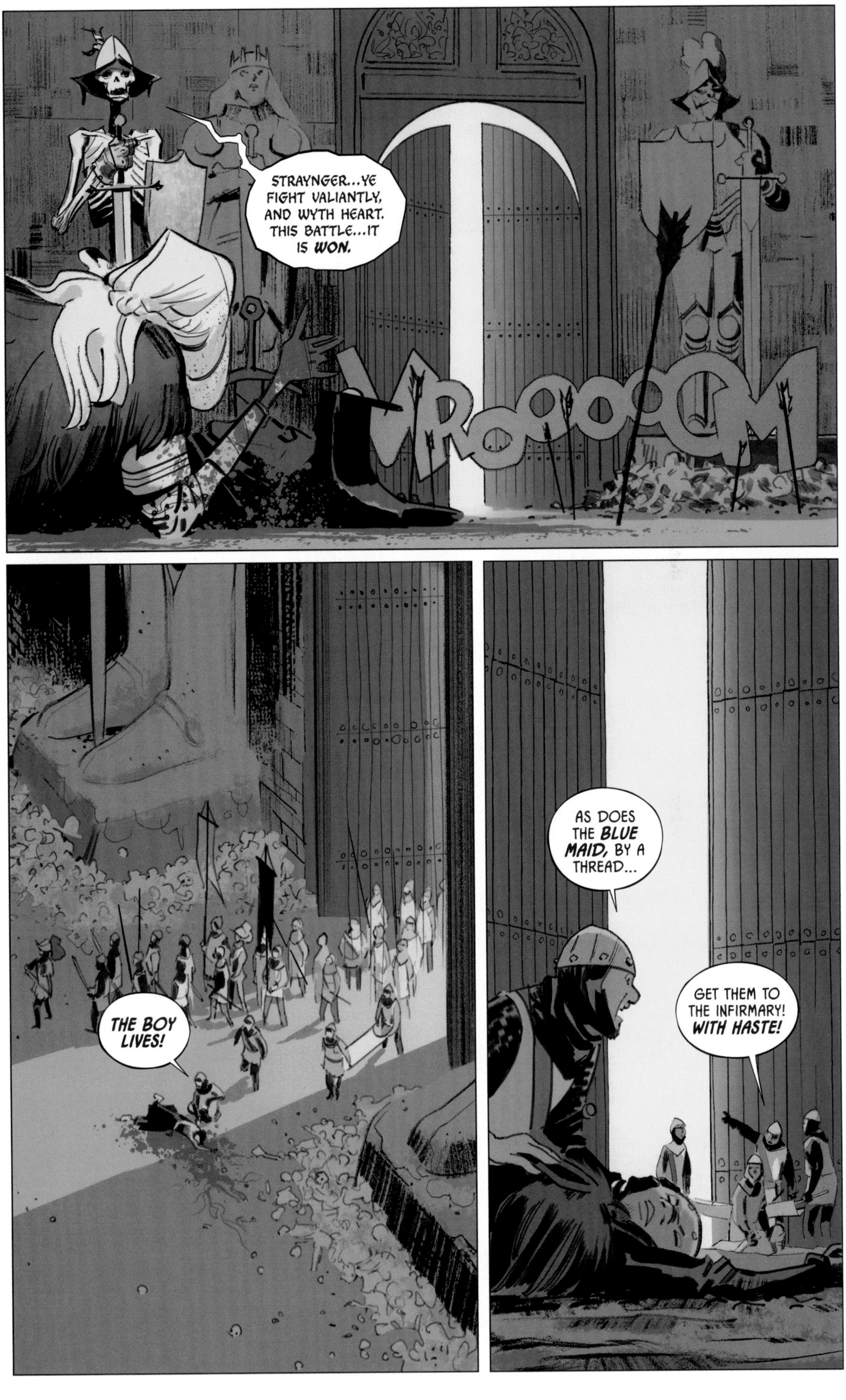
STRAYNGER...YE FIGHT VALIANTLY, AND WYTH HEART. THIS BATTLE...IT IS WON.
VROOOOOM
THE BOY LIVES!
AS DOES THE BLUE MAID, BY A THREAD...
GET THEM TO THE INFIRMARY! WITH HASTE!

Later.

THE *INDIGO DAEMON* IS LIKEWISE VALIANT. AND THIS WITCH HATH RESTOR'D ME.

WITCH. YES. THAT I AM, GOOD SIR.

YOU'RE RIGHT, CAPTAIN...THIS WOMAN IS THE *BRAVEST* I'VE EVER KNOWN.

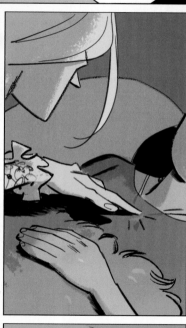

AND SHE'S WAKE'D ME *MORE THAN ONCE*, IT SEEMS...

MMFF...

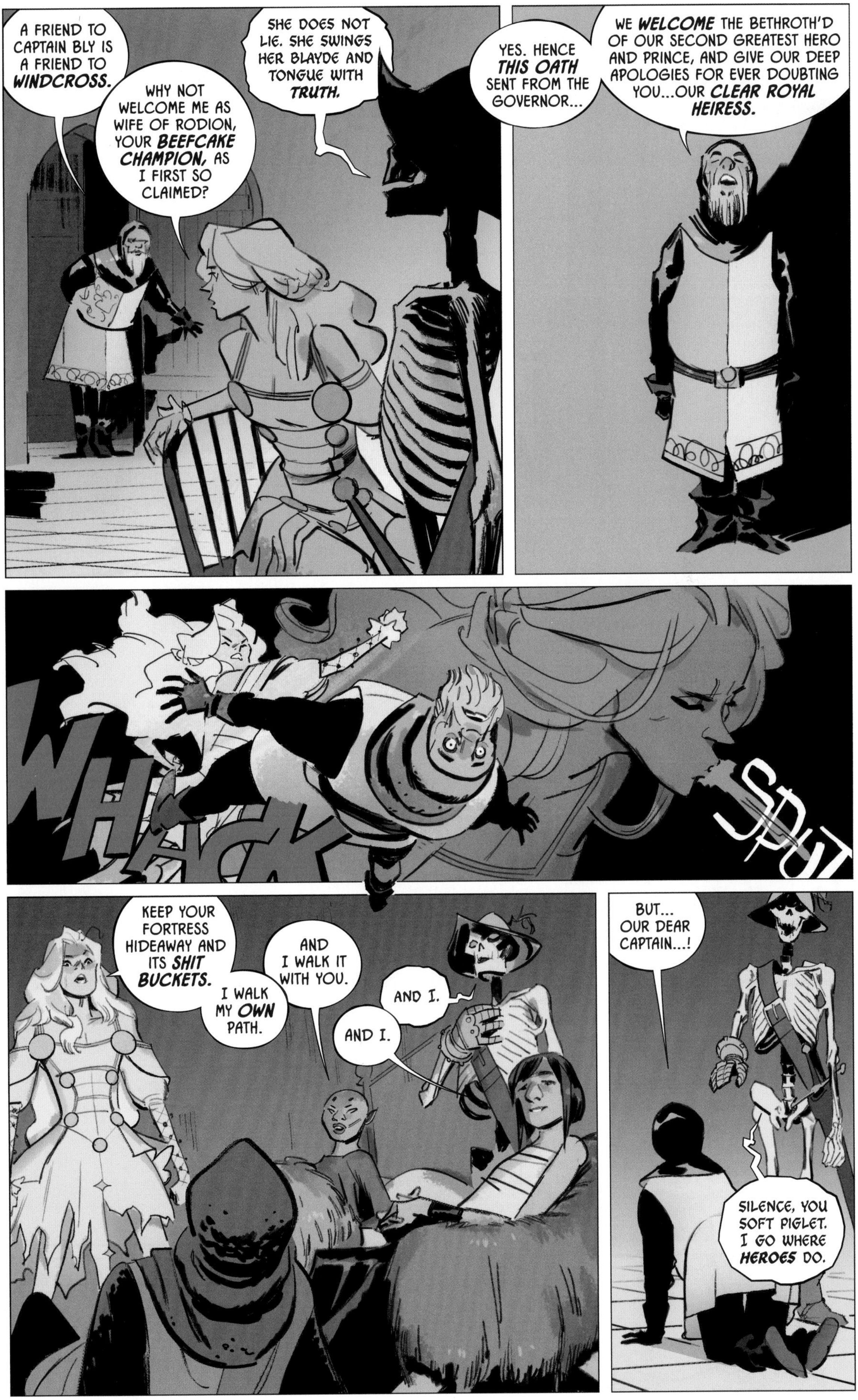
A FRIEND TO CAPTAIN BLY IS A FRIEND TO WINDCROSS.
WHY NOT WELCOME ME AS WIFE OF RODION, YOUR BEEFCAKE CHAMPION, AS I FIRST SO CLAIMED?
SHE DOES NOT LIE. SHE SWINGS HER BLAYDE AND TONGUE WITH TRUTH.
YES. HENCE THIS OATH SENT FROM THE GOVERNOR...
WE WELCOME THE BETHROTH'D OF OUR SECOND GREATEST HERO AND PRINCE, AND GIVE OUR DEEP APOLOGIES FOR EVER DOUBTING YOU...OUR CLEAR ROYAL HEIRESS.
WHACK
SPUT
KEEP YOUR FORTRESS HIDEAWAY AND ITS SHIT BUCKETS.
I WALK MY OWN PATH.
AND I WALK IT WITH YOU.
AND I.
AND I.
BUT... OUR DEAR CAPTAIN...!
SILENCE, YOU SOFT PIGLET. I GO WHERE HEROES DO.

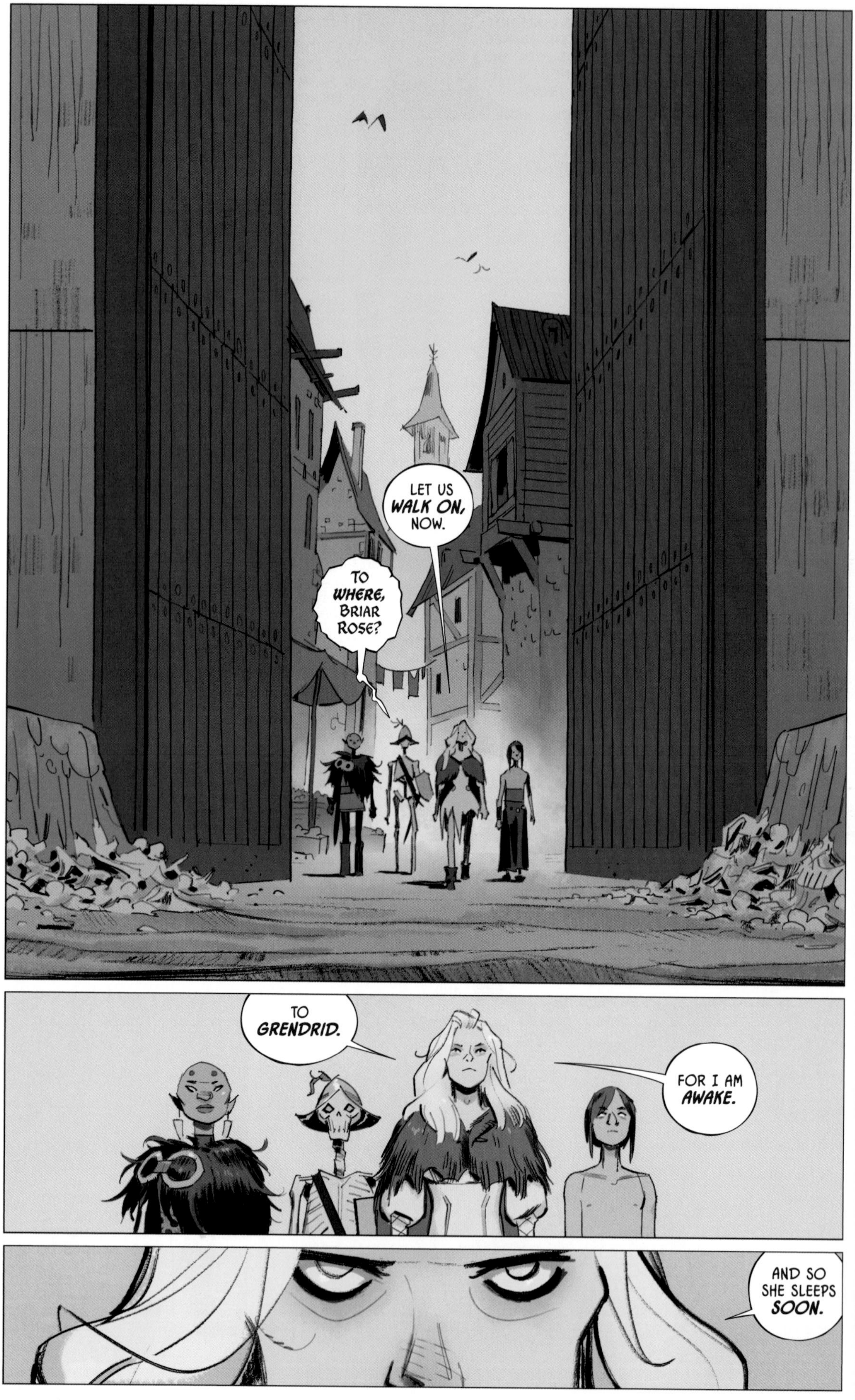
LET US WALK ON, NOW.
TO WHERE, BRIAR ROSE?
TO GRENDRID.
FOR I AM AWAKE.
AND SO SHE SLEEPS SOON.

To Be Continued...

COVER GALLERY

Featuring artwork by
Germán García
Germán García & Matheus Lopes
Jenny Frison
Stephanie Hans
Frany
Tiffany Turrill
Dan Mora
Raúl Allén
Toni Infante
Yanick Paquette & Matheus Lopes

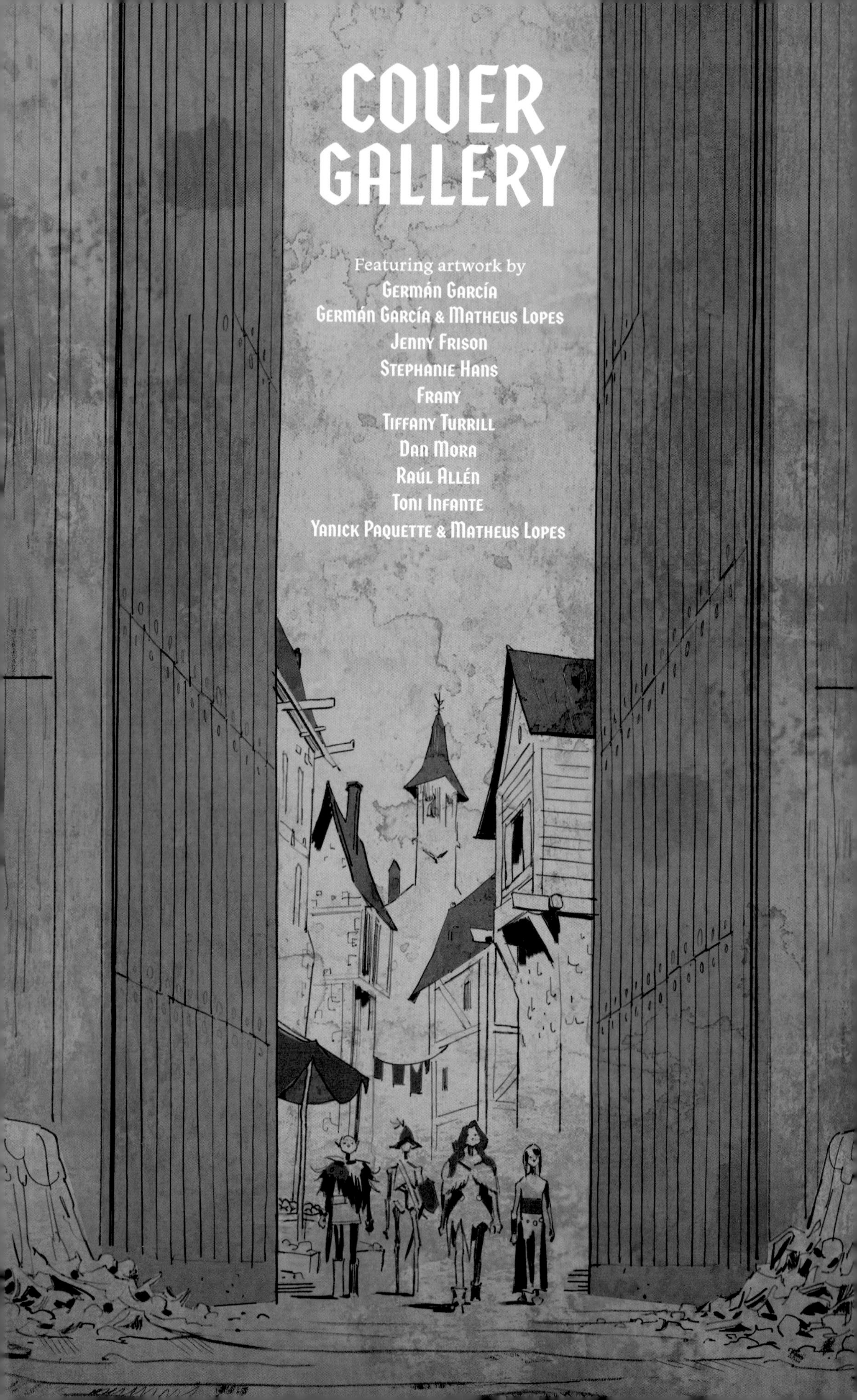

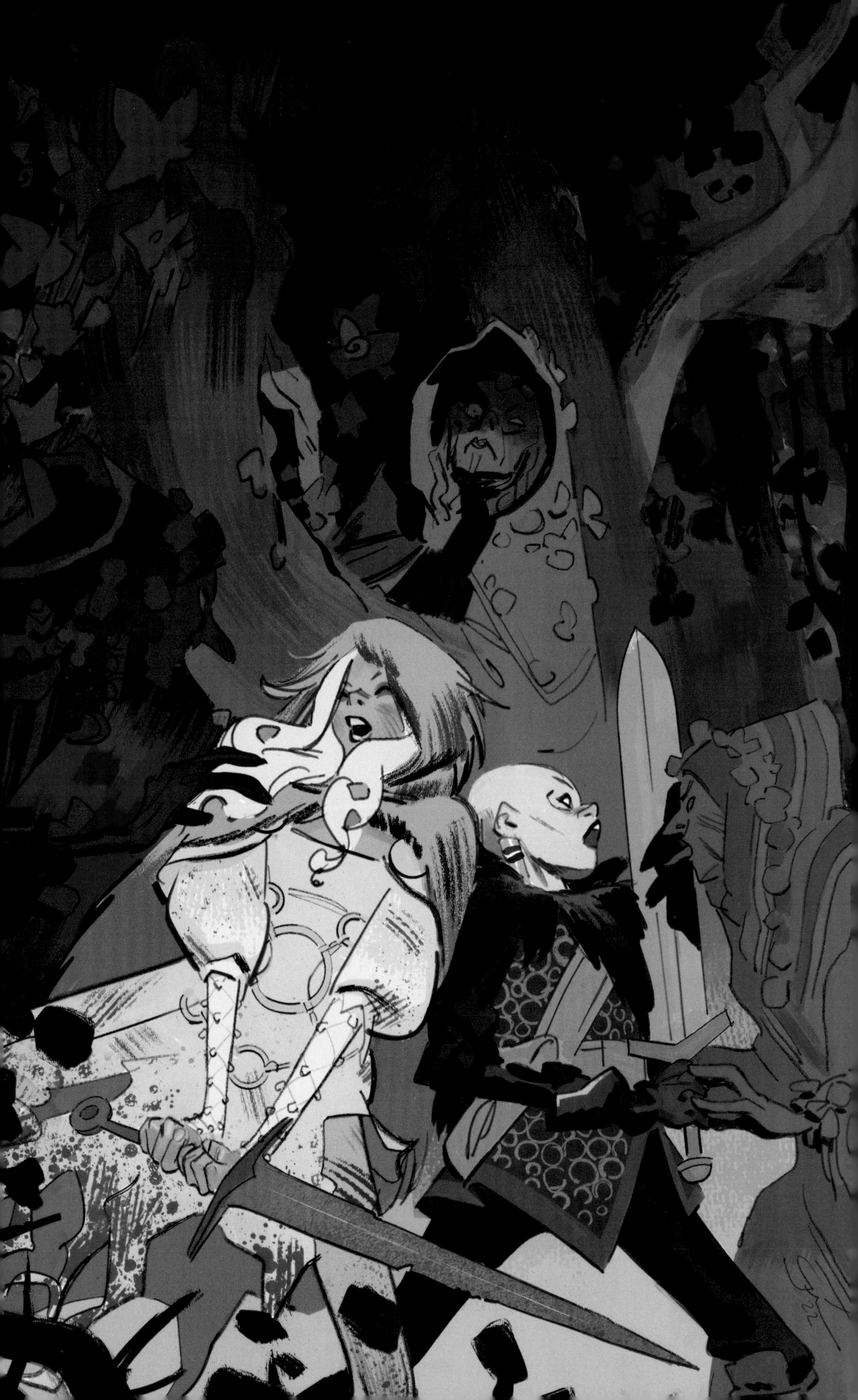

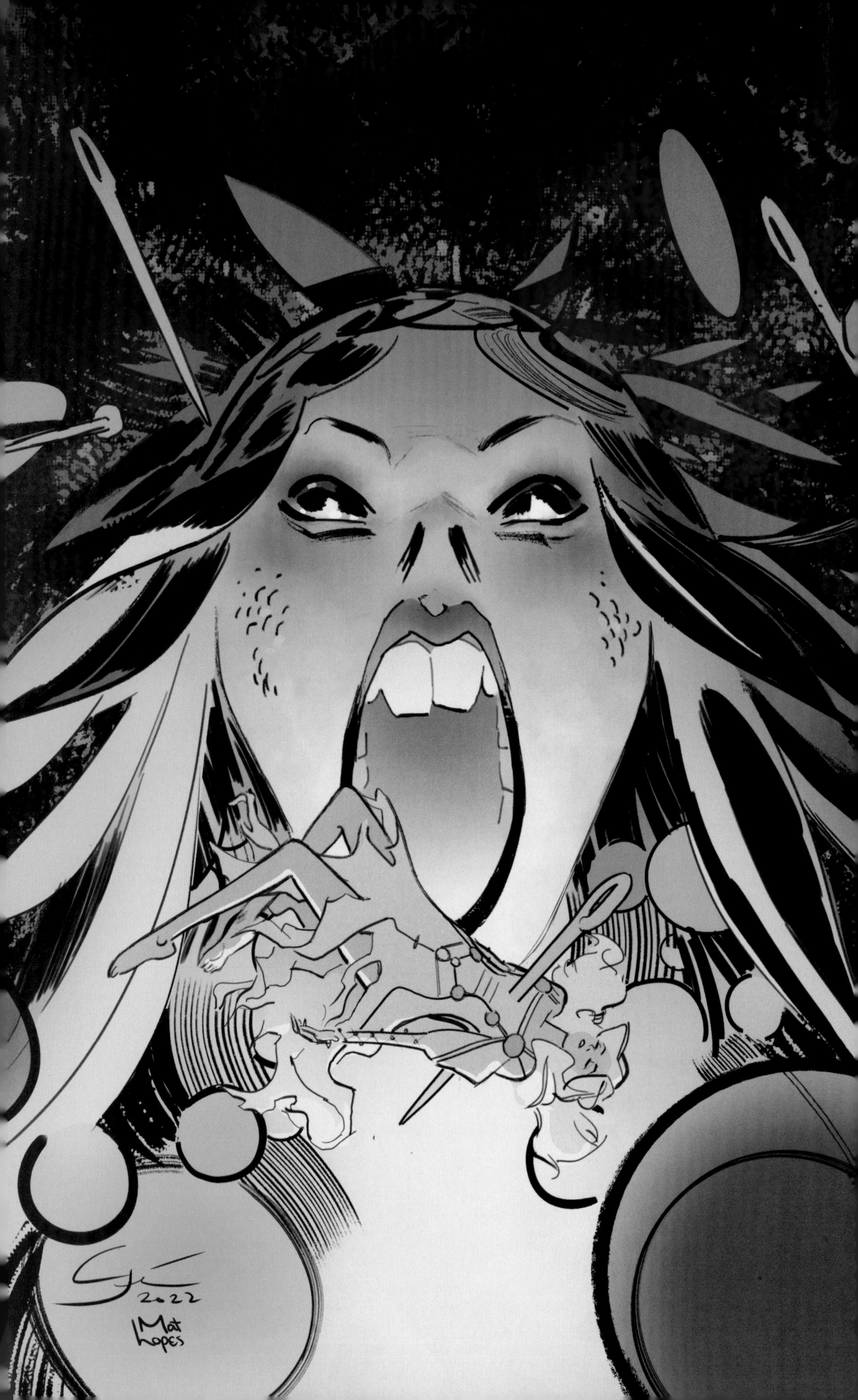
2022
Mat Lopes

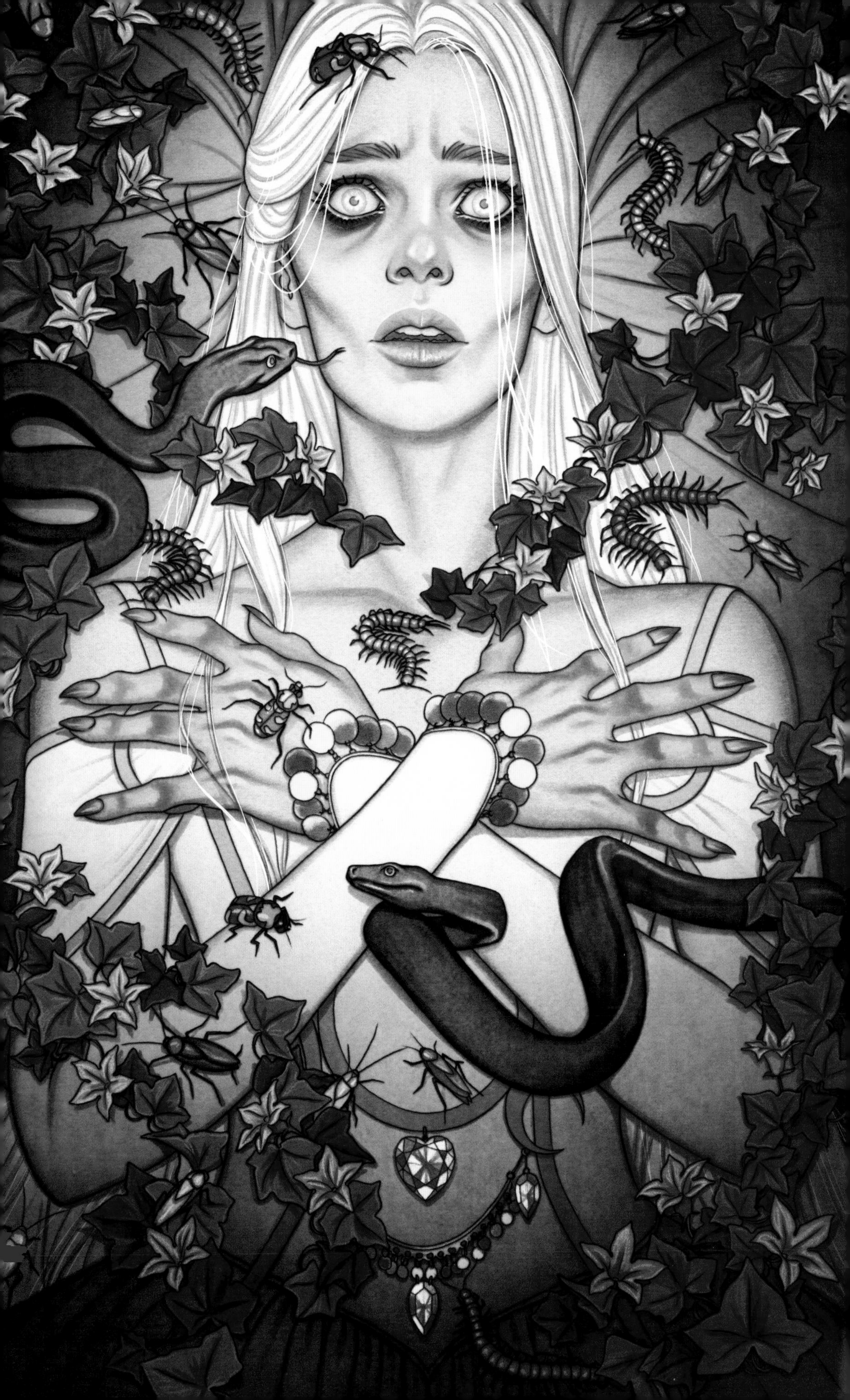

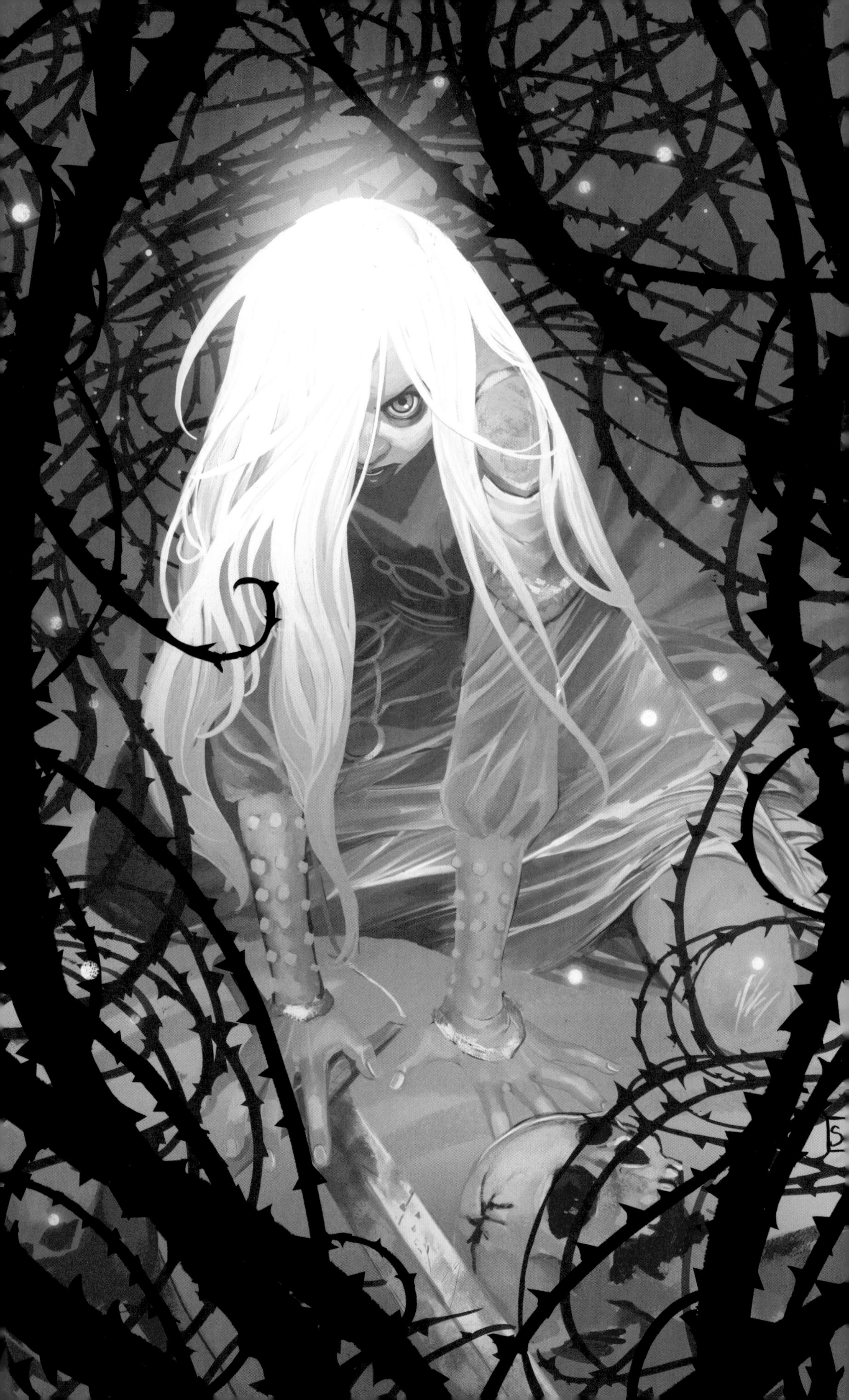

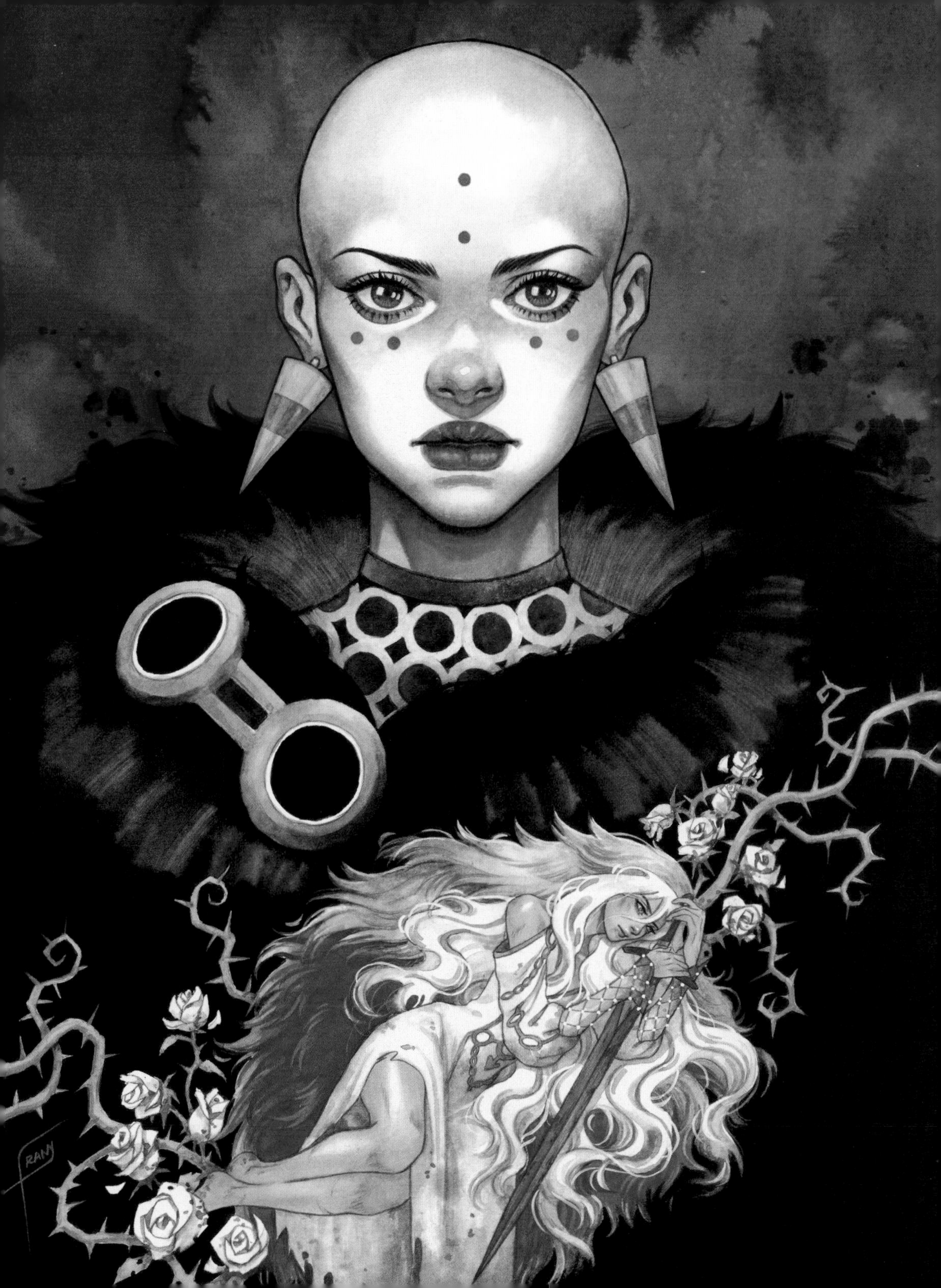

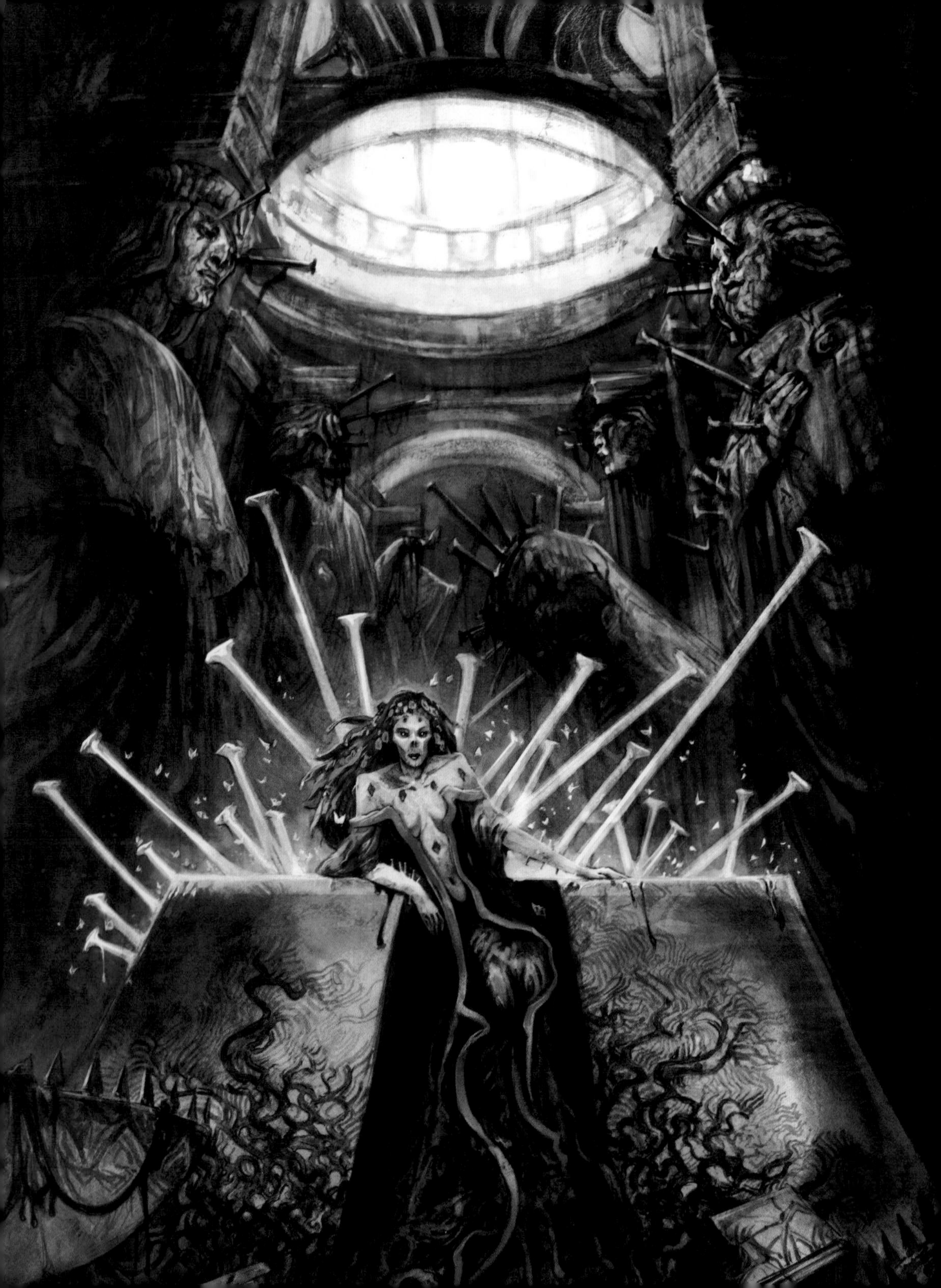

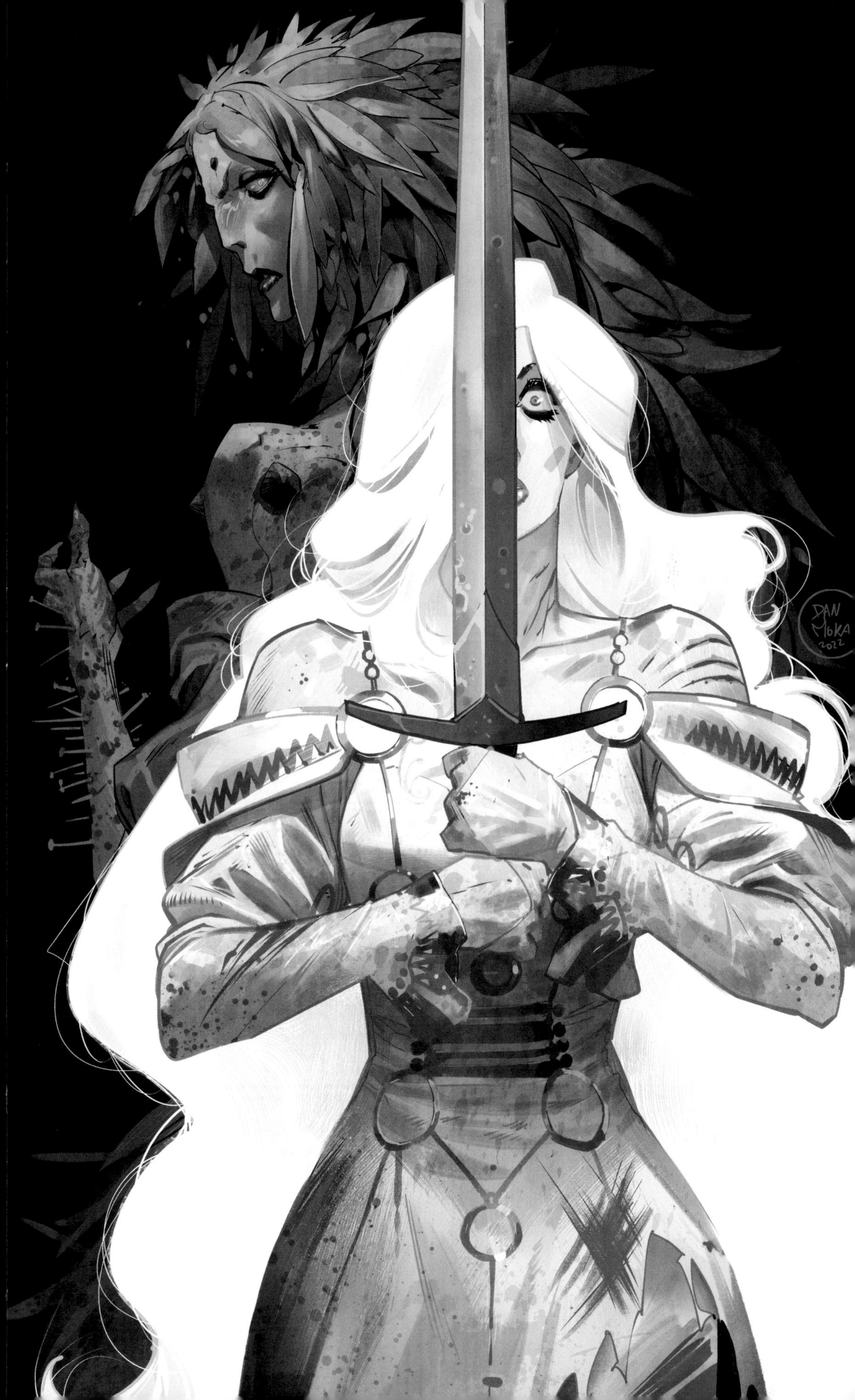

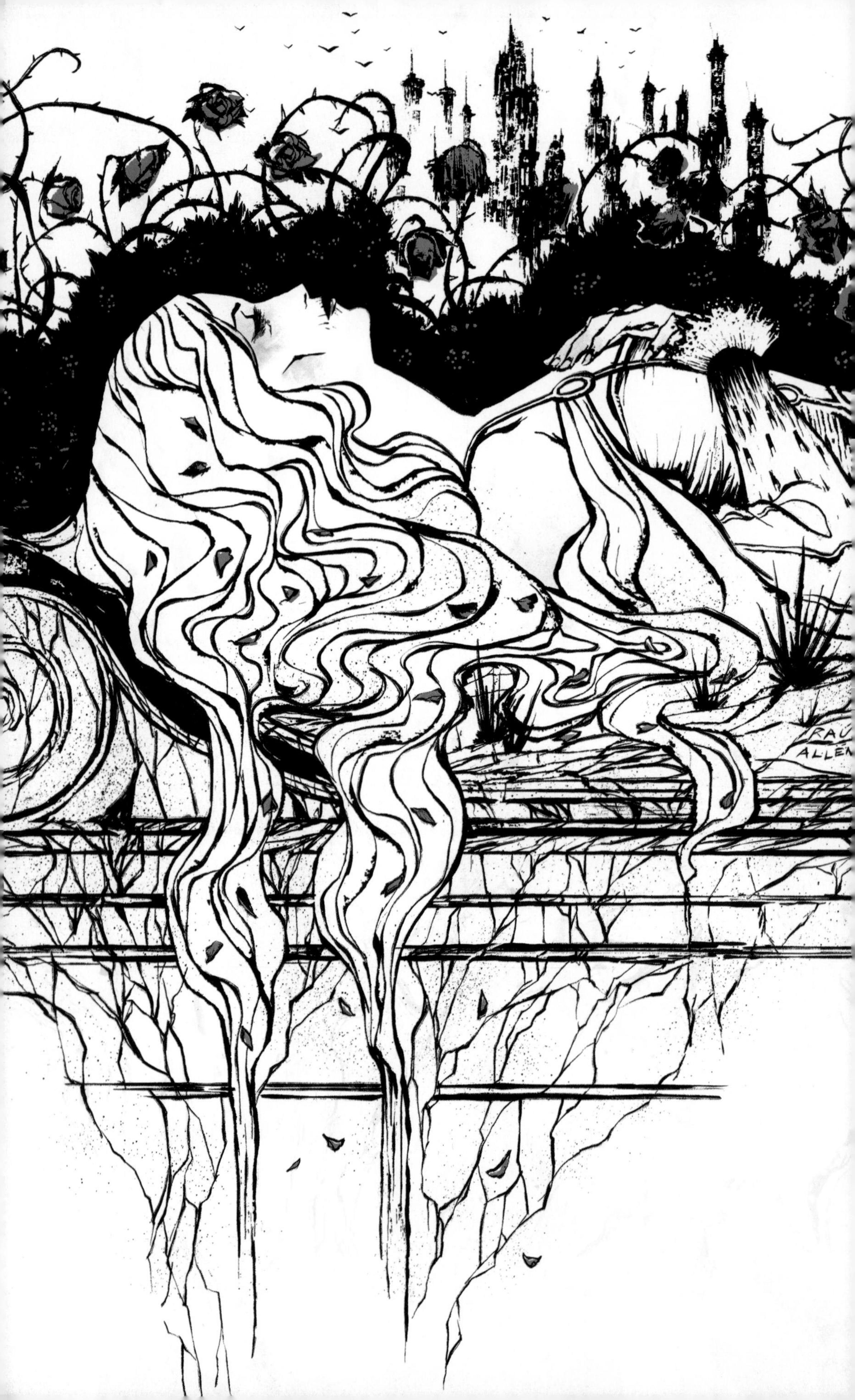

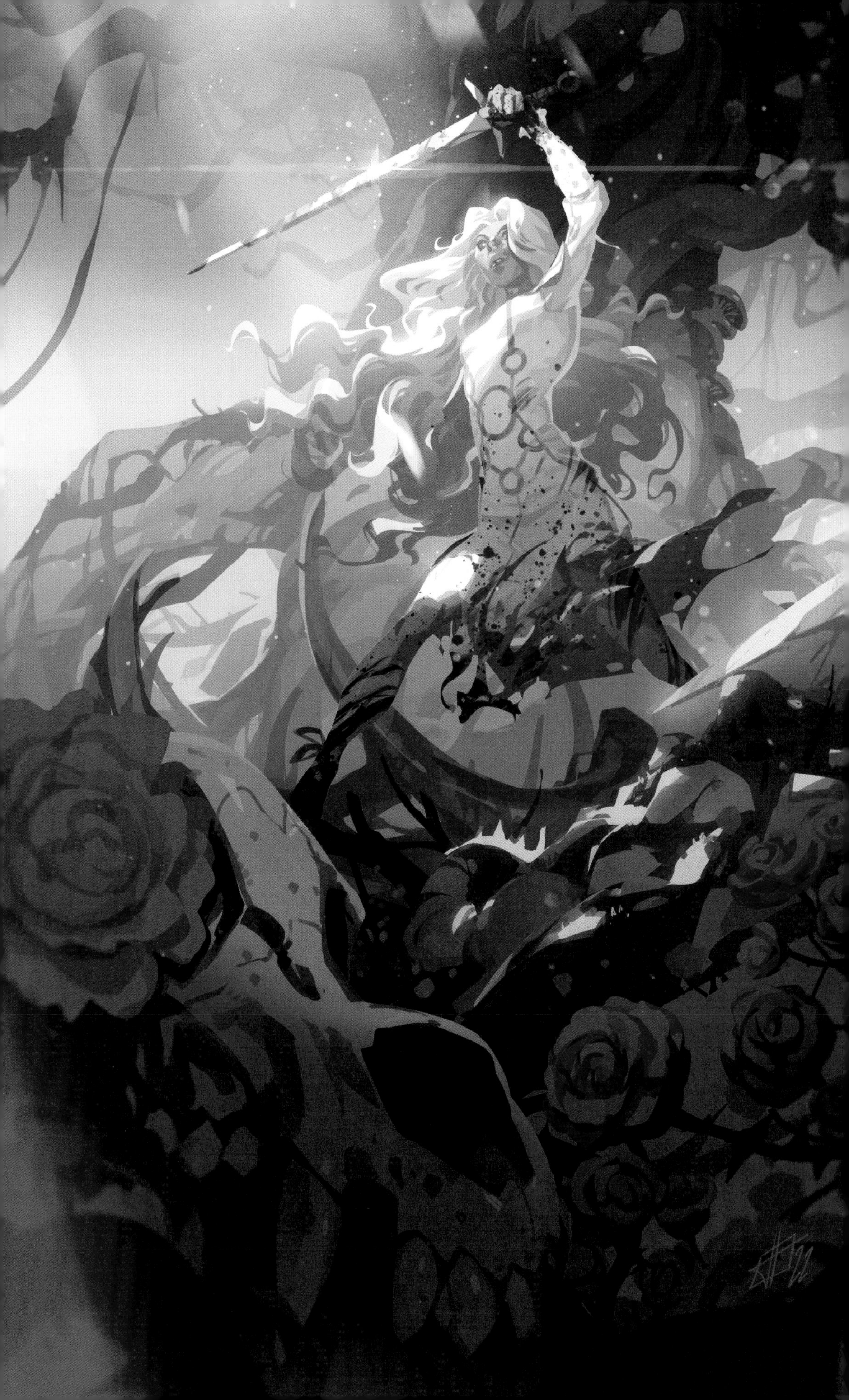

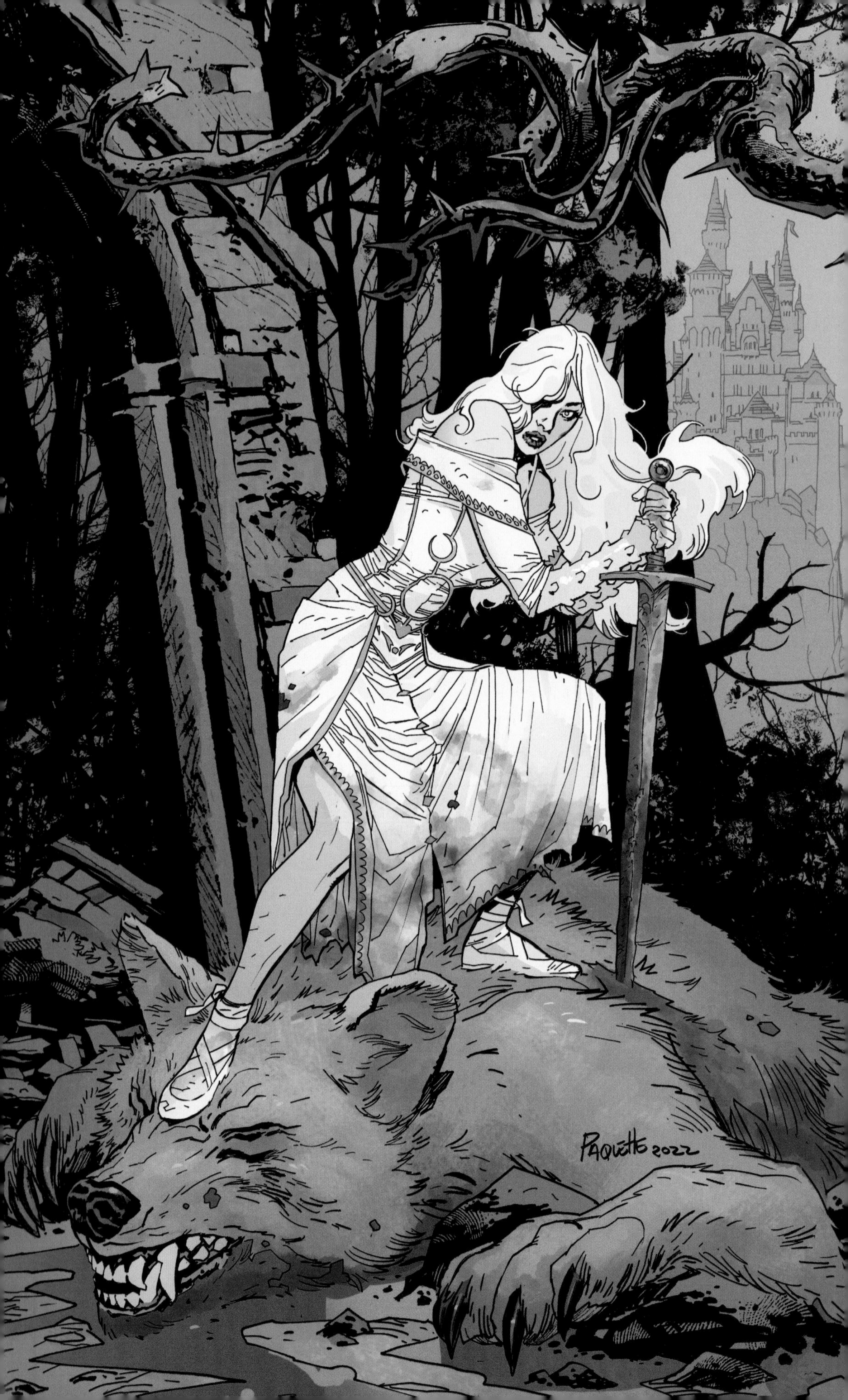
PAQUETTE 2022

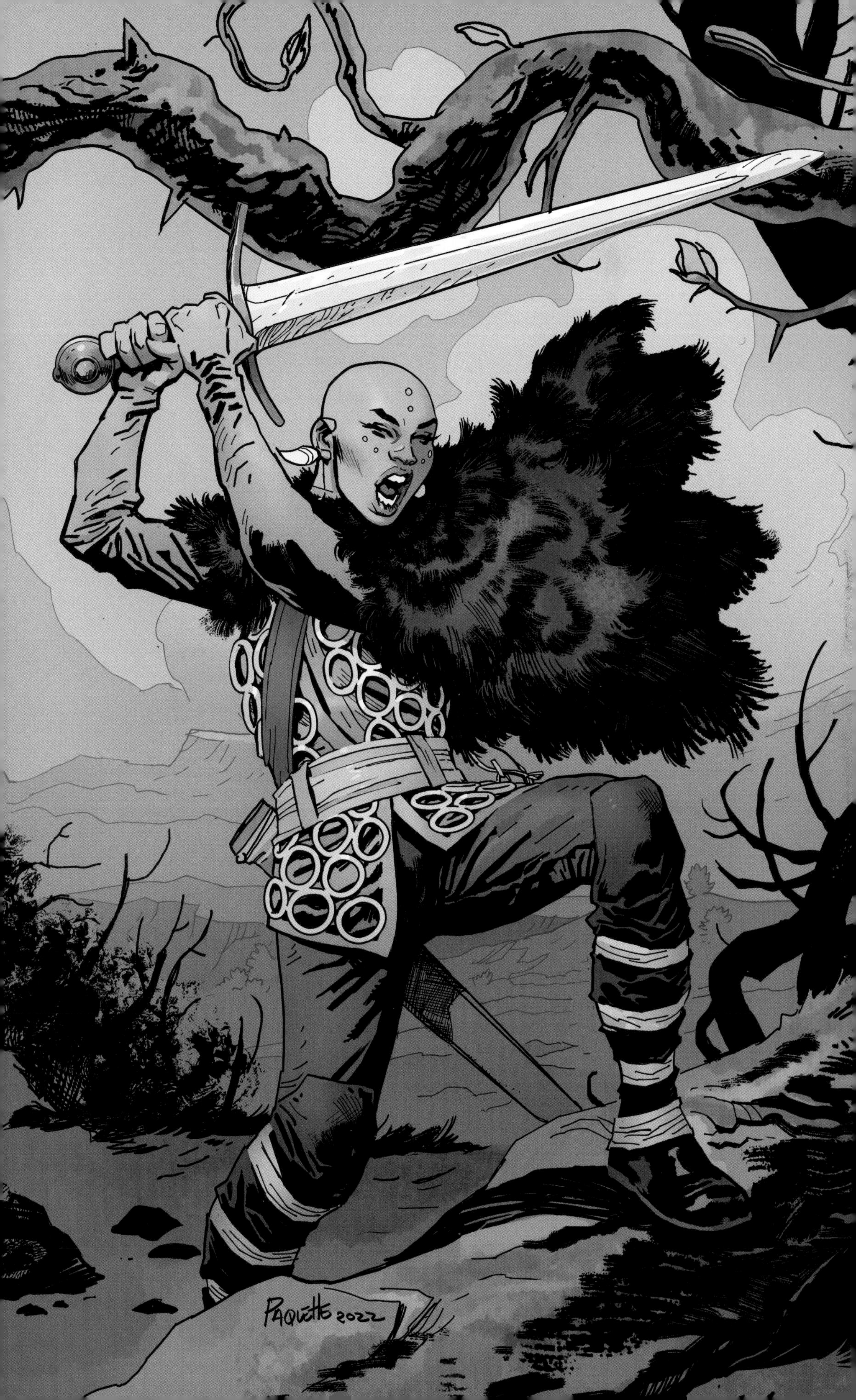
PAQUETTE 2022

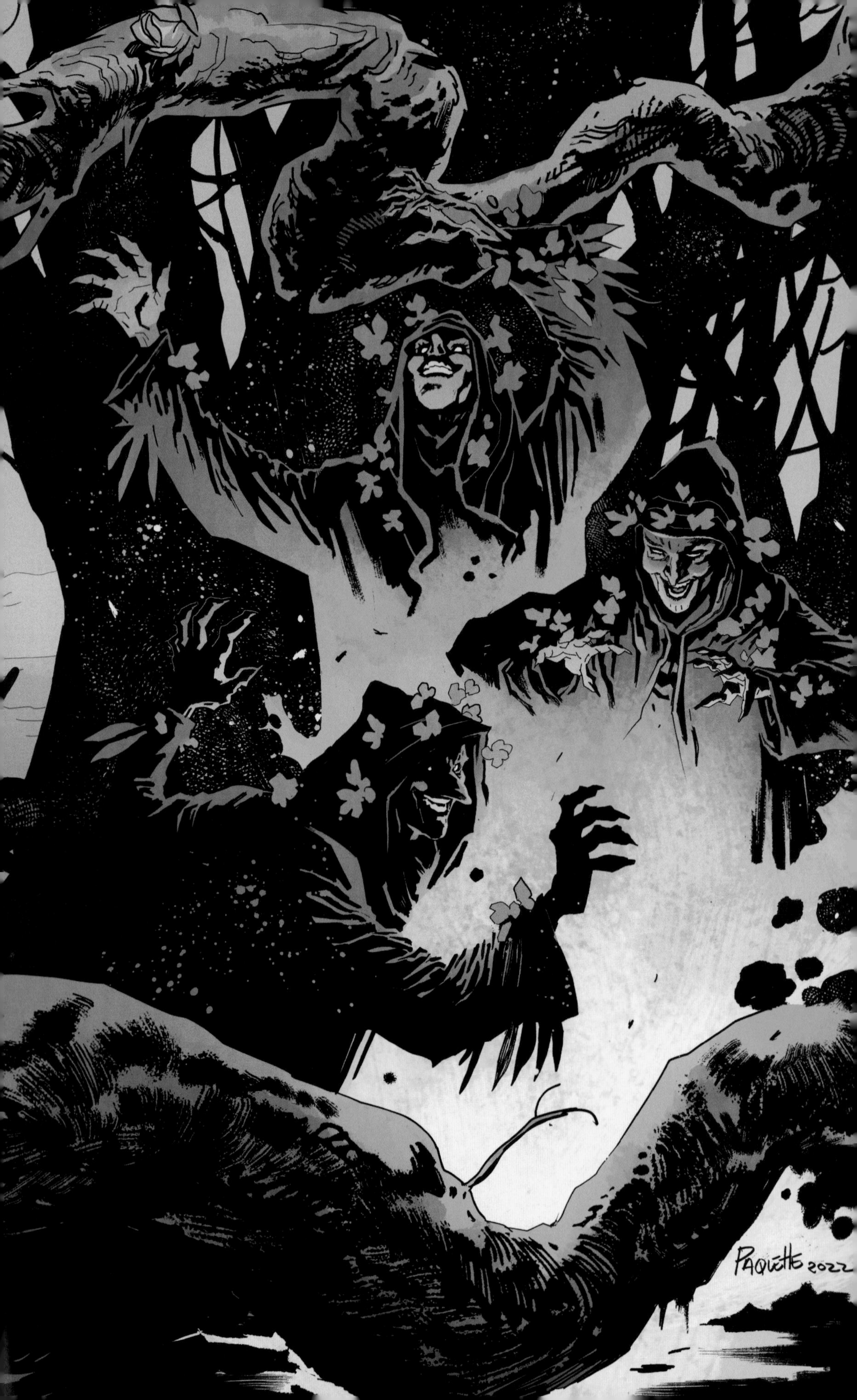
PAQUETTE 2022

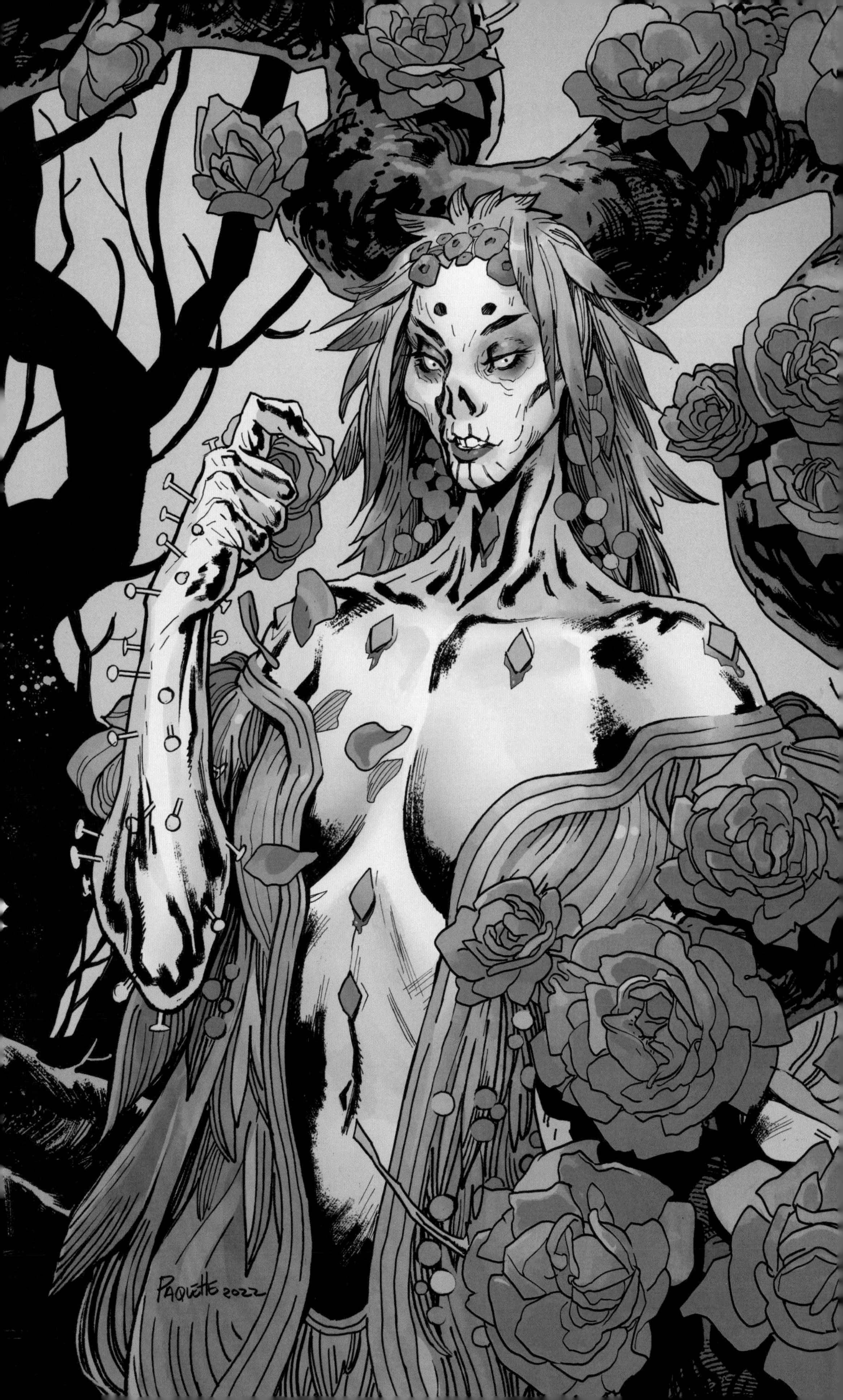
PAQUETTE 2022

CHARACTER DESIGNS
BY GERMÁN GARCÍA

BRIAR

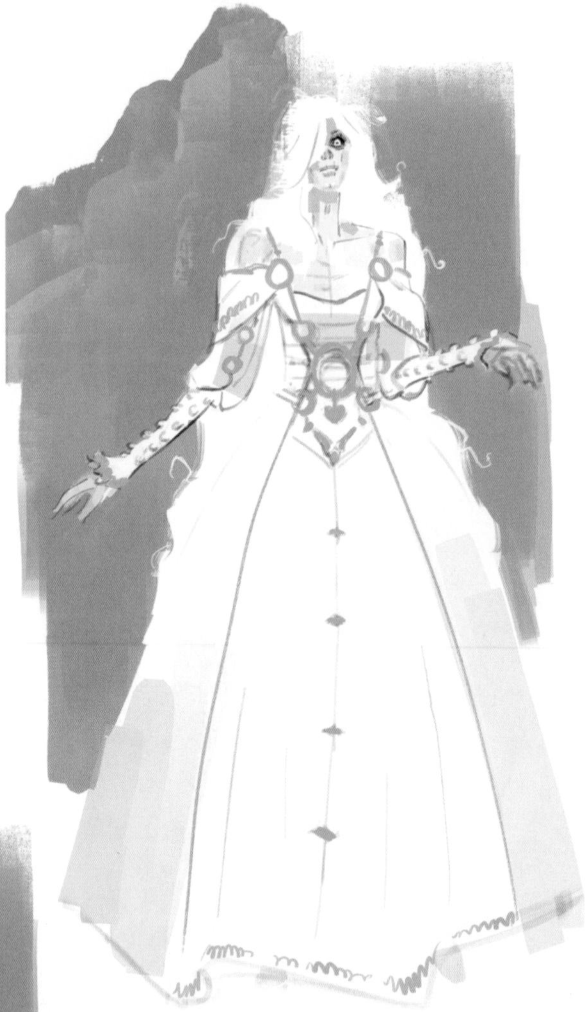

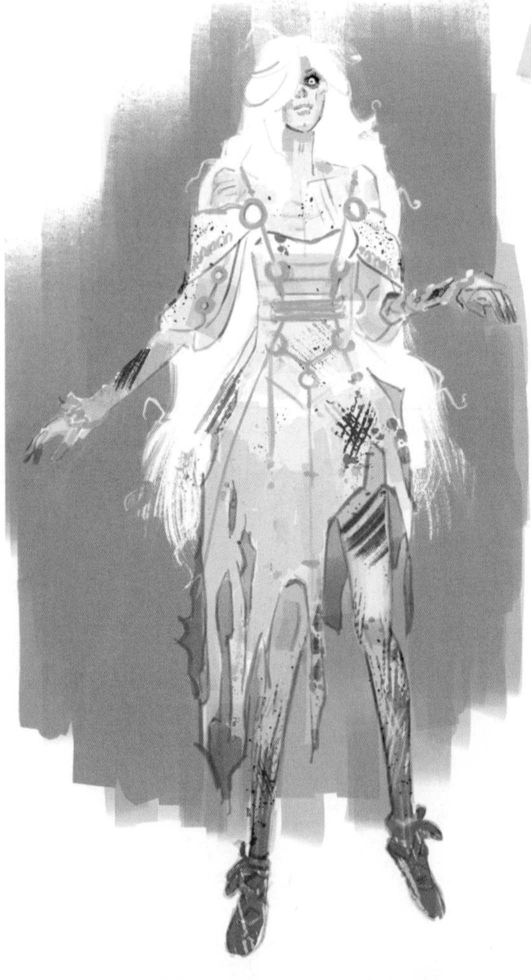

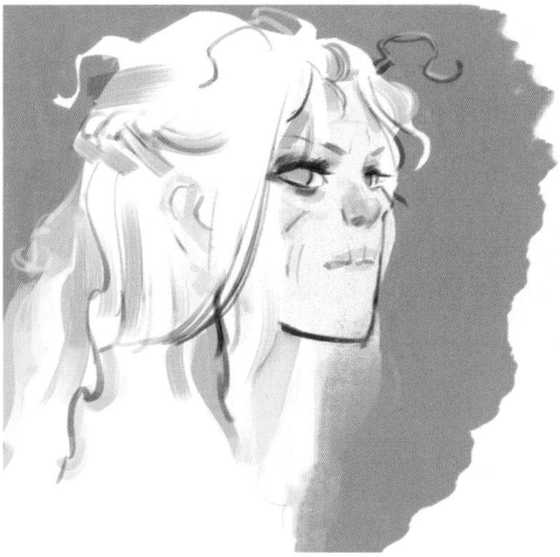

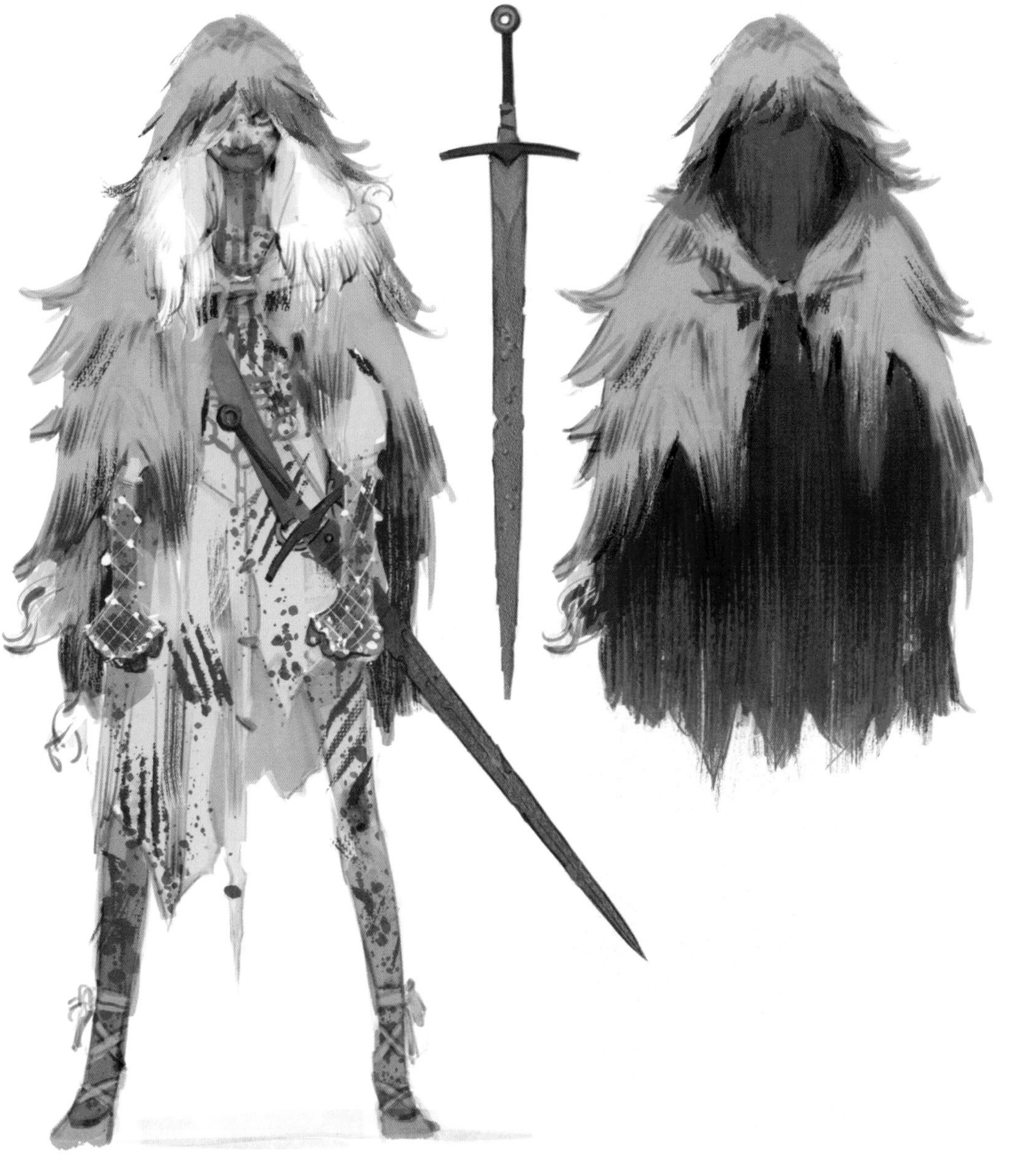

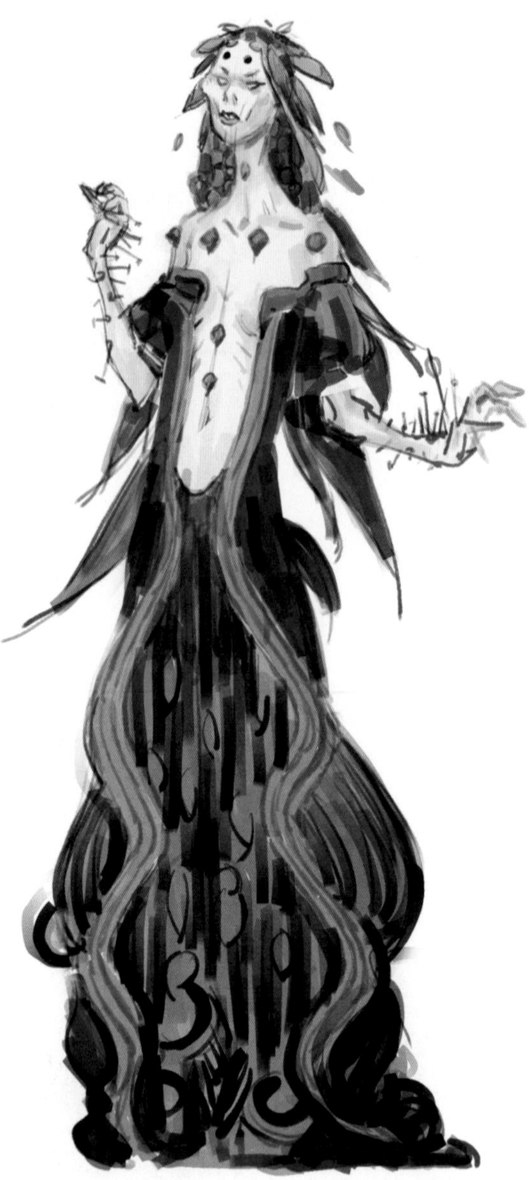

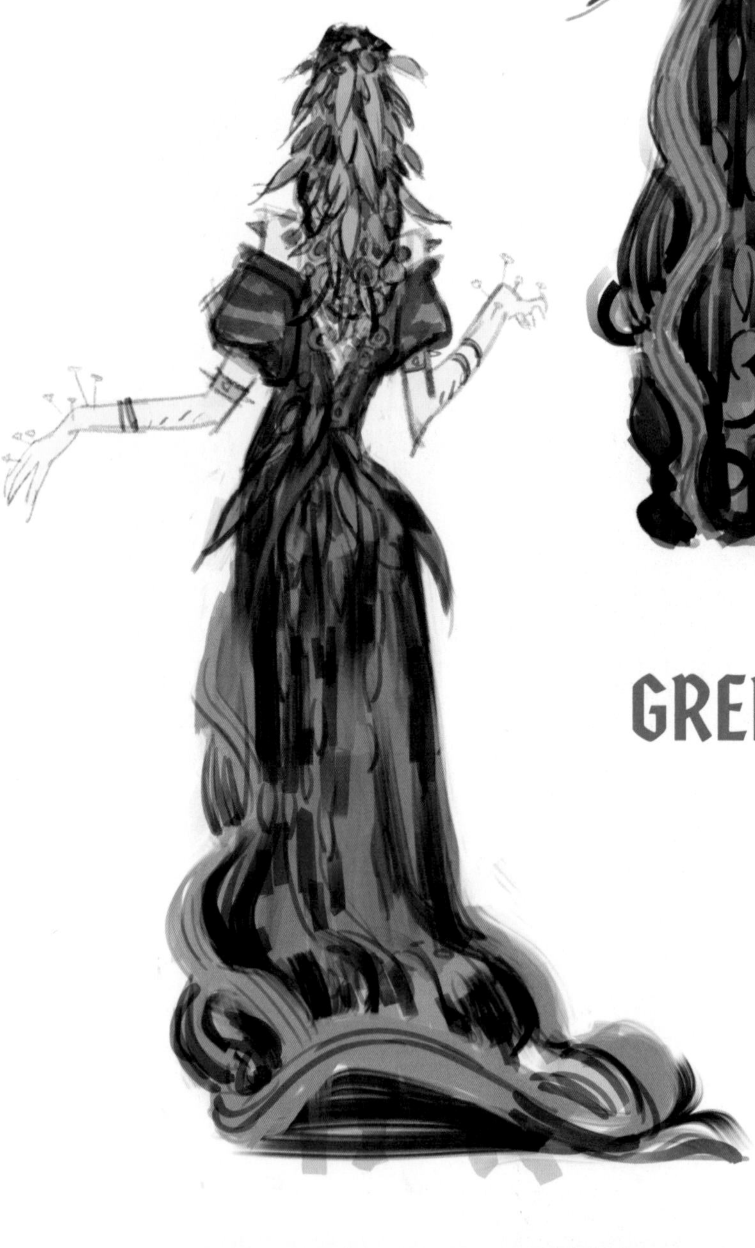

GRENDRID

SPIDER

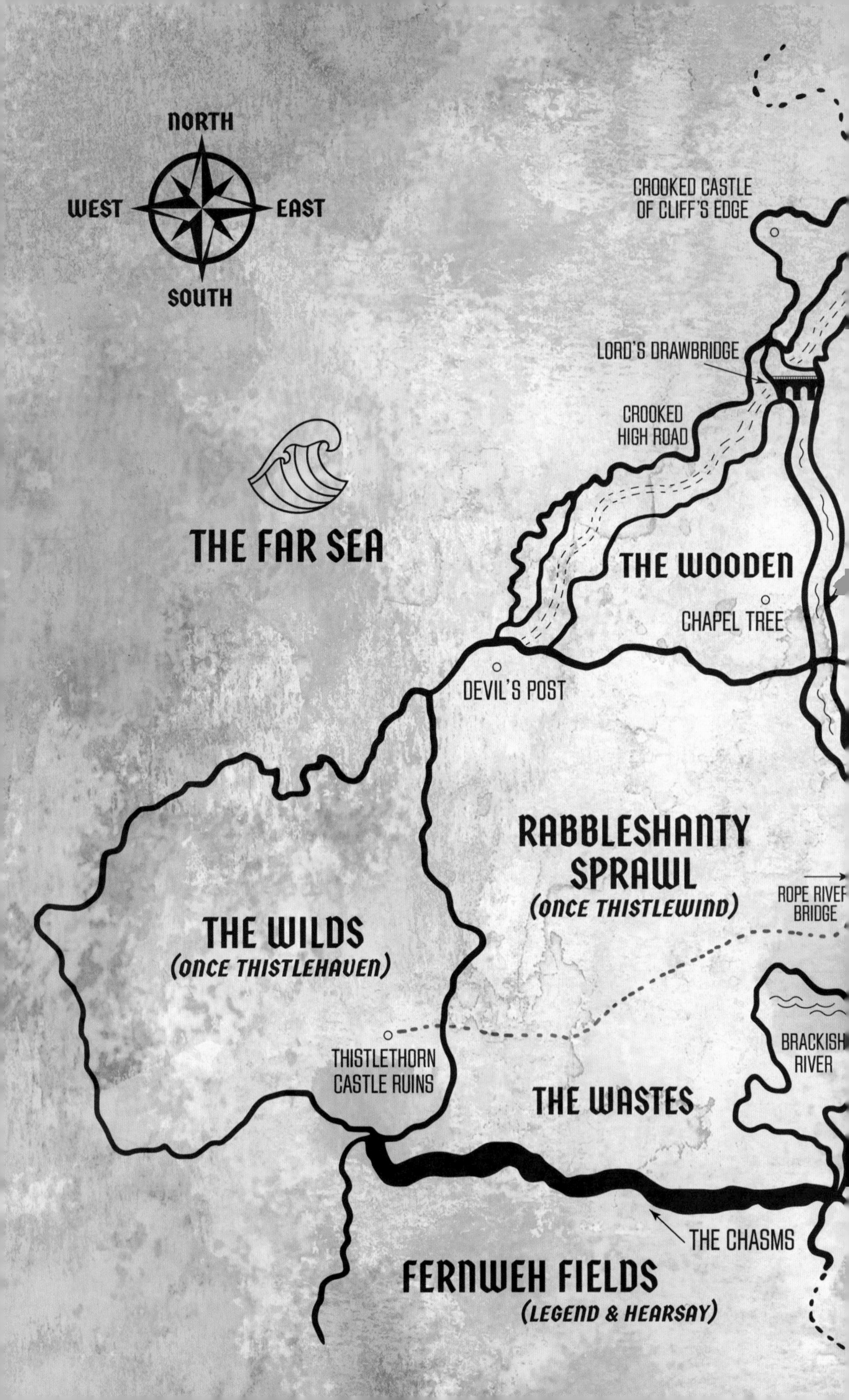
NORTH
WEST
EAST
SOUTH
CROOKED CASTLE OF CLIFF'S EDGE
LORD'S DRAWBRIDGE
CROOKED HIGH ROAD
THE FAR SEA
THE WOODEN
CHAPEL TREE
DEVIL'S POST
RABBLESHANTY SPRAWL
(ONCE THISTLEWIND)
ROPE RIVER BRIDGE
THE WILDS
(ONCE THISTLEHAVEN)
BRACKISH RIVER
THISTLETHORN CASTLE RUINS
THE WASTES
THE CHASMS
FERNWEH FIELDS
(LEGEND & HEARSAY)

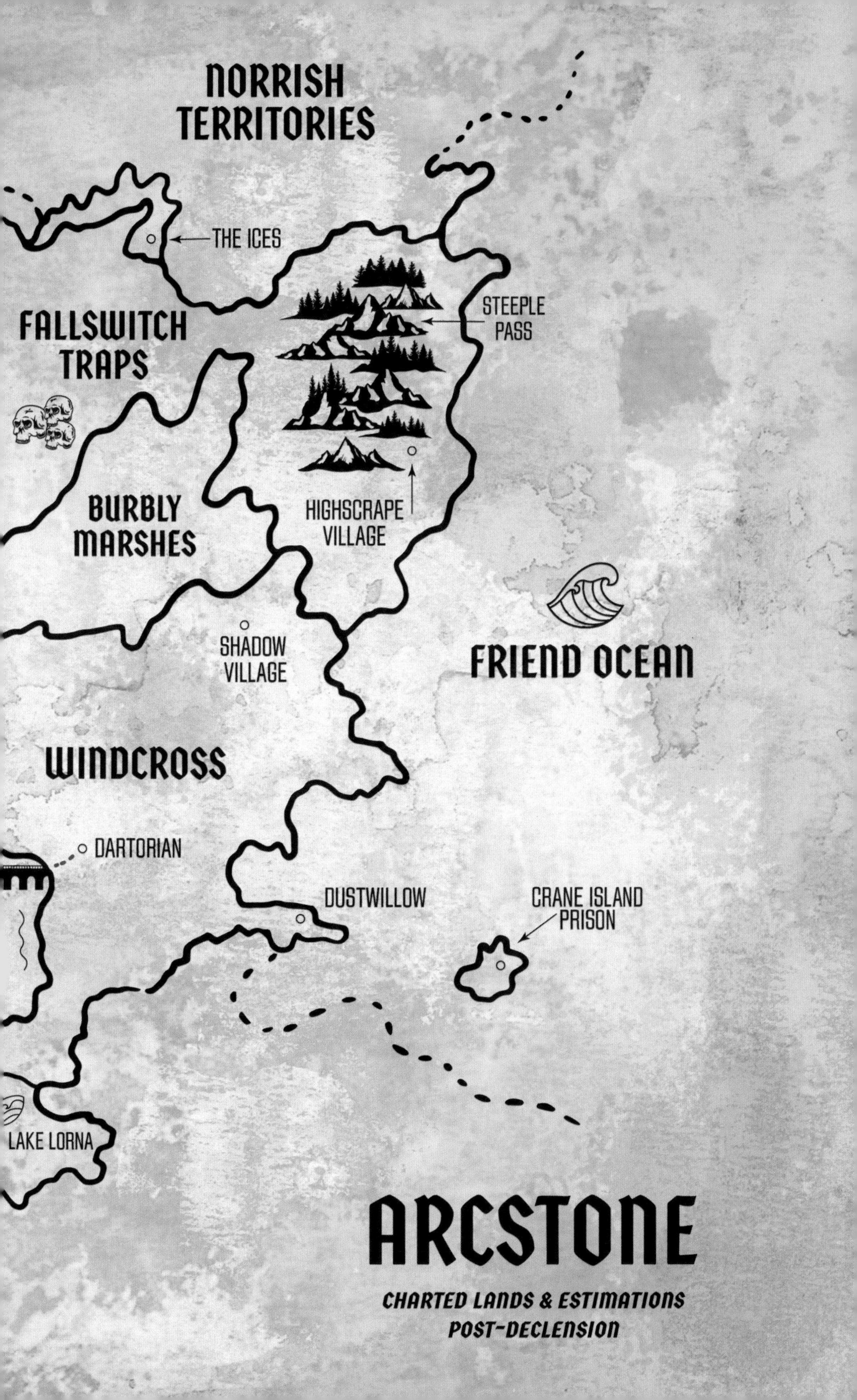
NORRISH TERRITORIES
THE ICES
FALLSWITCH TRAPS
STEEPLE PASS
BURBLY MARSHES
HIGHSCRAPE VILLAGE
SHADOW VILLAGE
FRIEND OCEAN
WINDCROSS
DARTORIAN
DUSTWILLOW
CRANE ISLAND PRISON
LAKE LORNA
ARCSTONE
CHARTED LANDS & ESTIMATIONS
POST-DECLENSION

CHRISTOPHER CANTWELL is the current writer of the ongoing series *Star Trek:Defiant* for IDW Publishing's new Star Trek comic book initiative, as well as *Hellcat* for Marvel Comics. Cantwell has additionally written *Iron Man*, *Doctor Doom*, *United States of Captain America*, *Namor: Conquered Shores*, and *Gold Goblin* for Marvel, as well as *Regarding the Matter of Oswald's Body* and *Angel* (BOOM! Studios), *The Blue Flame* (Vault), *She Could Fly*, and *Everything* (both from Berger Books and Dark Horse). Chris was also a co-creator, executive producer, and showrunner of AMC's *Halt and Catch Fire* and additionally served as an executive producer on the first season of the TV adaptation of Brian K. Vaughan and Cliff Chiang's *Paper Girls*. He is currently developing the return of *Max Headroom* to television for AMC.

GERMÁN GARCÍA is a comic book author from Asturias, Spain. After creating his comic book series, *Tess Tinieblas*, he broke out in the U.S. market as an artist drawing titles such as *X-Men*, *Action Comics*, and most recently *Barbarella/Dejah Thoris*, *Immortal Hulk*, and *Ka-Zar: Lord of the Savage Land*.

MATHEUS LOPES is a Brazilian colorist born in 1991. He is self-taught, and learned about his craft in online forums in 2008. After finishing high school, Matheus decided to forgo a formal college education, focusing on what he dreamed would become his profession: coloring comics. His first published gig came in 2011, and in July 2012 he secured his first ongoing project. He hasn't stopped coloring since.

ANDWORLD DESIGN is the design and production studio founded by veteran letterer Deron Bennett. The comic-based company's extensive list of clients includes BOOM!, Z2, Image, Dark Horse, Vault, IDW, Oni Press, AHOY, and DC Comics. They also produce typesetting, cover design, and illustration for Amazon Publishing as well. You can see their work on such acclaimed titles as *Something is Killing the Children*, *The Many Deaths of Laila Starr*, and *The Nice House on the Lake*. AndWorld's team of artists have garnered multiple Harvey, Ringo, and Eisner nominations.